GLQ: A Journal of Lesbian and Gay Studies

VOLUME 24 NUMBER 4 2018

The Queer Commons

Edited by Gavin Butt and Nadja Millner-Larsen

JOSÉ ESTEBAN MUÑOZ

Preface:

Fragment from the *Sense of Brown* Manuscript

395

NADJA MILLNER-LARSEN AND GAVIN BUTT

Introduction: The Queer Commons

399

CHRISTINA B. HANHARDT

"Dead Addicts Don't Recover": ACT UP's Needle Exchange and the Subjects of Queer Activist History

421

BETH CAPPER AND ARLEN AUSTIN

"Wages for housework means wages *against* heterosexuality": On the Archives of Black Women for Wages for Housework and Wages Due Lesbians

445

**JULIE TOLENTINO, VIVIAN A. CROCKETT, TARA HART,
AMIRA KHUSRO, LEEROY KUN YOUNG KANG, AND DRAGON MANSION**
The Sum of All Questions: Returning to the Clit Club
467

ERIC STANLEY
The Affective Commons:
Gay Shame, Queer Hate, and Other Collective Feelings
489

The Queer Commons Dossiers
AMALLE DUBLON
Second nature / 2nd Nature:
On Ultra-red, TLC, and Dependency
509

CENK ÖZBAY AND EVREN SAVCI
Queering Commons in Turkey
516

DIARMUID HESTER
The Anarcho-Queer Commons of Dennis Cooper's Blog,
The Weaklings: A Brief History
522

MACARENA GÓMEZ-BARRIS
How to Block the Extractive View
527

ASHON CRAWLEY
The Lonely Letters
532

ZACH BLAS
Jubilee 2033
538

Moving Image Review

BONNIE RUBERG

Queerness and Video Games: Queer Game Studies
and New Perspectives through Play

543

Books in Brief

LEON J. HILTON

Living On

557

JORDAN VICTORIAN

Kinking Race Pleasures

560

BRETT FARMER

Impermanent Longings

563

EMMA HEANEY

A Deviant Sexual Type Well before 1870

566

KARA THOMPSON

Unsettled Time, Sensuous Duration:
Methodologies of Native Becoming

569

RAMÓN A. GUTIÉRREZ

Sexual Unruliness in Colonial Latin America

572

About the Contributors

575

PREFACE: FRAGMENT FROM THE *SENSE* *OF BROWN* MANUSCRIPT

José Esteban Muñoz

*B*rown Commons is meant to signify at least two things. One is the commons of brown people, places, feelings, sounds, animals, minerals, flora, and other objects. How these things are brown, or what makes them brown, is partly the way in which they suffer and strive together but also in the commonality of their ability to flourish under duress and pressure. They are brown in part because they have been devalued by the world outside their commons. Their brownness can be known by tackling the ways that global and local forces constantly attempt to degrade their value and diminish their verve. But they are also brown insofar as they smolder with a life and persistence, they are brown because brown is a common color shared by a commons that is of and for the multitude. This is the other sense of brown that I wish to describe. People and things in the commons I am rendering are brown because they share an organicism that is not solely the organic of the natural as much as it is a certain brownness, which is embeddedness in a vast and pulsating social world. Again, not organic like a self-sufficient organism, but organic in that objects within that world touch and are copresent. The Brown commons is not about the production of the individual but instead about a movement, a flow, and an impulse, to move beyond the singular and individualized subjectivities. It is about the swerve of matter, organic and otherwise, the moment of contact, the encounter and all that it can generate. Brownness is about contact and nothing like continuous. Brownness is a being with, being alongside. The story I am telling about a sense of brown is *not* about the formation of atomized brown subjects but, instead, about the task, the endeavor, not of enacting a brown commons but, rather, about knowing a brownness that is our commonality. Furthermore, the brownness

GLQ 24:4
DOI 10.1215/10642684-6957730
© 2018 by Duke University Press

that we share is not knowable in advance. Brownness is not reducible to one object or a thing, so the commons of brownness is not identifiable as any particular thing we have in common.

While I am narrating an expansive brown commons that traverses the regime of the human, the politics that organize this thought experiment are primarily attached to the lives of human actants in larger social ensembles. I am drawn to the idea of a brown commons because it captures the way in which brown people's very being is always a being-in-common. The brown commons is made of feelings, sounds, buildings, neighborhoods, environments, and the nonhuman organic life that might circulate in such an environment alongside humans, the inorganic presences that life is so often attached to. But first and foremost I mean brown as in brown people in a very immediate way, people who are rendered brown by their personal or familial participation in south-to-north migration patterns. I am also thinking of people who are brown by way of accents and linguistic orientations that convey a certain difference. I mean a brownness that is conferred by the ways in which one's spatial coordinates are contested, the ways in which one's right to residency is challenged by those who make false claims to nativity. I also think of brownness in relation to everyday customs and styles of living that connote a sense of illegitimacy. Brown indexes a certain vulnerability to the violence of property, finance, and capital's overarching mechanisms of domination. Also, things are brown by law insofar as even those who can claim legal belonging are still increasingly vulnerable to profiling and other state practices of subordination.

People are brown in their vulnerability to the contempt and scorn of xenophobes, racists, and a class of people who are accustomed to savagely imposing their will on others. Nonhuman brownness is only partially knowable to us through the screen of human perception. But then *everything* I am describing as being brownness is only partially knowable. To think about brownness is to accept that it arrives to us, we attune to it only partially. Pieces resist knowing and being knowable. At best we can be attuned to what brownness does in the world, what it performs, and the sense of the world such performances engender. But we know that some humans are brown in that they feel differently, things are brown in that they radiate a different kind of affect. Affect, as I am employing it in this project, is meant to address a sense of being-in-common as it is transmitted, across people, place, and spaces. Brown affect traverses the rhythmic spacing between those singularities that compose the plurality of a brown commons.

Note

This text is excerpted from Muñoz's "The Brown Commons," a chapter from the *Sense of Brown*, edited by Joshua Chambers-Letson and Tavia Nyong'o, forthcoming from Duke University Press, by permission.

INTRODUCTION

The Queer Commons

Nadja Millner-Larsen and Gavin Butt

$\mathcal{F}$rom one vantage point, "the commons" today might look like the proverbial dodo, facing extinction as a result of neoliberal privatization across the globe. The conventional idea of the commons, as a resource managed by the community that uses it, might appear hopelessly anachronistic in the twenty-first century. At present, increasing amounts of so-called public spaces are actually PoPS (privately owned public spaces), with all the restrictions on access and use that implies; oil industry pipeline incursions threaten indigenous peoples' long-standing use of land and water; and communal spaces are lost to gentrification at alarming rates in cities from London and New York to Jakarta and Johannesburg. When a mere 3 percent of English land, for example, can currently be considered common, and community resources are either threatened or bulldozed, or retained only at the cost of being price-tagged, gated, and policed, it could be said that the commons are running out of time as a category of political economy (Caffentzis 2016: 96). Some might say that they are quite literally *out-of-time*, as an ailing residuum of a precapitalist historical period, and now all too vulnerable to expropriation or removal by rapacious present-day economic forces.

This sense of a commons under threat, or as historically receding, has been paralleled in recent years by the rising power of a populist political cadre in the United States and Europe, seen by some to be acting in the interests of a "common" people alienated by decades of globalization and centrist governments (Garcia 2016). Right- and left-wing populist politicians have fashioned different images of "the people" they claim to represent, but have been united in doing so by distinguishing them from an "elite" class. With the success of the Brexit poll and the US presidential election in 2016, such a politics has come to be variously accompanied by egregious enactments of racial, national, and gendered forms of violence and exclusion. We hardly need to write that in Donald J. Trump such a

GLQ 24:4
DOI 10.1215/10642684-6957744
© 2018 by Duke University Press

politics finds its most lurid expressions, whether in the form of executive orders or tweets, whose purpose is to denigrate or curtail the rights of, for example, Mexican, Sudanese, Haitian, or Iranian migrants; Muslims; Native Americans; women; and trans people. If the history of the commons is also a history of attempts to *enclose it* through fences or other boundaries, then Trump's rhetoric exemplifies how building walls has also come to be a particularly resonant trope for his supporters, among whom are a significant number of conservative white nationalists and supremacists. That the interests of *these* people are presented as those of *the* people within Trump's discourse should be immediately obvious when considering who it attempts to shut out, whether in keeping them on the wrong side of the president's proposed border wall or outside the bathroom door (as a result of a 2017 directive rescinding federal protections therein for trans people). Indeed, Trump's recourse to an ideological notion of a "common people" is yet another symptom of the fact that, as Cheryl Harris (1993) famously argued, whiteness is a form of property that wields its power through claims to a natural (e.g., common) order.

If both the commons and the political solidarity of commoners are being enclosed and distorted in such ways, why bother with the commons as an idea or a thing today? And why the *queer* commons? Answer: because queer activism—not to mention queer life—is a particularly rich resource for imagining, experimenting with, and enacting the improvisational infrastructures necessary for managing the unevenness of contemporary existence.[1] Moreover, while not always labeled as such, grassroots politics in the past decade or two, and queer activism in particular, looks to have been significantly shaped by commons-forming initiatives. As Peter Linebaugh notes (2014: 24), radical activism across the globe from the Arab Spring to Occupy has comprised varied attempts to "common" city squares, from Tahrir Square to Gezi and Zuccotti Parks, and has involved antihierarchical forms of sharing (of food, space, knowledge) and of making decisions. Indeed, much of the encampment politics of Occupy and Gezi were *already* queer and coalitional in their building of a body politic, as some of the contributors to this volume and others suggest.[2] Such collectivized, horizontal forms of organization have also been significant in recent queer activism, from very different groups like FIERCE! in New York and Gay Shame in San Francisco to queer anarchist communities, like those associated with Bash Back! or the Queeruption festivals throughout the 2000s.[3] In the context of the privatizing and commodification of the gay agenda in the twenty-first century—through the mobilization of an individual rights-based politics, the rise of the nonprofit industrial complex,[4] or the enclosing of formerly free Pride festivals quite literally behind pay walls—such groups have worked to build broader political commonalities and establish resources that serve queer communities marginalized by mainstream LGBT politics.

FIERCE!, for example, was founded in 2000 in response to increased criminalization of LGBT youth of color in the gentrifying areas of the Christopher Street Piers in New York City. As a membership-led organization, it seeks to be run *by*, as well as *for*, its users, in order to encourage leadership-in-common and to trouble the divide between a professionalized body of "staff" and "members." This is an organization that emerged in the wake of 1980s and 1990s urban regeneration projects that targeted queer publics and the housing insecure, among other vulnerable populations, in its privatizing drive to subject urban space to a regime of "new enclosures."[5] We should also mention here the trans and queer feminist energies that shape the work of groups like Sisters Uncut and DIY Space for London in the UK, which, though not explicitly or narrowly queer in their political orientation, are notable for mobilizing issues of queerness through campaigning work on domestic violence and decolonization, and through the production of shared social spaces. In general, such instances of "queer commoning"—if indeed that is what we can call them—can be taken as varied ameliorative responses not only to the failures of mainstream LGBT politics but also to twenty-first-century austerity and gentrification: namely, to cuts in the state provision of social services and social housing, and the vanishing of urban infrastructures for the production of contemporary culture.

Crises of capitalism demand such responses, but they also provoke reactionary impulses. As a "cluster of promises," the commons offer a "frame for belonging" in the present whose anachronistic quality appears appealing on all sides (Pardy 2009: 195).[6] And embedded in that sense of a commons under threat is the presumption that the commons did in fact once exist. Indeed, the contemporary strain of leftist thought on the commons certainly revivifies a particular historical formation of English land management predating the rise of capitalism, one whose organizational form, in Silvia Federici's (2011) terms, offers a "historical alternative to both State and Private Property," thus "enabling us to reject the fiction that they are mutually exclusive and exhaustive of our political possibilities." If left-wing political theorists look to the commons as a recoverable site ruined by the spoils of capital, right-wing appeals project a reparative desire for a putatively organic unity lost in the *longue durée* of modernization. It was in his remarkably prescient attempt to develop a Marxist theory of fascism between the world wars that Ernst Bloch articulated his concept of the noncontemporaneous as a contradiction itself produced via the uneven development of capitalism. Such contradictions can be put to either progressive or regressive purposes—as witnessed in the rise of so-called new populism(s) in recent years. The commons might thus usefully be understood as what Bloch (1991: 101) called a "crooked remnant" of the past whose anticapitalist dimension must be harnessed for a critique of "the now." Furthermore, the work of more recent thinkers, including Jean-Luc Nancy, J. K. Gibson-Graham, and J. Kēhaulani Kauanui, press upon us the idea that we have never, in fact, been common, if we take the common to entail a multiplicitous "quality of relations" whose form of community is not singular, pregiven, or circumscribed by the property regimes of capital.[7] They make the argument, in quite disparate ways, that the very idea, even *ideal*, of a commons when instanced within historical formations is entangled with, or compromised by, relations of power that imperil it.[8] Given the contested historical, geographic, and ontological foundations of the commons discourse that these authors survey, we propose to think the commons, following the late José Esteban Muñoz (2009: 1), as an ideality "not yet here." In positioning the commons as a horizon not yet here—that in fact never has been here in any fixed way—the concept's conceptual power is orientated toward the potentiality of a future in which more might be had by the many rather than by the few.

This special issue of *GLQ* takes its lead from some of the initiatives discussed above in order to explore the tentative relation between the *common* and the *queer*. How might the category queer open up a discourse that has emerged as one of the most important challenges to contemporary neoliberalization at both the theoretical and the practical level? Of course, this has proved a difficult task, largely because, as Lauren Berlant (2016: 397) has recently pointed out, the "commons concept" remains "incoherent, like all powerful concepts." So by way of introducing this special issue, we have chosen to pose a number of perspectives on the very queerness of "the commons" and to speculate on how those perspectives might be productively thought through the prerogatives of sexuality studies. If, since the early 1990s, the term *queer*, as George E. Haggerty and Molly McGarry (2007: 1) have argued, has "seemed almost magically to animate both the streets and the academy," activism and critical theory, the club and the literary journal, we have—somewhat remarkably—found the same to be true for the discourse of the commons. Circulating among guerrilla gardeners, prison activists, in DIY spaces, as well as within political philosophy and ecological policy, the concept of the commons has activated a diversity of social, cultural, and critical practices.

Genealogies of the (Queer) Common

Recent cultural theory has variously foregrounded the commons as a resource with nonexclusive rights of access or use, and it has turned to radical ontologies of the common in order to reconsider the essential multiplicity of personhood—a multiplicity (arguably) at the root of queer theory's refutation of the singular subject. Meanwhile, queer studies has also deepened its account of political economy by taking on the sexual economies of neoliberalism, global migration, and the intimacies of social reproduction.[9] But even while the discourse of the commons has developed in concert with feminist theorizations of labor and antiwork politics, the relationship between queer theory and queer life, on the one hand, and accounts of communization, on the other, have typically been held apart.[10] This segregation further disarticulates queer liberation struggles from that of anticapitalist politics and hinders efforts to sustain fugitive models of social reproduction already in practice.[11]

This is all the more curious for, as many of the contributions to this issue attest, sex is *already* central to the discourse of the commons from the perspectives of both its promoters and detractors. On the side of the former, for example, Federici's work has placed sexual demarcation at the root of the commons discourse. Federici's writing, and the activist struggles from which it emerged—the wages for housework movement and the Zerowork collective—provides us with an invaluable set of tools for the issue.[12] The groundbreaking *Caliban and the Witch* traced how the devaluation of women's labor (and communal knowledges) were a direct result of the loss of the commons in the enclosure of the open fields system. Federici (2014: 97) has thus made the extraordinary claim that the long, bloody process that Karl Marx called "primitive accumulation" had the effect of robbing women of communal lands while producing the female body as itself a common "natural resource." This recasting of the history of primitive accumulation, and of reproduction as a site of value creation and accumulation, also accounts for the politicization of multiple forms of sexuality in the middle ages, predating Michel Foucault's assignment of the discursive production of sex in the seventeenth century.[13]

At the center of political philosophy's "return to the commons" has been Michael Hardt and Antonio Negri's influential book *Commonwealth*. Hardt and Negri here famously posed a turn to the singular "common" as opposed to "the commons." The focus on the common emerged from an analysis of the shift in the capitalist economy from industrial production to biopolitical, or immaterial, forms of production alongside the generalization of precarious working conditions. For Hardt (2010a: 135–36), this entailed a shift in the hierarchy of forms of property that has allowed the common to take a central place in economic relations: the productivity of immaterial goods depends on their reproducibility rather than their exclusivity, so their value increases the more it is shared, or "commoned." But Hardt and Negri (2009: 62–63) also lean on the category queer to articulate their concept of the multitude: "The biopolitical event," they write, "is always a queer event, a subversive process of subjectivization that, shattering ruling identities and norms, reveals the link between power and freedom, and thereby inaugurates an alternative production of subjectivity."

Certainly, these thinkers understand the discourse of the commons as one that presents a challenge—or at least an alternative—to the property relations of global capital, and one that might therefore offer us a useful framework for rethinking identity formations beyond what Judith Butler (2005: 136) has called "the self-sufficient 'I' as a kind of possession." If the beginnings of proletarianization are at the root of sexual demarcation, then we might also see the project of abolishing the wage contract (central to those activist struggles in which Federici has been embedded, and Hardt and Negri draw on) as a precondition for abolishing normative sexual identities.[14] Indeed, *Commonwealth* situates the queer critique of identity as a crucial ground to launch the project of the abolition of identity at the core of the common's "abolition of property and the abolition of the state" (Hardt and Negri 2009: 333–34)—a critique mobilized across numerous strains of "communization theory."[15] But beyond mere critique, Hardt and Negri, like other Autonomist thinkers, are indebted to the black radical tradition's conceptualization of revolutionary transformation as essentially abolitionist—a project of both tearing down and building up that is crucial to any queer engagement with the discourse of the commons.[16]

On the side of the commons' detractors, Garrett Hardin's infamous "Tragedy of the Commons" (1968) is also cut through with preoccupations regarding sexual reproduction and the ruination of public resources. For Hardin, the category of the open pasture serves as a placeholder for a certain "sex panic" induced by a racialized and gendered anxiety over the purported excesses of the US welfare state.[17] This is an anxiety that, as Beth Capper and Arlen Austin discuss in their contribution to this issue, prefigures the "welfare queen" myth produced and popularized in the Reagan and Clinton presidencies. This image of the oversexed and unwed black mother (one recently resurrected by Trump[18]) promoted the fantasy that, as Angela Mitropoulos (2012: 192) has argued, "welfare had catastrophically supplanted the labour market as a source of income, just as it had displaced the normative family as the appropriate site of care and support." With the welfare queen as its figurehead, the notion of a "culture of dependency" trumpeted by a neoliberal war on the poor reveals a deep preoccupation with forms of intimacy on the part of the state—a complex domopolitics that has been expertly traced by queer scholars of neoliberalism including Dean Spade, Lisa Duggan, David Eng, and Lauren Berlant, among others.[19] Moreover, as Spade has shown, these antipoor preoccupations went hand in hand with gentrification and the expansion of imprisonment in the United States. This sex panic (prefigured by Hardin) has resulted in a literal enclosure of life in the prison system and the continued targeting of the poor, sex workers, migrants, people with disabilities, those of color, and trans people.[20] Contemporary thinkers have paid close attention to how "the escalating onslaught of violent, state-orchestrated enclosures following neoliberalism's ascent to hegemony has unmistakably demonstrated the *persistent* role that unconcealed, violent dispossession continues to play in the reproduction of colonial and capitalist social relations in both the domestic and global contexts" (Coulthard 2014: 9).

In his contribution to this volume, Eric Stanley traces the devastating effects of such violent neoliberal policies for the city of San Francisco. Writing about the campaigns of Gay Shame against the dispossessions caused by white cis-normative urban privatization in the 2000s, Stanley highlights the complicity of LGBT organizations and municipal authorities in developing "public" spaces requiring the enforced removal of undesirable bodies. Drawing out the importance of critiques of settler colonialism for trans/queer activist responses to gentrification, Stanley also calls our attention to another significant aspect of thinking the common as a category distinct from the private or the public. Indeed, as Marina Vishmidt (2015) points out, "the category of 'the public' . . . was only ever established through contracts of exclusion (women, racialised or migrant others, the poor)" and "access to 'public goods' has never been simply defined in terms of universal rights . . . resources are allocated on the basis of particular kinds of legal status, themselves the result of the classification of people into ethno-nationalistic categories."[21] Such a perspective makes clear—again—how the accumulation and demarcation of difference is central to the development of capitalism, and the enclosure and reenclosure of the commons on which it depends. Considering the discourse of a queer commons thus demands an examination of how identity formations continue to be produced and reproduced through racialized and gendered "property statuses" that accompany legal infrastructures such as the marriage bond, but also function through the historical organization of "chattel slavery, land theft, and genocide" (Spade 2011: 31).

The category of the commons is further tricky to mobilize because it is not, in some contexts, *necessarily* incompatible with the interests of capital. As many critiques of Hardt and Negri's thesis have pointed out, if cognitive capitalism produces conditions of communization, so too does it create new conditions for capital accumulation. The more policy-oriented leftist discourses of the commons (such as those of Elinor Ostrom and David Bollier) view the commons not as a determinate negation of the state and the market but as a way to temper some of neoliberalism's most rampant forms of marketization. At a more nefarious level, the discourse of the commons has also been appropriated by various corporate and governing bodies—from the World Bank to the UN—to justify, for example, the "protection" of lands previously managed by those who lived on them.[22] To take a particularly violent example, the Israeli state has turned to the category of public land to justify the continued dispossession of Palestinian commons.[23] As Ash Amin and Philip Howell (2016: 5-6) have written, issues of migration, of "the free movement of labor, not to mention the rights of refugees and exiles have become . . . source[s] of grievances over entitlements to shrinking common-pool resources." A politics of the commons, they argue, can be quite easily mobilized in the service of neoliberal/neoconservative interests where any "'common' reduced to the 'public' becomes wholly complicit" in such practices.

Such systems of appropriation dovetail with another important critique of the commons central to our endeavor. A number of articles included here point to the problem of the discourse's tendency to occlude forms of land dispossession central to settler colonialism. Both the concept's "capitalocentrism" and its tendency to overlook the particularities of indigeneity arise from the centrality of the theory of primitive accumulation to the "resuscitation" of the commons.[24] As capital's foundational drama, Marx's theory proposed a formative link between violent acts of dispossession ("conquest, enslavement, robbery, murder") and the emergence of capitalist accumulation. In the forced removal of commoners (peasants, women, indigenous peoples) from their land, once collectively maintained territories and resources are opened up for enclosure (and privatization). This process establishes the precondition for the institution of capitalist relations, which produces a "class" of workers "free" to enter the wage relation in order to ensure their survival—a process otherwise known as proletarianization. In privileging the production of the proletarian worker, this narrative tends to occlude forms of access, use, and dispossession that both pre- and postdate capital's origin story. Both Glen Coulthard and Federici provide an important conceptual shift in thinking the history of capitalism away from the perspective of the (white cis) male waged worker toward that of the colonized. Coulthard (2014: 12) cautions against a "blanket 'return to the commons'" when "the 'commons' not only belong to somebody—*the First Peoples of this land*—they also deeply inform and sustain Indigenous modes of thought and behavior that harbor profound insights into the maintenance of relationships within and between human beings and the natural world built on principles of reciprocity, nonexploitation and respectful coexistence." Such an approach to the commons would not only downplay histories of colonial dispossession but also risk overlooking the kinds of practices that might actually invoke a repatterning of the social in an ethical and just way.

The centrality of land—as a site of belonging, topography, or ordering of space—to the discourse of the commons might in fact aid us in recentering issues of indigenous sovereignty into queer responses to state power.[25] In this issue, Macarena Gómez-Barris identifies what she calls "an extractive view" of land and territory that "empties the land of Native peoples . . . to assert the legitimacy of dominant modes of seeing that divide nature from the human." Exploring the photography of Laura Aguilar, a queer Chicana artist who pictures her body in the landscapes of New Mexico and California, Gómez-Barris elucidates the artist's queer challenge to this "view" of such lands. In using her naked body to echo the folds and contours of the landscape, Aguilar shows us "that it is still (in)visibly saturated with Indigenous and Mestiza presence." And in their analysis of resistance to the gentrification plans announced in 2013 for Gezi Park, Istanbul, Cenk Özbay and Evren Savcı draw attention to the difficulties of modern-day claims to commons ideals once "uneven histories of dispossession" of a particular space or territory are unearthed. Indeed, part of the task of establishing a queer commons, they argue, is to "intervene in the erasures neoliberalism performs on collective memories of public space," thereby allowing potentially competing claims and grievances—historic and contemporary—to animate and inform future uses made of it. All these contributors agree that such a difficult reckoning with past uses (and abuses) of space, in relation to present-day realities, is an ethical and political requirement for any queer commons worth pursuing. Rather than dismiss the discourse altogether, Coulthard (2014: 8) argues that "when placed in dialogue with feminist, anarchist, queer and postcolonial traditions, it can be useful for analyzing the relationship between white settler states and indigenous peoples."

A similar rewiring of the commons concept's problematic reliance on a normative idea of the resource might also be possible when entered into a dialogue with queer studies. Many engagements on the part of environmental justice movements tend to think of the commons as one or another "natural resource"—from land to air, oceans, or forests. For Hardt, there are two contrasting versions of the common resource—if ecological movements tend to envision commons as inherently limited and thus in need of protection, those focused on social forms of the common (movements for net neutrality, for example) tend to see their object as a limitless sphere of production. Nevertheless, even while Hardt (2010b: 266) argues that both forms of the common "defy and are deteriorated by property relations," they are dominated by the concept of the resource. Such an understanding of the commons, in Linebaugh's (2008: 279) terms, is "misleading at best and dangerous at worst[, for] the commons . . . expresses relationships in society that are inseparable to nature. It might be better to keep the word as a verb, an activity, rather than as a noun, a substantive. But this too is a trap. Capitalists and the World Bank would like us to employ commoning as a means to socialize poverty and privatize wealth." The rejection of a notion of the commons as an object to be found in the world dovetails with the Midnight Notes Collective's contention that commons are actually relations of solidarity—a contention that echoes the influence of more anarchist practices such as mutual aid and prefiguration (Caffentzis 2016: 101).

But we would caution against dispensing with the resource version of the concept quite so fast—for it has been a great province of queer activism and queer life more broadly to transform what is normatively perceived as lack (of capacity, able-bodiedness, decorum, or representation) into a shared resource.[26] Douglas Crimp's argument, for example, in "How to Have Promiscuity in an Epidemic" (1987) revalued sex as itself a resource to be mined, valued, proliferated, celebrated—and creatively managed by its community of users—during the continuing AIDS crisis. The beginnings of the AIDS crisis figure strongly in what few previous mentions of a "queer commons" predate this volume.[27] Both Kevin Floyd (2004) and Gavin Brown (2015) have looked to gay cruising sites in areas such as Christopher Street or Jackson Heights in New York and sites of "common ground" like "forests, heath and beaches," respectively, where queer uses of space revalue them as resources that are not reducible to property ownership (Brown 2015: 208). In these pages, Amalle Dublon's examination of Ultra-red's *Second Nature* offers us a reading of sex's unrepresentability as an *aesthetic resource* for the production of a queer pastoral imaginary. Exploring the sexual commons of black and Latinx queers in Griffith Park, Los Angeles, Dublon critiques the ideals of pastoral art that have contributed to received imaginaries of the commons and foregrounds instead Ultra-red's "contrarian noise" of sexual contact and policing.

The late 1980s and early 1990s is an era that looms large for other contributors to this volume. Christina Hanhardt, and the collective of writers comprising Julie Tolentino, Leeroy Kun Young Kang, Tara Hart, Vivian A. Crockett, Amira Khusro, and Dragon Mansion, consider the troublesome question of how, if at all, a queer commons might be representable, especially as a heterogeneous and maligned body politic. For Hanhardt, in her detailed study of the needle exchange programs of ACT UP, the problem is one of how, if at all, differently maligned groups within a single activist organization could join political forces. The maligning of addicts as a "throwaway class" of persons causes Hanhardt to speculate on the "lumpen" character of ACT UP's political constituency—as an under- or nonclass. Tolentino et al. draw on Stefano Harney and Fred Moten's important thinking on "the undercommons" to characterize the kinds of sensual, sexual, and social connections made at New York's sex-positive Clit Club throughout the

1990s. The club became renowned for its openness to varied forms of gender presentation and oft-decried sexual practices, as well as welcoming people from racial groups and economic backgrounds otherwise denigrated by other gay clubs and negatively affected by policing and gentrification in New York City at the time. In trying to "get with the undercommon sensuality," the authors collectively draw on Harney and Moten's ideas about a fugitive blackness to riff the multifarious and somewhat unmanageable object that Clit Club appears to be when viewed through the retrospective lenses of "history" and "scholarship."

These examples of queer organizing—and pleasure—also underscore the fact that the commons discourse is not only about envisioning new models of public, collective, or common ownership. It is also, importantly, about transforming the modes of social reproduction on which such mechanisms depend, for, as Federici (2011: 6) points out, "the 'commoning' of the material means of reproduction is the primary mechanism by which a collective interest and mutual bonds are created." In this sense, the verb form "commoning" also refers to a performative project (Joseph 2017: 212). As Rana Jaleel (2013) has usefully argued in one of the few previous efforts to articulate a queer politics of commoning, this "would place the politics of social regeneration alongside queer efforts to belong to, care for, and be dependent on others in ways that endure."

Beth Capper and Arlen Austin turn to a slightly earlier history in order to take up the politics of social reproduction. In their examination of two specific autonomous groups within the 1970s Wages for Housework movement—Wages Due Lesbians and Black Women for Wages for Housework—Capper and Austin take up two lines of inquiry that further trouble any reading of Federici's feminism as narrowly heteronormative. First, they probe Federici's provocation about how coming out as a lesbian might be understood as a kind of "going on strike" (in refusing reproductive labor). Second, they explore nonnormativizing claims on the figure of the housewife by black feminist activists agitating for political alliances between black sex workers and domestic laborers. Braiding both of these together, Capper and Austin return to the scene of 1970s feminism in order to identify within it political tendencies from which to articulate a queer "uncommon" theory and praxis.

While many political theorists of the common discussed above draw on Marxian categories to articulate ongoing forms of what David Harvey (2003) calls "accumulation by dispossession," those more indebted to the trajectories of critical race theory, queer theory, ethnic studies, black studies, and cultural studies more broadly have reclaimed the category of *dis*possession as a site of radical un/ reworlding in the face of ongoing crisis. Muñoz's own articulations of a "brown commons" are indebted to this strain of critical thinking that includes, among others, the work of Lauren Berlant, Moten and Harney, and J. Jack Halberstam and Tavia Nyong'o. In common with Berlant (2016: 395), these thinkers all emphasize "*non*sovereign relationality"—a radically *dis*possessed self—as "the foundational quality of being in common," and recast politics itself as a site that is, fundamentally improvisational, potentially antagonistic, and even extralegal.[28] In this volume, Ashon Crawley draws on this trajectory of contemporary thought in his experimental address to thinking and feeling the queer relationality of black Pentecostalism. Here he uses the form of an epistolary exchange between "A" and "Moth" as a way to allegorize "the renunciation of the subject for the entangled folds of blackness" as itself a revaluation of dispossession. As Crawley (2017: 24–25) writes, in another context, "Otherwise names the subjectivity in the commons, an asubjectivity that is not about the enclosed self but the open, available, enfleshed organism."

Contributors to this issue thereby draw on multiple trajectories to provide analyses equally attuned to the material conditions of colonial dispossession and the possibilities of a nonaccumulative repossession through the trajectories of queer worlding. Yet our best resource for such a project is still the work of Muñoz, the only scholar to date who has repeatedly brought the queer and the common together in his late thinking on the punk rock commons and the brown commons.[29] Muñoz's scholarship offers us an important engagement with another genealogy of the commons concept—that developed by Jean-Luc Nancy. In this late work, Muñoz describes queerness as a mode of "being-with" emergent in the forms of encounter that animate punk rock sociality. The queer commons, for Muñoz, is a nonexploitative utopian collectivity that is nevertheless grounded in punk's politics of the negative. By mining Nancy's concept of the singular-plural, Muñoz develops a notion of community as one that is aleatory, improvisatory, and essentially multiplicitous rather than homogenized and holistic. Crucially this community is always in the process of becoming, orienting itself toward future, potential queer worlds (Muñoz 2013b: 96).

Muñoz's summoning of the singular-plural calls on us to creatively explore radical ontologies of the common from the scene of the punk club to that of the network. This call is answered in this issue by contributions from Zach Blas and Diarmuid Hester, who explore social, technological, and imaginary communities made possible through encounters within DIY queer networks.[30] Punk is a touchstone for Blas and Hester, as it is for Muñoz, underscoring its importance as a generative cultural moment and set of cultural practices for thinking through the shape of a queer commons, specifically in the figuring or creating of anarchist or quasi-anarchistic, self-organizing communities.[31] Riffing on Derek Jarman's dystopian imagining of a punk future in his 1978 film *Jubilee*, Blas renders a twenty-first-century update of this vision, looking forward to 2033: the date of the internet's silver jubilee. Blas's point is to imagine a future for queer sociality *after* the internet, indeed "contra-internet," as he terms it, where an "infrastructural commons" exists beyond the corporatized web. Hester explores the fraught autonomy of a queer commons in his exploration of the blog of a gay poet and novelist, Dennis Cooper. Looking back over the removal of Cooper's blog by Google in 2016, he highlights the vulnerability of queer contacts to corporate erasure while reminding us of their ability to persist in the most inhospitable of places.

The attempt to conceptualize a new discourse of commoning signals, at bottom, a search for alternative models of organizing life beyond those produced by the state and the market. This is a question that has remained at the heart of queer studies since its inception. Reestablishing dispossession at the core of the commons concept as a central feature of our critical engagements with contemporary capitalism opens up the possibility of developing a critique that is equally attentive to the foundational "we" of personhood as it is to the climate(s) within which we navigate our social lives.

Always Been Common

To return to the present conditions from where we began this introduction, right-wing populism defines the "common people" as a culturally homogeneous grouping whose interests are posed in contrast to those of "others" whose false threat of encroachment is continuously reimagined as a fantasy of the unruly exterior. Trump's rhetorical reversals pose the nation as a "surrounded fort" facing threats from all manner of outsides—the migrant, the black, the brown, the queer. But as Harney and Moten (2013: 17) begin *The Undercommons*, this is not, in fact, a "false image." The "fort" really is "surrounded, is besieged by what still surrounds it, the common beyond and beneath—before and before—enclosure." The wall must be built because the common has already made its way through it before enclosure, the bathroom must be privatized because it has already been made public. We have never been common and we have always been common, but our task remains: to disturb "the facts on the ground with some outlaw planning" (ibid.).

"We cannot represent ourselves. We can't be represented," write Harney and Moten (ibid.: 20). These words have reverberated for us in multiple ways as we have put this issue together. It is, in part, why we have solicited multiple forms of writing from our contributors, from long-form scholarly essays and collectively authored writings mixing analysis with community testimony to shorter writings presented here in a "Dossier." In the latter, contributors have written speculative futural imaginings, tightly focused case studies, and experimental epistolary exchanges. Our hope is that across this collection of diverse works, the promise of the "we" of a queer commons might begin to be heard, even if, ultimately, it is infested with dissensus and in excess of what these pages contain. The queer common is not yet here, but it has also already been happening in the "experiment of the hold," in the "engaged dispossession" of study, in the queer encampments from Gezi Square to Oakland, and in the underground networks of hormone exchange.[32]

We begin this special issue with an excerpt from Muñoz's forthcoming book *Sense of Brown*, which the author was working on at the time of his death in 2013, and which is a crucial complement to his work on punk and critical utopianism. Growing out of Muñoz's work on the queer world-making practices of queer artists of color, he formulates an understanding of a *brown* commons as ways of being-together forged by people surviving, even thriving, in the face of racist, neocolonial, and capitalist forms of subjugation and control. Importantly, this politicized "sense" of brown here is not only avowedly intersectional across categories of identity—of ethnicity, linguistic use, gender, sexuality, class—but also *more than human*. It is an affective continuum arising out of people *and* things, "of feelings, sounds, buildings, neighborhoods, environments, and nonhuman organic life." Moreover, it is made up of relations *between* these things, encounters among them that cannot be known in advance. "Brownness is about contact. . . . [it] is a being with, being alongside."

The brown commons also entails a particular turn to the material of the past. As "an homage to the history of Brown Power," this is a commons born from an insurrectionism embedded in "the sense of brown in the Chicana walk out of 1968" and in the brown of "the brown berets." This is a relationship to the liberationist past that is not enclosed by nostalgia. Rather, Muñoz turns to the past to make "the point that the world is not becoming brown but has been brown." It is in this materialist spirit that contributors to this issue approach the past—not as a site from which to imagine a commons free from social antagonism but in order to wrestle with the material traces of insurrectionism from which to build urgent political imaginaries for the present. From the dance floor of the Clit Club to the tracts of Wages Due Lesbians and Black Women for Wages for Housework, to the runway rage of Gay Shame and the coalition building of ACT UP's needle exchange—these histories challenge us "to touch queer and trans history," in an attempt not to authorize or master it as a grand narrative but to aid us in realizing a critical utopianism borne from the realization "that one is not starting anything but [is] instead fortunate enough to be a participant in something vaster, something common."[33]

Notes

1.   Lauren Berlant (2016: 394) has recently addressed the role of the commons in the context of "the infrastructural breakdown of modernist practices of resource distribution, social relation, and affective continuity." At such moments of crisis, the political, as Berlant suggests, comes to be understood as the reinvention of infrastructures for managing the violent contingencies of contemporary life. Alternative infrastructural practices of association and care have been one of the great provinces of queer life and activism.

2.   See Özbay and Savcı, this issue. See also Jaleel 2013; Pérez Navarro 2016; Vivian 2013; and Millner-Larsen 2013.

3.   On Queeruption, see Brown 2007. On Bash back!, see Baroque and Eanelli 2011.

4.   See Spade 2011: 28.

5.   This is the Midnight Notes Collective's term (1990). On the impact of "Quality of Life" campaigns on queer sociality, see Delany 1999.

6.   Maree Pardy (2009) uses these terms to describe the affective texture of multiculturalism.

7.   Federici (2012) has warned that the concept of "community" must be intended not "as a gated reality," or as a social grouping based on race, ethnicity, religion, or exclusive interests, "but rather as a quality of relations, a principle of cooperation and of responsibility to each other and to the earth, the forests, the seas, the animals."

8.   As Jean-Luc Nancy (1991: xxxix) has warned, "The community that becomes *a single* thing (body, mind, fatherland, Leader . . .) necessarily loses the *in* of being-in-common." Where J. K. Gibson-Graham, Jenny Cameron, and Stephen Healy (2016: 196) contend that "the community that commons is not pregiven . . . [but] constituted through the process of commoning," such modalities of being-in-common are occluded in the kind of community touted by the populist right. To frame the noncontemporaneity of the commons within a discourse of nostalgia is, ultimately, yet another form of enclosure, for, as J. Kēhaulani Kauanui (2013) has argued, the concept is itself "historically racialized and gendered." By tracing the discourse's entanglement in the history of the North American expropriation of indigenous land by English settlers, Kauanui shows that the commons is *not* an ideal space outside the violence of property relations.

9.   See, especially, Eng 2010; and Duggan 2003. The *GLQ* special issue "Queer Studies and the Crisis of Capitalism" (Rosenberg and Villarejo 2012) provides an important set of tools in this regard.

10.   While less widely acknowledged, Autonomist discourses of the commons are also

indebted to the black radical tradition as well as feminist Marxism(s). See James, Lee, and Chaulieu 1974.

11. We are thinking here of the networks of care that have flourished in queer communities in the absence of state provisions as well as the fugitivity of "undercommon appositionality" that Stefano Harney and Fred Moten (2013) locate in the practice of black study. The trajectories traced here would be impossible without the important work of Harney and Moten which we discuss further toward the end of this introduction.

12. In *Wages against Housework*, Federici ([1975] 2012) famously points to the fact that neither heterosexuality nor homosexuality eliminate work. Both, for her, imply particular working conditions, where if homosexuality signifies worker control of the means of production, it cannot in itself realize the goal of overcoming the wage relation.

13. "The witch trials provide an instructive list of the forms of sexuality that were banned as 'non-productive': homosexuality, sex between young and old, sex between people of different classes, anal coitus, coitus from behind (reputedly leading to sterile relations), nudity, and dances. Also proscribed was the public, collective sexuality that had prevailed in the middle ages" (Federici 2014: 194). Carolyn Dinshaw's (1999) work on medieval sexualities is also instructive here.

14. Hardt and Negri echo the argument of Théorie Communiste, that the abolition of the value-form would require a process of self-abolition. See Mattin 2013: 53–67. It should be noted that the discourse of self-abolition often overlooks the "standpoint," in Harney and Moten's (2013: 93) words, "of those who had already been abolished and remained."

15. Much communization theory (Tiqqun and the Invisible Committee, Théorie Communiste, and others) is critical of Hardt and Negri's position, but the role of self-abolition in the contestation of capital is nevertheless central to this radical strain of contemporary thought, and one that has recently been mobilized within queer anarchism and Marxist feminism(s). On the potential intersections of communization theory and "anti-essentialist critiques of raced and gendered identities—gender abolitionist feminism, queer insurrectionism, and Afro-pessimism" (Palace 2012), see *LIES: A Journal of Materialist Feminism*. On communization theory more broadly, see Noys 2012.

16. Angela Davis (2005: 73) describes W. E. B. DuBois's concept of an "abolition democracy" as not only "a negative process of tearing down, but it is also about building up, about creating new institutions." On abolition as "already and of necessity the struggle for the promise of communism, decolonization, and settler decolonization," see Jared Sexton (2016: 593). On Italian Autonomism's relation to the black radical tradition in general, and the work of C. L. R. James in particular, see Harney and Moten 2013: 65.

17. For more on the logic of the sex panic, see Duggan 2006: 71–76.

18. See Chang 2017.

19. Dean Spade (2011: 112–19) describes how the Reagan presidency mobilized this

mythic image as part of its campaign to dismantle social assistance programs in the 1990s.

20. See Spade 2011: 53–55.

21. For a parallel argument on gender as property in the field of critical legal studies, see Katyal 2017.

22. See Caffentzis 2016: 99.

23. See Wolfe 2013: 257–79.

24. See Harvey 2003. On the "capitalocentrism" of the commons concept, see Gibson-Graham, Cameron, and Healy 2016.

25. On indigenous sovereignty and land use, see Byrd 2011.

26. Thanks to Park McArthur, Constantina Zavitsanos, and Jeannine Tang for helping us to articulate this point.

27. Here, Lauren Berlant and Michael Warner's foundational essay "Sex in Public" (1998) is a resource on the radicality of queer sexual culture, as is Warner's (2014) important work on counterpublics.

28. For more on the extralegality of revolutionary politics, see Harney and Moten 2013: 18.

29. This special issue of *GLQ* was initially conceived by Gavin Butt and José Esteban Muñoz in 2013. As has been widely acknowledged, Muñoz's untimely death that year robbed contemporary study of a uniquely dynamic and campaigning voice. It also brought to a sudden end his pioneering work on the commons. This issue, we hope, albeit belatedly, recognizes the generative importance of Muñoz's work in this area. The guest editors dedicate this special issue to his memory.

30. Blas is part of a collective of writers who have also previously considered the "queer commons." See Barrett et al. 2016.

31. See Butt 2016.

32. On "the experiment of the hold," see Harney and Moten 2013: 99. "Engaged dispossession" is Halberstam's term (2013: 5). On genderhacking, see Mary Maggic's DIY biohacking project, "Open Source Estrogen" (2015), Ryan Hammond's "Open Source Gendercodes (OSG)" (2016), and Preciado 2013. Contemporary biohacking projects also have roots in queer activism's campaigns for access to knowledge from the beginnings of the AIDS crisis.

33. All above quotes in this paragraph are taken from Muñoz 2013a.

References

Amin, Ash, and Philip Howell. 2016. "Thinking the Commons." In *Releasing the Commons: Rethinking the Futures of the Commons*, edited by Ash Amin and Philip Howell, 1–17. New York: Routledge.

Baroque, Fray, and Tegan Eanelli, eds. 2011. *Queer Ultraviolence: Bashback! Anthology.* San Francisco: Ardent.

Barrett, Fiona, Zach Blas, Micha Cárdenas, Jacob Gaboury, Jessica Marie Johnson, and Margaret Rhee. 2016. "QueerOS: A User's Manual." *Debates in the Digital Humanities*. dhdebates.gc.cuny.edu/debates/text/56.

Berlant, Lauren. 2016. "The Commons: Infrastructures for Troubling Times." *Environment and Planning D: Society and Space* 34, no. 3: 393–419.

Berlant, Lauren, and Michael Warner. 1998. "Sex in Public." *Critical Inquiry* 24, no. 2: 547–56.

Bloch, Ernst. 1991. *Heritage of Our Times*. Translated by Neville Plaice and Stephen Plaice. Berkeley: University of California Press.

Brown, Gavin. 2007. "Mutinous Eruptions: Autonomous Spaces of Radical Queer Activism." *Environment and Planning A: Economy and Space* 39, no. 11: 2685–98.

———. 2015. "Marriage and the Spare Bedroom: Exploring the Sexual Politics of Austerity in Britain." *ACME: An International E-Journal for Critical Geographies* 14, no. 4: 975–88.

Butler, Judith. 2005. *Giving an Account of Oneself*. New York: Fordham University Press.

Butt, Gavin. 2016. "Being in a Band: Artschool Experiment and the Post-Punk Commons." In *Post-Punk Then and Now*, edited by Gavin Butt, Kodwo Eshun, and Mark Fisher, 57–83. London: Repeater.

Byrd, Jodi A. 2011. *The Transit of Empire: Indigenous Critiques of Colonialism*. Minneapolis: University of Minnesota Press.

Caffentzis, George. 2016. "Commons." In *Keywords for Radicals: The Contested Vocabulary of Late-Capitalist Struggle*, edited by Kelly Fritsch and Claire O'Connor, 93–101. Chico, CA: AK Press.

Chang, Clio. 2017. "Trump Is Resurrecting the Myth of the Welfare Queen." *Splinter News*, October 16.

Coulthard, Glen. 2014. *Red Skin, White Masks: Rejecting the Colonial Politics of Recognition*. Minneapolis: University of Minnesota Press.

Crawley, Ashon. 2017. *Blackpentecostal Breath: The Aesthetics of Possibility*. New York: Fordham University Press.

Crimp, Douglas. 1987. "How to Have Promiscuity in an Epidemic." *October* 43: 237–71.

Davis, Angela Y. 2005. *Abolition Democracy: Beyond Empire, Prisons, and Torture*. New York: Seven Stories.

Delany, Samuel. 1999. *Times Square Red, Times Square Blue*. New York: New York University Press.

Dinshaw, Carolyn. 1999. *Getting Medieval: Sexualities and Communities, Pre- and Postmodern*. Durham, NC: Duke University Press.

Duggan, Lisa. 2003. *Twilight of Equality? Neoliberalism, Cultural Politics, and the Attack on Democracy*. New York: Beacon.

———. 2006. "Sex Panics." In *Sex Wars: Sexual Dissent and Political Culture*, edited by Lisa Duggan and Nan D. Hunter, 71–76. New York: Routledge.

Eng, David. 2010. *The Feeling of Kinship: Queer Liberalism and the Racialization of Inti-macy.* Durham, NC: Duke University Press.

Federici, Silvia. [1975] 2012. "Wages against Housework." In *Revolution at Point Zero: Housework, Reproduction, and Feminist Struggle*, 15–22. Oakland, CA: PM.

———. 2011. "Feminism and the Politics of the Commons." *The Commoner: A Web Journal for Other Values*, January 24. www.commoner.org.uk/wp-content /uploads/2011/01/federici-feminism-and-the-politics-of-commons.pdf.

———. 2012. "Feminism and the Politics of the Commons." In *The Wealth of the Commons*, edited by David Bollier and Silke Helfrich. Amherst, MA: Levellers. wealthofthecommons.org/essay/feminism-and-politics-commons

———. 2014. *Caliban and the Witch: Women, the Body, and Primitive Accumulation.* 2nd rev. ed. Brooklyn: Autonomedia.

Floyd, Kevin. 2004. *The Reification of Desire: Toward a Queer Marxism.* Minneapolis: University of Minnesota Press.

Garcia, Catherine. 2016. "Putin Praises Trump for 'Representing the Common People.'" *The Week*, October 27. theweek.com/speedreads/658069/putin-praises-trump -representing-common-people.

Gibson-Graham, J. K., Jenny Cameron, and Stephen Healy. 2016. "Commoning as a Post-capitalist Politics." In *Releasing the Commons: Rethinking the Futures of the Com-mons*, edited by Ash Amin and Philip Howell, 192–212. New York: Routledge.

Haggerty, George E., and Molly McGarry. 2007. Introduction to *A Companion to Lesbian, Gay, Bisexual, Transgender and Queer Studies*, edited by George E. Haggerty and Molly McGarry, 1–14. Chichester, UK: Wiley-Blackwell.

Halberstam, J. Jack. 2013. The Wild Beyond: With and for the Undercommons." In *The Undercommons: Fugitive Planning and Black Study*, by Stefano Harney and Fred Moten, 5–12. Brooklyn: Autonomedia.

Hardin, Garrett. 1968. "The Tragedy of the Commons." *Science* 162: 1243–48.

Hardt, Michael. 2010a. "The Common in Communism." *The Idea of Communism*, edited by Costas Douzinas and Slavoj Žižek. London: Verso.

———. 2010b. "Two Faces of Apocalypse: A Letter from Copenhagen." *Polygraph* 22: 265–74.

Hardt, Michael, and Antonio Negri. 2009. *Commonwealth.* Cambridge, MA: Harvard University Press.

Harris, Cheryl. 1993. "Whiteness as Property." *Harvard Law Review* 106, no. 8: 1709–91.

Harney, Stefano, and Fred Moten. 2013. *The Undercommons: Fugitive Planning and Black Study.* Brooklyn: Autonomedia.

Harvey, David. 2003. *The New Imperialism.* Oxford: Oxford University Press.

Jaleel, Rana. 2013. "A Queer Home in the Midst of a Movement? Occupy Homes, Occupy Homemaking." In *Periscope: Is This What Democracy Looks Like?*, edited by A. J.

Bauer, Cristina Beltran, Rana Jaleel, and Andrew Ross. what-democracy-looks-like
.org/a-queer-home-in-the-midst-of-a-movement-occupy-homes-occupy-homemaking/.

James, C. L. R., Grace C. Lee, and Pierre Chaulieu. 1974. *Facing Reality.* Detroit, MI:
Bewick Editions.

Joseph, Miranda. 2017. "Community, Collectivity, Affinities." In *A Companion to Critical
and Cultural Theory,* edited by Imre Szeman, Sarah Blacker, and Justin Sully,
205–21. Hoboken, NJ: Wiley-Blackwell.

Katyal, Sonia K. 2017. "The Numerous Clauses of Sex." *University of Chicago Law
Review* 84, no. 1: 389–494.

Kauanui, J. Kēhaulani. 2013. "Nothing Common about 'The Commons': Settler Colonialism and the Indigenous Politics of Land Dispossession." Paper presented at Brown
University, Providence, RI, October 9.

Linebaugh, Peter. 2008. *The Magna Carta Manifesto: Liberties and Commons for All.*
Berkeley: University of California Press.

———. 2014. *Stop, Thief! The Commons, Enclosures, and Resistance.* Oakland, CA: PM.

Mattin. 2013. "Improvisation and Communization." In *Undoing Property,* edited by Mary-
sia Lewandowska and Laurel Ptak, 53–67. Berlin: Sternberg.

Midnight Notes Collective. 1990. "The New Enclosures." *Midnight Notes* 10. www
.midnightnotes.org/newenclos.html.

Millner-Larsen, Nadja. 2013. "Demandless Times." *WSQ* 41: 113–30.

Mitropoulos, Angela. 2012. *Contract and Contagion: From Biopolitics to Oikonomia.*
Brooklyn, NY: Autonomedia.

Muñoz, José Esteban. 2009. *Cruising Utopia: The Then and There of Queer Futurity.*
New York: New York University Press.

———. 2013a. "The Brown Commons: The Sense of Wildness." Paper presented at
Eastern Michigan University, March 25.

———. 2013b. "'Gimme Gimme This . . . Gimme Gimme That': Annihilation and Innovation in the Punk Rock Commons." *Social Text,* no. 116: 95–110.

Nancy, Jean-Luc. 1991. *The Inoperative Community.* Edited by Peter Connor. Minneapolis: University of Minnesota Press.

Noys, Benjamin, ed. 2012. *Communization and Its Discontents.* Brooklyn, NY:
Autonomedia.

Palace, Sky. 2012. "'To Be Liberated from Them (or through Them)': A Call for a New
Approach." *LIES: A Journal of Materialist Feminism* 1: 209–14.

Pardy, Maree. 2009. "The Shame of Waiting." In *Waiting,* edited by Ghassan Hage,
195–209. Carlton, Aus.: Melbourne University Press.

Pérez Navarro, Pablo. 2016. "'Where Is My Tribe'? Queer Activism in the Occupy Movements." *Interalia: A Journal of Queer Studies.* www.interalia.org.pl/en/artykuly/on_a
_rolling_basis/where_is_my_tribe_queer_activism_in_the_occupy_movements.htm.

Preciado, [Paul] B. 2013. *Testo Junkie: Sex, Drugs, and Biopolitics in the Pharmacopor-
nographic Era.* Translated by Bruce Benderson. New York: Feminist Press.

Rosenberg, Jordana, and Amy Villarejo, eds. 2012. "Queer Studies and the Crisis of Capitalism." *GLQ* 18, no. 1.

Sexton, Jared. 2016. "The *Vel* of Slavery: Tracking the Figure of the Unsovereign." *Critical Sociology* 42, nos. 4-5: 583-97.

Spade, Dean. 2011. *Normal Life*. Brooklyn, NY: South End.

Vishmidt, Marina. 2015. "The Manifestation of the Discourse of the Commons in the Field of Art." Paper presented at KUNCI Cultural Studies Center, Yogyakarta, Indonesia, March 30. kunci.or.id/articles/marina-vishmidt-commons-in-the-field-of-art/.

"Vivian". 2013. "Queer Activism and the Gezi Riots: What You Didn't Know." *Autostraddle*, July 1. www.autostraddle.com/queer-activism-and-the-taksim-gezi-riots-what-you-didnt-know-182975/.

Warner, Michael. 2014. *Publics and Counterpublics*. New York: Zone Books.

Wolfe, Patrick. 2013. "Recuperating Binarism: A Heretical Introduction." *Settler Colonial Studies* 3, nos. 3–4: 257–79.

"DEAD ADDICTS DON'T RECOVER":

ACT UP's Needle Exchange and the Subjects of Queer Activist History

Christina B. Hanhardt

On June 18, 2017, former and present-day members of the New York City chapter of the AIDS Coalition to Unleash Power (ACT UP) reunited for the conference "Thirty Years of ACT UP/NY: Hidden Histories and Voices, Lessons Learned." Members had commemorated the founding of ACT UP before, in 2007 and 2012, when they came together in protest to show that AIDS—and ACT UP—were far from over. But the 2017 event was different. It took the form of a series of panels and videos meant to correct what many of those gathered consider a popular but distorted history of the group. As Bob Lederer, the main organizer of the day's event and a longtime member of ACT UP, explained:

> This conference represents an important reclamation of lost movement history . . . Too many books, films, and articles about ACT UP have omitted or barely mentioned the powerful campaigns and actions on HIV/AIDS issues focused on women, people of color, drug users, young people, and the Global South, and the role played by members of these communities in the coalitions that mounted those often-successful efforts. Many ACT UP histories falsely report that the group disbanded in the early '90s, when in fact it has persisted and continues to win victories up until today.[1]

In addition to campaigns addressing immigration, women's health, and incarceration, a recurrent theme was ACT UP's early participation in needle exchange programs (NEPs), which distribute free syringes and have been shown to reduce HIV transmission among injection drug users. In early 1990 the new mayor of New

GLQ 24:4
DOI 10.1215/10642684-6957758
© 2018 by Duke University Press

York, David Dinkins, suspended a pilot NEP sponsored by the city's health department. ACT UP New York members continued exchanges in an act of civil disobedience, a role chapters played in cities across the United States.

The 2017 ACT UP commemoration hoped to re-enter projects like needle exchange into the historical record where they are otherwise missing, such as in David France's award-winning 2012 documentary *How to Survive a Plague*, and 2016 book by the same name. Although the film won accolades and brought attention to ACT UP, activists and scholars critique France's narrow focus on the Treatment and Data Committee of ACT UP New York and white gay men (Cheng 2016). Jim Hubbard and Sarah Schulman's much more expansive documentary *United in Anger: A History of ACT UP* (2012) and Deborah Gould's book, *Moving Politics: Emotion and ACT UP's Fight against AIDS* (2009), are more inclusive and do not lionize the leadership of a select group, but neither do they provide focused attention on all of ACT UP's many campaigns.[2] With the exception of *The Life and Death of ACT UP/LA* (2017), by Benita Roth, which dedicates a substantial section to ACT UP Los Angeles's relationship to Clean Needles Now, few studies of ACT UP detail needle exchange. Instead, it mostly appears in studies of public health, HIV/AIDS, or direct action activism that are not focused on ACT UP alone, or in commentary that thematizes how ACT UP has been remembered (Chavez 2012; Cohen 1999; Gould 2012; Juhasz 2012; Lune 2007; Shepard 2010, 2015).

Without a doubt, no single source could fully contextualize a group whose number of actions, subcommittees and chapters, offshoots, cultural productions, short- and long-term collaborations, and conflicts and successes is so staggering. But the challenge of detailing needle exchange in ACT UP's history is significant because many ACT UP members consider it a key means by which the group's focus extended beyond white gay men, and they cite ACT UP's use of civil disobedience, arrest, and trial as essential to the later municipal approval of NEPs. Moreover, this rich history of an expansive, militant, and creative approach to fighting the stigma of HIV/AIDS is also what inspires many to count ACT UP as one of the most important *queer* activist groups in the United States during the 1980s and 1990s, even as ACT UP was not identified as a lesbian, gay, bisexual, and/or transgender (LGBT) organization. Why has needle exchange been so difficult to include? And how does it fit within queer activist history?

The present article provides a brief look at ACT UP New York's participation in needle exchange, not only to address its representational absence, but to show how contestations over social movement history reflect political differences within those movements that continue to structure how they are remembered. The main participants in "Thirty Years of ACT UP/NY" were not those featured in

France's documentary, and included many who were active in ACT UP in the late 1990s and 2000s (as opposed to the oft-highlighted late 1980s and early 1990s). It also included people who worked in coalition with the group rather than claimed membership in it and who were involved for short periods or only active in a caucus; and most all in attendance continue to do multi-issue political organizing. In this interpretation of ACT UP, the group is not bound by formal membership or fixed within a single period; it is also shaped by a larger activist context. These include feminist, antiracist, socialist, and prisoner solidarity organizing, but also the activism of documentation, most especially the collection of videotaped footage and printed ephemera and making of documentaries and other forms of creative production (indeed, a taped message from member Maxine Wolfe was featured at the event). The fact that all the anniversaries cited in this article's opening represented ACT UP and its history as still in-the-making signals that the group might be best understood not only via traditional historical study, in which scholars focus on the members, aims, and actions of an organization, but as a political formation whose identity was and continues to be under contestation.

The Queer Commons

The idea that ACT UP's history is part of a shared project of continued remaking is one reason it provides an ideal opportunity to consider the theme of this special issue—the *queer commons*. In fact, ACT UP already has a privileged place in the few published references to the term, which tend to invoke the group's commitment to public access, such as efforts to democratize medical knowledge or claim the streets for direct action, as well as ACT UP's majority gay and lesbian membership, who, nonetheless, treated that identity as oppositional and open (Barnett et al. 2016; Floyd 2004). Central to these conceptualizations is the idea of queer *world-making*, especially as theorized by José Esteban Muñoz (1999: 195), "in which performances—both theatrical and everyday rituals—have the ability to establish alternative views of the world." Gavin Brown's (2009) theorization of the *queer commons* is also based on everyday life and an anticapitalist practice. A geographer, Brown draws on J. K. Gibson-Graham's study of "diverse economies" that challenge or at least reorganize the logics of the capitalist system, and he names examples such as public sex sites, queer do-it-yourself collectives, and gay institutions. In sum, these models treat *queerness* as both a diversity of sexual/ gender minority identities as well as a nonidentity based in variable analyses of outsiderness, and they describe the *commons* as an ideal of anticapitalist collectivism, albeit not prescriptive of one political ideology.

But the terms *queer* and *commons* index other debates within LGBT and left activism during the years in which ACT UP took on needle exchange, from 1989 to 1992, that continue to define central differences of interpretation and method in social movements and the study of them, especially how to name the subjects and delimit the form of political activity. The 1980s saw the relative mainstreaming of lesbian and gay movements, as over two decades of political organizing transformed some modes of sexual deviancy into affirmative identities nominally recognized in popular culture, the marketplace, and the law. At the same time, this assimilation was uneven, and excluded those who, because of race and class in particular, remained outside the promises of partial economic and legal integration. As a result, alongside a mainstream movement, radical and subcultural LGBT politics continued to gather steam, even as the popular social movement record often narrates this period as one of declension or, at best, as a stalemate between liberal and radical, policy and culture.

But the distinctions between the two sides of these oppositions were never absolute, and the second terms of each were far from homogeneous. *Radical* might signal militancy within gay liberalism; membership in a socialist party or anarchist formation; or a call to expand identity, reject identity, or dismiss what was increasingly called identity politics. Similarly, *culture* might be the making of art; the expression of nonnormative gender or sexuality; or the adoption of communal ideals as prefigurative practice, necessary accommodation, or apolitical retreat. This was no more so the case than in the discussion of the emergent term *queer* and debates about the state. Theories of social construction informed the rise of what was called *queer theory* by the 1990s; activists also took on *queer* as a personal and group label. As Lisa Duggan ([1991] 1995) outlines, queer theory's antifoundationalism sometimes clashed with activist goals that depended on the consolidation rather than destabilization of identity.

The urgency of these debates was due in no small part to the presidency of Ronald Reagan, whose cuts to social welfare programs were coupled with the rise of the Religious Right and its explicit condemnation of homosexuality. Lesbian and gay activists divided between those who focused solely on lesbian and gay rights and those who found common struggle with others affected by Reagan's promises of privatization, most especially the racialized poor. Reagan's refusal to acknowledge AIDS provided one link between these efforts, but activist strategies were by no means uniform. Tensions emerged not only between supposedly assimilationist gays and lesbians and anti-assimilationist queers, or between liberal policy advocates and radical activists, but also *among* the vast landscape of activists who rejected the status quo but disagreed on how to interpret and challenge it.

By 1990, the effects of Reagan's attack on the social safety net had left activists scrambling, as they balanced filling in some of the gaps of lost services while demanding their reinstatement. Activists debated then and later about whether mutual-aid type efforts had the potential to be an affirmative alternative to diminishing or disciplinary state programs, or if embracing them was simply another symptom of what would become more broadly known as neoliberalism. At stake would be the question not just of the state as giver of rights or punishment but of its role in managing the distribution of resources along the road to greater liberation. In other words, these were conflicts about the substance of the *commons* and reflected many lines of political difference, including anarchist or communist affiliations, or between those who did or did not work with or count themselves as part of communities affected by HIV with the greatest distance from access to resources—namely, in New York City in 1990, low-income and poor African Americans and Latinos.

As a result, activists debated who the subjects of political action were and how to account for race, sexuality, gender, and class structure together. Queer theory and activism posed points of entry, but in the early 1990s at least, the dominant approach to what was increasingly called queer activism was based on analyses of norms focused on regulating sexual object choice in a way that too often ignored the disciplining of other aspects of sexuality, pleasure-seeking, or kinship models. In addition, queer theory's challenges to liberal humanism often engaged with the question of agency at a distance from left social movement strategy. In 1997 the political scientist Cathy Cohen highlighted the limits of a queer politics centered on the primacy of the (often tacit) opposition of heterosexual and homosexual and that did not take into account the operation of race and class. She offered an interpretation of *queer* as based on one's *relation to power* that emphasized how the stigmatization of different forms of kinship, sexuality, and pleasure was not restricted to homosexuality in isolation. Significantly, Cohen uses the case study of HIV/AIDS activism to frame what would become a field-defining essay. She opens with an anecdote about racism at the Gay Men's Health Crisis (GMHC), the organization to which ACT UP was founded as a militant alternative; she concludes with a discussion of needle exchange and prison projects as promising sites of "principled transformative coalition work" in which ACT UP participated (Cohen 1997: 461).

Current directions in queer studies and activism continue to turn away from the primacy of LGBT identity to look at the regulatory function of health, ability, rationality, and responsibility. One line of inquiry is a queer take on anarchism, from Jack Halberstam's, Tavia Nyong'o's, and Muñoz's writings on *wildness* to Dean Spade's and Reina Gossett's discussions of "participatory governance" and prefigurativism (Halberstam 2014b; Nichols 2012; Gossett et al. 2014). Given the central place of anarchism in theorizations of the commons, it is worth further highlighting what anarchist theory offers to two of the key debates I have just outlined here: defining the subjects of queer politics and modeling antistate activism. Halberstam's (2014a) not-a-manifesto for the "queer and the wild" invests the *disorderly* with transformative potential. This conceptualization resonates with a description of the *lumpenproletariat* as the most revolutionary for having the least to lose, by Mikhail Bakunin ([1873] 1992), a nineteenth-century anarchist. Frantz Fanon ([1965] 2005) described a similar position for the *lumpenproletariat* in the anticolonial context, and the Black Panthers took up the concept in the United States in their advocacy for those who traded in the economies of the street. Bakunin was rejecting Marx, who had described the *lumpenproletariat* as "tricksters," "brothel keepers," and "beggars," among a much longer list—in sum, "the society of disorder, prostitution and theft"—with no class consciousness or organization, and, ultimately, counterrevolutionary (Marx [1852] 1994). In general, scholars have theorized the *lumpenproletariat* as a position of difference counter to a unified class-based category (Stallybrass 1990) and as a placeholder for the "unassimilable heterogeneity" (Thoburn 2003) and outsiderness that *queer* too has often represented (see also Hanhardt 2012).

By naming these commonalities between two of the most dominant political categories on the left used to stand in for those considered hypermarginal or categorically illegible, I want to point to a rich if complicated genealogy for understanding what has been called the "throwaway class" that ACT UP organized through needle exchange.[3] In addition, although prefigurativism is not restricted to anarchism, it is often associated with it as a key means to cast group care as a model for political futures.

After providing a brief history of ACT UP New York's turn to needle exchange, the remainder of this article focuses on three themes central to the considerations of a queer commons as I have mapped it here. First, I look at how ACT UP identified those whom it sought to organize in needle exchange, and the use of the category *addict*. I then examine how debates over city space provide a helpful angle on some of the tensions about drug use inherent to needle exchange. From there, I discuss the practice of needle exchange as political promise. In 1992 NEPs were formalized into municipal programs, including the Lower East Side Needle Exchange Program, which was soon renamed the Lower East Side Harm Reduction Center (1993). Today, many public health advocates and queer activists alike invoke needle exchange as a cornerstone of harm reduction—an approach that seeks to reduce the harms of high-risk activities by rejecting prohibition, shame, or punishment. Thus, in the article's conclusion, I ask after the place of harm reduction as well as the dynamics of coalition and recuperation in queer social movement historiography.

ACT UP New York's Needle Exchange

Needle exchanges were first formalized in the 1980s in response to the spread of hepatitis, and then HIV. One of the first organized exchanges was the Interest Group for Drug Users, known colloquially as the Junkiebond (in English, the Junkie Union), first established in the Netherlands as a collective of heroin users (Lune 2007; Friedman et al. 2007).[4] Although NEPs steadily developed across northern Europe and other parts of the world during that decade, they were slow to take hold in the United States. The criminalization of drug paraphernalia combined with a 1988 congressional ban on the use of federal dollars for needle exchange meant that most early efforts were illegal and informal. Nonetheless, throughout the 1980s, activists developed roving or temporary exchanges across the United States. In the Northeast US, the National AIDS Brigade was an early leader, as its founder Jon Parker set up emergency exchanges in New Haven and Boston.

The majority of those involved in ACT UP New York at the time were gay men, many white and middle class, even as the group was outspoken in its critique of the unjust racial and economic politics of health care. When research demonstrated that the HIV infection rate of drug users in major cities was outpacing that of gay men (categories treated in the literature as separate) and that low-income African Americans and Latinos were by far the most affected, needle exchange presented both an opportunity and a challenge for ACT UP to expand its identity across race and class lines. As the artist Zoe Leonard (2010) noted years later, "We were also really interested in building coalition and understanding that this wasn't just happening to us, it wasn't just happening to gay people; this kind of systematic negligence was happening to numerous other communities around the country. So needle exchange was a really smart way to get out a lot of those things all at the same time." When New York disbanded its short-lived, city-approved pilot program, ACT UP members, often joined by Parker, adopted the strategy of syringe distribution as civil disobedience, getting arrested and going to trial in order to challenge the ban. In February 1990 ACT UP's efforts officially began, and soon the group was also providing a main source of funding and labor for New York's illegal exchanges.

The initial energy came from two subgroups: ACT UP members who used drugs or identified as in recovery (many of whom were part of a briefly lived Addicts Rights Caucus) and members of the Majority Action Committee (MAC), named to reflect the fact that the majority of those affected by HIV/AIDS were people of color; but it also included the participation of a range of interested ACT UP members (ACT UP n.d.a; Clear 2015; Elovich, n.d., Lune 2007).[5] One of the group's leaders was Richard Elovich, who publicly identified as a former injection drug user, and others included Donna Binder, Gregg Bordowitz, Allen Clear, Heidi Dorow, Zoe Leonard, Debra Levine, Juan Mendez, Kathy Otter, Monica Pearl, Gay Wachman, and Dan Williams, among others. They quickly realized that to do this work, they needed to challenge the stigma about injection drug use inside and outside ACT UP, as well as some of the racial and class assumptions held by other ACT UP members (Clear 2015; Juhasz 2012; Levine, 2010; Saalfield and Navarro 1991; Shepard 2002; Vazquez-Pacheco 2002).

Internally, one of their first activities was to create a glossary to help educate ACT UP members. The glossary included the names of relevant organizations and public health officials as well as definitions for *majority* and *minority*, *addictophobia*, *genocide*, and *Tuskegee Experiment* (Navarro et al. n.d.). It defined *genocide* ("the deliberate and systematic extermination of a national, cultural, racial or ethnic group") and *Tuskegee Experiment* ("infamous incident in which US health officials allowed 40 black male prisoners infected with syphilis to go untreated in order to monitor the disease") because these were two of the main terms of debate *outside* the organization. Some progressive black city leaders charged needle exchange as "genocide" for providing tacit support for drug use, and, as a then still-unproved HIV-prevention strategy, racist medical experimentation like that at Tuskegee. In turn, ACT UP's external actions focused on the importance of needle exchange rather than drug prohibition in HIV prevention. As Cohen (1999) has shown, the economic and social devastation of the drug economy in communities of color, combined with select antidrug moralism, made some black community leaders, especially council and church members, wary of a program that seemed to provide approval for drug use. In addition, the needle exchange's origins in a municipal public health program made it even more suspicious. And although Mayor Dinkins was one of the earliest politicians to take AIDS seriously, he had won the Democratic primary saying that he would suspend the program as he ran against the more law-and-order incumbent Ed Koch, who, as mayor, had actually come around to supporting needle exchanges.

Black and Latino advocates were also among those in support of NEPs. The Association for Drug Abuse Prevention and Treatment (ADAPT) and its director, Yolanda Serrano, were among those responsible for New York's original pilot NEP;

Serrano also served as the vice president of the Hispanic AIDS Forum and as sec-retary of the Latino Commission on AIDS, and was a member of the Health and Human Services HIV Planning Council of New York (Sullivan 1993). Black gay leaders in the Minority Task Force on AIDS in New York, as well as activists in an expanding national network of HIV/AIDS activist groups organized by and for LGBT people of color, also worked tirelessly to challenge what Cohen (1999) theo-rized as the "secondary marginalization" of drug users and gay people within main-stream black political mobilizations, including the growing AIDS service industry.

Moreover, for many black HIV/AIDS activists, vulnerability to AIDS was seen as inseparable from the disproportionate conditions of poverty, criminaliza-tion, and violence faced by black people in the United States, rather than a disease linked solely to one's identity or experience as gay *or* drug using.[6] In this context, genocide was not just the rhetoric of mainstream politicians but also a long-stand-ing charge of radical activists who argued the state had pushed heroin and crack into poor black and Latino communities during the very years that drug criminal penalties increased. This was a position shared by some white gay activists as well; nonetheless, more often, radical activism addressing racial and economic segrega-tion in the city cast white gay people on the *other* side of genocide claims, espe-cially in coterminous debates about gentrification (Hanhardt 2013).[7] And although not all of ACT UP's needle exchange members were white gay men, many were. As a result, when ACT UP decided to respond to the discontinuation of the pilot program by illegally distributing needles in neighborhoods of color, they had to balance how to acknowledge the racism of the War on Drugs and the broader racial politics of health and residential segregation in New York while pushing against black and Latino leaders' charges of genocide.

"Who Are the Fags? Who Are the Junkies?"

Elovich cited fellow ACT UP needle exchange member, the artist Gregg Bordowitz, in the title to his 1992 essay "Who Are the Fags? Who Are the Junkies? Where Are the Services?" Elovich explained, "These categories are used to divide us. That false question is still being used to fracture the AIDS community, to obscure our own issues of substance abuse and to reinforce the idea that people who shoot drugs are alien and criminal. . . . The result is that addicts, especially active addicts, are not seen by legislators, or even health care providers, as deserving of services." In its early years, ACT UP, like many needle exchange advocates at the time, used the word *addict* rather than *user* as a noneuphemistic term that empha-sized the biological aspects of addiction. Elsewhere in the essay, Elovich mocked approaches that he felt minimized the harsh realities of addiction, describing them as "conference room" talk. Along with naming the right to health care, housing, and self-determination, ACT UP often explained that the actions of the addict—to seek a fix no matter the risk and to prioritize drugs above all else—were non-cultural and nonracial features that were also the factors that led to heightened HIV risk. As the group emphasized in a 1990 press briefing: "Visit a room where alcoholics and addicts in recovery gather, and you will see people from all walks of life, all colors, all classes acknowledging their powerlessness to manage this crippling disease on their own" (Elovich 1990).

This was, of course, the dominant language of recovery, but in detailing the identity of *addict* as deracinated—important for destigmatization—this explanation sometimes risked sustaining the two sets of vulnerabilities as separate and obscuring the racialized features of the term *addict* itself. To be clear, ACT UP's needle exchange materials consistently noted that uneven access to health care and housing differentiated one's risk. In a booklet that ACT UP provided for the second National People of Color AIDS Activist Conference in 1991, they adopted the term "user" and explained that addiction is "'produced,' maintained, and experienced largely through social and environmental factors," and thus needle exchange is a political, not just a public health, solution. They also emphasized that the primary problems posed by drug use were a result of the structural blocks imposed by stigma, poverty, and criminalization and not because of drug use itself; they concluded, "by assuming that drug use automatically leads to disability is assuming, again, that drug users can have no control over their use." (ACT UP 1991).[8] Ultimately, ACT UP's NEP proponents argued that criminalizing needles was a carceral solution to a public health problem and that the plans of progressive opponents of needle exchange—"drug treatment on demand"—was all talk if not joined by a budget. (ACT UP was also suspicious of methadone because it addressed heroin rather than needle use—crack and methamphetamines can also be injected—and was often detached from other recovery efforts.) Given the racialized contours of criminalization and access to health care, in these definitions race might be considered a central determinant of marginality, even if sometimes left tacit.

It is worth noting, though, that ACT UP's early publicly stated goals for needle exchange were in many ways to discourage drug use and to treat needle exchange as key to removing blocks to recovery. In this way, ACT UP's efforts did at least in part (or by strategic rhetoric) share with their critics the assumption that certain forms of drug use were undesirable. The differences between needle exchange advocates and opponents rested more on ideas of addiction's cause and the proper response to it, along a broad ideological spectrum: from interpretations of addiction as resulting from psychological injuries wrought by larger social structures (homophobia, racism) to it being an expression of individual failure; from addiction as a prohibiting choice to being an un/acceptable choice; from addiction as a problem of failed self-management to a feature of all drug use.

Not all members of ACT UP's needle exchange shared the same views; in an interview years later, the harm reduction activist Donald Grove described the dominance of twelve-step recovery logics in ACT UP's early NEPs, and that it often felt at odds with what was still then an emergent harm reduction discourse that aimed to treat drug use as value neutral, even if to variable effect (Grove 2008). The end result was that the strategy of organizing addicts was distinct from organizing gay men: for many in ACT UP, addiction was difficult to solve rather than acceptable, and the main goal was to give addicts an opportunity to be ex-addicts. In fact, one of the primary slogans of ACT UP's NEP was "Dead Addicts Don't Recover"; although this was a retort to toothless calls for drug treatment on demand, it worked to keep central the goal of recovery (ACT UP n.d.c). The link between gay men and addicts was less common cause or identity than overlap—as in, many gay men were addicts—and activists invoked personal experiences that the ostracism of homophobia led to addiction that, in turn, led to risky choices. In the contexts in which ACT UP adopted the language of *user*, it emphasized respecting the choice to use drugs; this was similar to but different from the tension between *gay* versus *men who have sex with men* (MSM), another emerging terminological divide in public health during those years. Although *user*, like *MSM*, was intended as a value-neutral term to emphasize practice over identity, *user* became a term of agency, like the affirmative identity *gay*, which, by extension, held the possibility for political participation, while addict, like MSM, remained at the time more associated with personal practice and medical and social subjugation than an emergent political identity.

To return to some of the other terms from the glossary, *majority* and *minority* highlighted the disproportionate risk of HIV for people of color by providing (along with their definitions) examples of use in a sentence: "The *majority* of HIV infected persons in the US are people of color" and "The health care system in the US has always discriminated against 'minorities'" (Navarro et al. n.d.). Here *minority* occupies the category of population, while *majority* measures the risks faced by that position, yet *addictophobia* ("irrational fear and ignorance of people who are chemically dependent") focused on a negative response to the users themselves. In sum, all these examples demonstrate an unresolved understanding of how and what structures of power and identity determine one's vulnerability to HIV/AIDS and one's status as a subject of activism.

At the time, the activist use of the word *queer* was just beginning to gather widespread recognition as a stand-in for gay militancy and anti-assimilationism. This association was largely because of the activities of the group Queer Nation, which was founded by fellow ACT UP New York members in March 1990, soon after ACT UP began its needle exchange. But the tensions I have described here foreshadow what would be the contradictory uses of *queer* in that and future decades: as a coalition of disparate subjects (gay men, addicts) versus as a new outsider identity that would encompass these subjects (queers) or as an analytic or practice for understanding the shifting systems that make and bind identities into hierarchical place. The last option would be the hardest to conceptualize and realize in both queer theory and politics, in part because of the uneven geography, broadly conceived, that provided the stage on which these ideas would be made.

The Places of Needle Exchange

In fact, the tension between *gay* and *addict* reflects over two decades of gay activism that distinguished gay people from drug users, alongside whom they had been long policed. In the 1970s and 1980s efforts to destigmatize and decriminalize homosexuality emerged in tandem with new policing strategies directed at so-called social disorder. Broken windows policing and concepts of a permanent underclass, both based in culture of poverty research, targeted drug users as a leading source of urban threat and decline. During these same years, though, municipal boosters, real estate developers, and even some activists selectively hailed the new visibility of certain lesbian and gay populations—namely, those white and middle class—as bringing promise to "slums" and other sites of urban disrepair. Although many LGBT activists worked against these alignments, others collaborated with groups like the Guardian Angels, a vigilante anticrime group founded in 1979, finding common cause in the fight against unregulated street life (Hanhardt 2013, 2016).

ACT UP's needle exchange adopted entirely different spatial and political affinities. For example, on March 6, 1990, members of ACT UP staged an exchange at the intersection of Essex and Delancey Streets in New York's Lower East Side, ready to get arrested. Not only did the police charge ten for needle possession, but the Guardian Angels, far from collaborating with them, counterdemonstrated across the street, chanting "No drugs! No needles!" (Lambert 1990).[9] The neighborhoods of needle exchange—like Harlem and the Lower East Side in Manhattan, Bushwick and East New York in Brooklyn, and the East and South Bronx—were poor and working class, a majority Latino and/or African

American, and outside the normative spaces of white gay activism. These were also the places of long-standing LGBT organizing among people of color and left political activity that had taken on issues like gentrification, policing, and drug use. For example, in the 1970s the Bronx-based group White Lightning (1974) allied with the Young Lords and Black Panthers in the fight over Lincoln Hospital in the Bronx, and they linked the politics of drugs to landlord neglect and real estate speculation. ACT UP needle exchange activists, too, sought to tease out these concerns by recognizing the problem of poverty and listing among the rights of drug users access to housing and health care. But since they were in large part fighting for a new public health policy many of their biggest allies were progressive public health advocates, and so they also drew on epidemiological research to emphasize the harm unmanaged addiction caused *to* neighborhoods.

Artists, many involved with ACT UP and sometimes sponsored by the GMHC, helped provide the justification for needle exchange, by showing how it worked and highlighting the challenges of where to locate them. Video artists made experimental and more formally conventional documentaries, including Hilery Joy Kipnis and Jean Carlomusto's *Up in Arms over Needle Exchange* (1988), Catherine Saalfield and Ray Navarro's *Bleach, Teach, and Outreach* (1989), and Elovich's (with Bordowitz) *Clean Needles Save Lives* (1991), and collected footage of protests, actions, trials, and NEPs in action.[10] For example, in *Bleach, Teach, and Outreach* founders of the original pilot exchange, such as Serrano of ADAPT, highlight needle exchange as an economic necessity, emphasizing that poverty, not preference, leads to dirty needle use, while Chuck Eaton, coordinator of the original city exchange, shows the wide variety of health services provided. ADAPT staff members such as John Robles and Michael Bethea excoriate community members who turn to vigilante groups to deal with their anger toward "junkies," and they call instead for people to organize and collaborate in the provision of services. They also highlight some of the spatial conflicts that adhered to the early days of needle exchange and that prohibited the equal use of a public service: politicians demanded that NEPs not be placed near schools even as public health agencies had been purposely located near them for decades. The first NEP in Lower Manhattan near City Hall was, as they explain, set up to fail, since it was close to courts, jails, immigration, and the FBI, making it risky for already criminalized and vulnerable populations, and to those whose appearances, sometimes disheveled, brought further scrutiny.

The videos address an audience inclusive of drug users, but, like other advocacy materials, also described NEPs by detailing their benefits not only for users but also for a surrounding community of *non*-users and how exchanges restore order to chaotic urban environments and encourage neighbors to care for rather than fear each other. This was often cast in the language of reducing harm for the community: meaning, to minimize the injury addiction caused to families, neighborhoods, and public spaces. Although NEP activists actively opposed anti-drug policing strategies, the idea that the problems to be targeted were undesirable behaviors that injured neighborhoods is one example of the sticky status of "self-management" in needle exchange. And although the opposition to needle exchange tended to demonize individuals, the aforementioned genocide argument spoke to a longer history of state aggression and not only localized neglect. In this way, ACT UP, along with other early needle exchange advocates, struggled to scale the gap between individual suffering and racism and poverty in general, on a spatial and conceptual frame. Here it is important to repeat that ACT UP did not act alone nor hold these views in isolation; the eventual success of NEPs and the lingo used to justify them owed much to collaborations with organizations like ADAPT as well as with a larger network of advocates, providers, and activists, including the very people who depended upon needle exchange services. This diverse scene, often visually captured in the video footage of protests shot by ACT UP members, demonstrates that needle exchange was far from a white-dominated political vision, and that a broad constellation of activists was key to many coalitions of which ACT UP was but one member and not always at the center. This was also the case with feminist and media activism among ACT UP members, many of whom were also involved in needle exchange (Cheng 2016).

Nonetheless, ACT UP's needle exchange did not always manifest its transformative promise. Groups of a majority of white activists confronting progressive black leaders in public settings caused tension between ACT UP and some black gay activists who were sympathetic to needle exchange but invested in building relationships with other black leaders for future mobilizations. In addition, some questioned ACT UP's tendency to practice needle exchange in very large groups of mostly white people in neighborhoods with a majority of people of color, fearing that it would bring heightened visibility to users and increase their vulnerability to policing. ACT UP members acknowledged these issues themselves—Clear later noted that the risks of carrying syringes were more heightened for people of color—and they innovated informal yet effective modes of dispersed exchanges across the city (Clear 2015; Lune 2007; Williams 2004). But the geography of needle exchange—the distance of a Bronx location from ACT UP's Lower Manhattan meeting spot; the vexed dynamics of white bodies moving through low-income communities of color—suggested that ACT UP's NEPs would be short-lived, an outcome also due (perhaps in even larger part) to what would be the *success* of the coalitional campaign to demand NEPs supported by the city.

Needle Exchange as Politics in Service

To repeat, among the black and Latino leaders who were opposed to needle exchange, some were antigay and few were themselves out, injection drug users. But it was also the case that few injection drug users of color were members of ACT UP, or, if so, they rarely chose to "come out" as users. The most outspoken member of ACT UP who publicly identified as a former injection drug user was Elovich, who was white, middle class, and later became a public health researcher. On the other hand, many members of ACT UP were identified as in recovery, often for the use of alcohol or noninjected drugs. The fear of the stigma of being an active injection user could be strong in the context of a dominant culture of recovery, as least during the exchange's earliest years. The late Rod Sorge, an intellectual and strategic leader of ACT UP's NEP, and Brian Weil, a participant and photographer, both obscured their active use. In a later interview, Elovich explained that among the things that still "haunted" him were those who "couldn't trust us to say that they were using heroin." He explained the situation of one woman of color who led a major organization: "It's not just hypocrisy. [She] died of AIDS. And there was all this courage amongst the women she organized—mostly sex workers and women who were using crack—to come out and tell their stories. But [she] was supporting her whole family; . . . [she] was afraid. Because she was paying out of cash. She was afraid of her insurance knowing. She was afraid, as a woman running an organization that it would be taken away from her" (Elovich 2007).[11]

The uneven punishments of publicly identifying as a drug user were also a debated feature of ACT UP's strategy of going to trial.[12] Of the eight people who went to trial after they were arrested on the Lower East Side in March 1990—Bordowitz, Elovich, Williams, Levine, Otter, Parker, Pearl, Velma Campbell, Cynthia Cochran, and Phillip Flores—the majority were members of ACT UP; others were involved in the National AIDS Brigade (Sullivan 1991). One ACT UP member, Dan Williams, later remembered that he was one of the few black people involved in ACT UP's needle exchange and that this shaped the dynamics of arrest. He recalled, "There are issues about getting arrested—especially if you're a black guy. I know black guys in ACT UP, who would never get arrested, because they were afraid of what was going to happen to them." Clear, who is white, also avoided arrest with needle exchange despite having been arrested for other actions, because of a fear that handing out syringes would bring a moral turpitude charge, for which a green-card holder like Clear might be deported (Clear 2015; Williams 2004).

A year later, the defendants were acquitted at trial after using a justification defense, and the judge agreed that the harm ACT UP sought to avoid was greater than the harm in breaking the law and thus justified. While the main harm, of course, was the then-considered death sentence of HIV, for ACT UP, survival was also a condition of participating in politics, and the high odds of HIV among drug users was seen as an organizing problem. Sorge wrote: "New York City's IV drug users who have AIDS or are HIV positive are not living with AIDS. For them, HIV is a death sentence. Their day-to-day struggles for basic necessities preclude any possibility of mobilization or political action or community building to demand access to drug and medical treatment. Needle exchanges can be a departure point for a user's process of empowerment and can even serve therapeutic purposes for active and former users involved in needle distribution." He continued later in the essay, "What is often overlooked or ignored by critics of needle distribution is the interaction that takes place during the encounter. It is this interaction between the giver and receiver of the needle that is the significant component of needle exchange, especially when encounters are repeated, and trust—maybe even friendship—is established" (Sorge 1990). In this way, ACT UP articulated a politics to include the exchange between those in recovery and those using (or non- and active users), an often informal gesture, that might involve not only conversations about accessing drug treatment but also everyday life pleasures, desires, and needs (Clear 2015).

Activists argued that the state's refusal to provide NEPs forced advocacy for them to be political mobilizations but that in their scene of administration other possibilities were made. Thus NEPs offered the possibility of entering into a political identity, but access to that might be limited for those with a less self-managed addiction. This was different from democratizing claims to expertise or deprivatizing scientific knowledge, as in other demands to make HIV-positive people experts in their own care. In these early years, unmanaged addiction was rarely seen as a viable place from which to organize, and it presented problems for how to analyze drug use across race and class lines. Moreover, if choice was the work of the activist, it left open the question of whether *addicts* as opposed to *users* (and those identified as in recovery) could be *activists*?

The interpersonal dynamics between those who were known to use in ACT UP and those who did not sometimes were strained; they might butt heads, not only about strategy, but also in the different rhythms of activism versus getting high, or about whom to trust (Lune, 2007). In both New York and Los Angeles, the ACT UP needle exchange subgroups had serious conflicts over money management. In LA, members of the needle exchange were asked to explain whether they were actually a part of ACT UP or merely "using" its name and resources. Clean Needles Now in Los Angeles eventually detached from ACT UP because of these dynamics (ACT UP/LA 1993; Roth 2017). In New York, Williams was accused of stealing funds and ended up leaving the group. He later took responsibility for his role in this financial conflict, explaining that he was struggling with alcohol, and he noted with some humor that he had participated in the trial high. But he also added that after the trial he left ACT UP altogether, and later found himself homeless and living far from the social worlds he occupied with ACT UP, contrasting his current life in black communities as far from his former life in Chelsea, a gay-identified neighborhood in Manhattan.

These conflicts in the early years of NEPs might be understood in part within debates about the complicated pleasures and choices behind the decision to use drugs or drink. Needle exchange was seen as a way to minimize risk so as to maximize life, and it was rarely seen as a way to achieve pleasure without pain. It is telling that almost none of the needle exchange videos show images of people shooting up or high, unlike the safer-sex videos of that time, which included explicit sex scenes. Clear, who was a member of the collective Impact Visuals, decided not to photograph users, since it felt voyeuristic: "I mean, in a demonstration, it's a different thing or when you're photographing activism within ACT UP, it's a different thing. But if you're photographing people's lives on the street, that's a different thing altogether." That said, although activists tended to dismiss scholarly or advocacy approaches that they thought romanticized or exploited addiction, they did try to imbue their activities with what Benjamin Shepard (2010: 150) describes as a "playfulness" that often incorporated poetry and creative healing. And they saw the informal scene of provision to provide at least some of the groundwork for new political possibilities.

Dead Addicts Don't Recover: What Is the Harm of Harm Reduction?

The status of needle exchange quickly changed as the 1990s continued. During the 1980s, privatization had been met by a do-it-yourself (DIY) subeconomy; Clear described needle exchange as an extension of this "DIY ethos" (Shepard 2010: 150). But by the mid-1990s, needle exchanges became increasingly acceptable in many US cities as, with no small measure of reluctance, mayors described them—as did John Daniels of New Haven—as necessary "band-aids" (Navarro

1991). In that decade, services were increasingly managed by a growing nonprofit sector, and by 1993, following New York's approval of needle exchange, many of the city's NEPs had transformed into nonprofits focused on *harm reduction.*

Harm reduction is a broad approach that seeks to minimize the harms of high-risk practices by rejecting disapprobation and coercion. Its definition is far from uniform, and includes the use of PrEP, supervised injection sites, methadone maintenance, or even counseling. Today many activists dedicated to *transformative justice*—alternatives to carceral solutions for a range of social problems—also invoke harm reduction.[13] This has also sometimes involved the integration of service provision in social movement building or casting "self-care" as a top priority. As a result, it is important to consider not only the place of social justice in health but the ideal of health in radical activism. As this article has tried to ask, how might such an ideal constrain as much as it might open up when it is seen as the building block of responsible self-management? This would be a debated aspect of harm reduction: that reducing harm might make broader structures of inequality more acceptable and that it emphasizes the repair offered by self-governance. Early harm reduction strategies were often explained via more accepted acts, such as designated drivers or even political reformism—that it makes life livable in order to change it. But if *activism* is defined as a will to health, is there a place for not only the pleasures of risky sex but also the predictable *and* uncertain risks of getting high?

The history of ACT UP's needle exchange program is, in many ways, to borrow a phrase from the historian Colin Johnson, one of the "odds of queer [activist] history," of outsiders to an outsider movement, but also of those considered to have the lowest odds of making history. To repeat, as ACT UP would say while citing that as of 1989, 60–70 percent was a conservative estimate of how many drug users in New York already had HIV: "Dead Addicts Don't Recover" (ACT UP n.d.c). What does it mean, then, to quite literally recover "addicts" into queer social movement history? Many of ACT UP's most successful activities were those that reached out, in projects and campaigns and geographies sometimes outside ACT UP's formal bounds, as seen by its thirtieth anniversary lineup. This suggests, then, that social movement historiography is limited when defined by the formal terms of organizations or identities rather than the shifting, often informal and contingent, contexts in which much of the work gets done. But as this article has explored through the example of needle exchange, there are opportunities *and* limits to recovery within the history and the historiography of a queer politics of coalition. The activist Maxine Wolfe described ACT UP as "organizing the unorganized," (Sommella, 1997) and insofar as the name ACT UP includes the word *coalition*, the group did try to make a place for all affected by HIV/AIDS. But that, at times, meant adopting a model of activism that did not make a space for varied forms of participation or, at other times, risked a recuperation, or a recovery, of outsiderness into a model of political agency and identity that we might now call *queer* but that still sticks to certain models of marginality over others. This is neither to deny nor to minimize members of ACT UP who were women, people of color, and who were and have remained committed to antiracism. Instead, it is to acknowledge that ACT UP's work was done in formal and provisional relationships with a broad set of individuals and organizations who moved in and out of the group, making this history more than ACT UP's own (Chavez 2012; Cheng 2016; Juhasz 2012).

Recovery can offer important interventions into normative structures, be that of a social movement or historiography or the unequal vulnerabilities faced by those who use drugs. But it can also risk offering proscribed modes of self-realization or political identity as unspoken conditions of inclusion. When social movements and their history are described as an aggregation of individual actors, this approach can assume that people understand themselves as part of a political story or recuperate their actions and identities into frames of legibility that are not always of their own making. It can also mask the messiness and expressions of uneven power within movements; this is also the case in idealizing the notion of a commons.[14] The challenge, then, for queer social movement history is not only to cast a more inclusive or comprehensive look at the subjects and campaigns of activism that might be assumed part of this history, but to also examine how stigma and power operate to define the terms of movements and how they are remembered. As Ricardo Bracho, an activist and writer, warned in a 2001 essay about harm reduction and California's prisons, the "wants" of incarcerated men are not always met by harm reduction, and that among the things they "need" is "a social movement that would work against their *coercive* collectivization." Bracho's (2001) use of "coercive" was referring to the "lock, stock, store, warehouse, and survival modality" of life in prison, but he was also speaking in the essay to the "researcher, harm reductionist, or radical." This is not to romanticize addiction or diminish the unevenly distributed risks of death but to respond to the refrain "Dead Addicts Don't Recover" with: what else do those living want, need, and do?

Notes

Research for this article was supported by a Research and Scholarship Award from the University of Maryland Graduate School.

1. In 2007 ACT UP New York protested for single-payer health insurance and drug price controls at New York's Federal Building; in 2012 ACT UP joined with Occupy to demand a tax on Wall Street transactions and speculative trades to fund universal health care and a global response to AIDS (see actupny.org). For the 2017 conference announcement, see actupny.com/act-up-ny-to-hold-30th-anniversary-conference/ (accessed February 12, 2018). In this article, all references to ACT UP are to the New York chapter unless otherwise noted.

2. Hubbard discusses the challenges of working with such a massive visual archive in Re.Framing Activism 2012.

3. Quoted in the Lower East Side Harm Reduction Center's history of needle exchange and ACT UP: www.leshrc.org/page/history (accessed February 12, 2018).

4. Sources put the first exchange in Amsterdam or Rotterdam, between 1981 and 1983.

5. MAC members were also essential to ACT UP's housing activism; for example, Keith Cylar was a cofounder of the organization Housing Works, which later provided needle exchange (Schindler 2004; Shepard 2002).

6. Cohen (1999) shows how black lesbian and gay HIV/AIDS activism built on informal systems of mobilization already in place in black communities but that these activists also struggled with a less resource-rich infrastructure than that of AIDS organizations focused on white gay men.

7. Profiles of gay developers circulated in the press during the 1980s, reporting a phenomenon while promoting a stereotype (Hanhardt 2013).

8. In 1990 the Americans with Disabilities Act was implemented, and advocates debated its application for people with HIV and addictions.

9. In his interview, Clear suggests that this was not their regular distribution spot but a strategic choice for this action.

10. Along with Bordowitz, Zoe Leonard was among those who went to trial, and a full half of the budget for ACT UP's needle exchange in New York came from the writer David Wojnarowicz (ACT UP n.d.b).

11. No other published sources that I have located identify this activist as a heroin user or that she died of AIDS, so I have chosen to obscure her identity here.

12. ACT UP members also got arrested in Jersey City, New Jersey (Nieves 1991), among other cities.

13. The Native Youth Sexual Health Network innovated early harm reduction models that challenge systems of inequality, such as racism or settler colonialism. Prison abolitionist groups like Critical Resistance, INCITE: Women of Color Against Violence, and Generation Five, among many others, also draw on the principle of harm reduction to pursue community-centered rather than state-centered solutions.

14. J. Kehaulani Kauanui (2015) offers an important critique of the left romanticism of the commons, by tracing the early history of the concept and strategy as developed by English settlers as they expropriated indigenous lands in North America. She thus demonstrates that any contemporary effort to "reclaim the commons" involves "reifying and legitimating the original theft of those same lands." Kauanui argues that to bring this history into focus and engage it is to pose the possibility of "open[ing] spaces for non-native anarchists and others to work in solidarity with indigenous peoples—in a form of radical relationality—by acknowledging indigeneity rather than disavowing it."

References

ACT UP/Los Angeles (LA). 1993. Meeting minutes, October. ACT UP LA Files, ONE Institute, Los Angeles, CA.

ACT UP/New York. [1991?]. Booklet. Box 32, folder 11, ACT UP/NY Records, Manuscripts and Archives Division, New York Public Library, Astor, Lenox, and Tilden Foundations (hereafter NYPL).

———. n.d.a. Addicts Rights Caucus notes. Box 29, folder 5, ACT UP/NY Records, NYPL.

———. n.d.b. ACT UP Needle Exchange Program Budget Reallocation Proposal. Box 32, folder 11, ACT UP/NY Records, NYPL.

———. n.d.c. Flyers. Box 32, folder 11, ACT UP/NY Records, NYPL.

Bakunin, Mikhail. [1873] 1992. "Statism and Anarchy." In *Bakunin on Anarchy*, edited by Sam Dolgoff, 323–50. Montreal: Black Rose.

Barnett, Fiona, Zach Blas, Micha Cárdenas, Jacob Gaboury, Jessica Marie Johnson, and Margaret Rhee. 2016. "QueerOS: A User's Manual." *Debates in the Digital Humanities*. dhdebates.gc.cuny.edu/debates/text/56.

Bracho, Ricardo. 2001. "I Am a Nightmare Walking." *Harm Reduction Communication*, no. 11, 12–13. Clipping, Hank Wilson Papers, Box 18. Gay, Lesbian, Bisexual, and Transgender Historical Society of San Francisco.

Brown, Gavin. 2009. "Thinking beyond Homonormativity: Performative Explorations of Diverse Gay Economies." *Environment and Planning A* 41: 1496–510.

Chavez, Karma. 2012. "ACT UP, Haitian Migrants, and Alternative Memories of HIV/AIDS." *Quarterly Journal of Speech* 98, no. 1: 63–68.

Cheng, Jih-Fei. 2016. "How to Survive: AIDS and Its Afterlives in Popular Media." *WSQ* 44, nos. 1–2: 73–92.

Clear, Allan. 2015. Sarah Schulman interview, March 1. ACT UP Oral History Project. www.actuporalhistory.org/interviews/images/clear.pdf.

Cohen, Cathy. 1997. "Punks, Bulldaggers, and Welfare Queens: The Radical Potential of Queer Politics?" *GLQ* 3, no. 4: 437–65.

———. 1999. *The Boundaries of Blackness: AIDS and the Breakdown of Black Politics*. Chicago: University of Chicago Press.

Duggan, Lisa. [1991] 1995. "Making It Perfectly Queer." In *Sex Wars: Sexual Dissent and Political Culture*, edited by Lisa Duggan and Nan D. Hunter, 155–72. New York: Routledge.

Elovich, Richard. 1990. ACT UP press briefing, May 10. Box 15, folder 6, ACT UP/NY Records, NYPL.

———. n.d. Proposal for affinity group of recovering drug addicts to covertly disseminate needles.… Box 32, folder 11, ACT UP/NY Records, NYPL.

———. 1992. "Who Are the Fags? Who Are the Junkies? Where Are the Services?" *NYQ*, March 8. Clipping, Box 32, folder 11, ACT UP/NY Records, NYPL.

———. 2007. Sarah Schulman interview, May 14. ACT UP Oral History Project. www .actuporalhistory.org/interviews/images/elovich.pdf.

Fanon, Frantz. [1965] 2005. *The Wretched of the Earth*. New York: Grove.

Floyd, Kevin. 2004. *The Reification of Desire: Toward a Queer Marxism*. Minneapolis: University of Minnesota Press.

France, David. 2016. *How to Survive a Plague: The Inside Story of How Citizens and Science Tamed AIDS*. New York: Knopf.

France, David, dir. 2012. *How to Survive a Plague*. itunes.apple.com/us/movie/how-to -survive-a-plague/id579227341

Friedman, Samuel R., Wouter de Jong, Diana Rossi, Graciela Touzé, Russell Rockwell, Don Des Jarlais, and Richard Elovich. 2007. "Harm Reduction Theory: Users Culture, Micro-Social Indigenous Harm Reduction, and the Self-Organization and Outside-Organizing of Users' Groups." *International Journal of Drug Policy* 18, no. 2: 107–17.

Gossett, Reina, Dean Spade, and Hope Dector. 2014. "Prison Abolition and Prefiguring the World You Want to Live In." Barnard Center for Research on Women, bcrw .barnard.edu/videos/reina-gossett-dean-spade-part-1-prison-abolition-prefiguring -the-world-you-want-to-live-in/ (accessed May 28, 2018).

Gould, Deborah B. 2009. *Moving Politics: Emotion and ACT UP's Fight against* AIDS. Chicago: University of Chicago Press.

———. 2012. "ACT UP, Racism, and the Question of How to Use History." *Quarterly Journal of Speech* 98, no. 1: 54–62.

Grove, Donald. 2008. Interview with Sarah Schulman, July 1. ACT UP Oral History Project. www.actuporalhistory.org/interviews/images/grove.pdf

Halberstam, Jack. 2014a. "Notes on Wildness (This Is Not a Manifesto)." Lecture. hemisphericinstitute.org/hemi/en/enc14-5-minute-manifestos/item/2608-enc14 -5min-halberstam.

———. 2014b. "Wildness, Loss, Death." *Social Text*, no. 121: 137–48.

Hanhardt, Christina B. 2012. "Left Queer." *Scholar and Feminist Online* 11, nos. 1–2. sfonline.barnard.edu/gender-justice-and-neoliberal-transformations/left-queer/.

———. 2013. *Safe Space: Gay Neighborhood History and the Politics of Violence*. Durham, NC: Duke University Press.

————. 2016. "Broken Windows at Blue's: A Queer History of Gentrification and Policing." In *Policing the Planet: Why the Policing Crisis Led to Black Lives Matter*,
edited by Jordan T. Camp and Christina Heatherton, 41–61. New York: Verso.

Hubbard, Jim, dir. 2012. *United in Anger*. DVD. Kickstarter Edition.

Juhasz, Alexandra. 2012. "Forgetting ACT UP." *Quarterly Journal of Speech* 98, no. 1:
69–74.

Kauanui, J. Kehaulani. 2015. "Nothing Common about 'the Commons': Settler Colonialism and Indigenous Difference." American Studies Association Annual Meeting,
Toronto, Canada.

Kipnis, Hilery Joy, and Jean Carlomusto, dirs. *Up in Arms Over Needle Exchange*. MP3.
GMHC Records, NYPL.

Lambert, Bruce. 1990. "Ten Seized in Demonstration as They Offer New Needles." *New
York Times*, March 7.

Leonard, Zoe. 2010. Sarah Schulman interview, January 13. ACT UP Oral History Project. www.actuporalhistory.org/interviews/images/leonard.pdf.

Levine, Debra. 2010. Sarah Schulman interview, December 21. ACT UP Oral History
Project. fds.lib.harvard.edu/fds/deliver/417793019/wid00003c000128.pdf.

Lower East Side Harm Reduction Center [LESHRC]. 1993. Funding proposal. Box 435,
folder 2, Aaron Diamond Foundation Records, NYPL.

Lune, Howard. 2007. *Urban Action Networks: HIV/AIDS and Community Organizing in
New York City*. Lanham, MD: Rowman and Littlefield.

Marx, Karl. [1852] 1994. *The Eighteenth Brumaire of Louis Bonaparte*. New York: International Publishers.

Muñoz, José Esteban, 1999. *Disidentifications: Queers of Color and the Performance of
Politics*. Minneapolis: University of Minnesota Press.

Navarro, Mireya. 1991. "Yale Study Reports Clean Needle Help Check AIDS." *New York
Times*, August 1.

Navarro, Ray, Catherine Saalfield, and members of Majority Actions Committee, eds. n.d.
"Some Keywords Related to IV-Drug Use and AIDS." Box 32, folder 11, ACT UP/
NY Records, NYPL.

Nichols, Rob. 2012. "Toward a Critical Trans Politics: An Interview with Dean Spade."
Upping the Anti 14: 37-51.

Nieves, Evelyn. 1991. "Judge Acquits Four of Distributing Needles in an Effort to Curb
AIDS." *New York Times*, November 8.

Re.Framing Activism. 2012. "Jim Hubbard: Framing ACT UP Activists." reframe.sussex
.ac.uk/activistmedia/2012/11/jim-hubbard-framing-hiv-activists.

Roth, Benita. 2017. *The Life and Death of ACT UP/LA: Anti-AIDS Activism in Los Angeles
from the 1980s to the 2000s*. New York: Cambridge University Press.

Saalfield, Catherine, and Ray Navarro, dirs. 1991. "Shocking Pink Praxis: Race and
Gender on the ACT UP Frontlines." In *Inside/Out: Lesbian Theories, Gay Theories*,
edited by Diana Fuss, 341–69. New York: Routledge.

————. 1989. *Bleach, Teach, and Outreach*. Gay Men's Health Crisis Records, NYPL.

Schindler, Paul. 2004. "Keith Cylar, 45, AIDS Activist Co-Founded Housing Works." *Villager* 73, no. 50. thevillager.com/villager_50/keithcylar45.html.

Shepard, Benjamin. 2002. "Building a Healing Community from ACT UP to Housing Works." In *From ACT UP to the WTO: Urban Protest and Community Building in the Era of Globalization*, edited by Benjamin Shepard and Ronald Hayduk, 351–60. London: Verso.

————. 2009. *Queer Political Performance and Protest*. New York: Routledge.

————. 2015. *Rebel Friendships: "Outsider" Networks and Social Movements*. New York: Palgrave.

Sommella, Laraine. 1997. "This is About People Dying: The Tactics of Early ACT UP and Lesbian Avengers in New York City: Interview with Maxine Wolfe." In *Queers in Space: Communities, Public Spaces, Sites of Resistance*, edited by Gordon Brent Ingram, Anne-Marie Bouthillette, and Yolanda Retter, 407–37. Seattle: Bay Press.

Sorge, Rod. 1990. "Drug Policy in the Age of AIDS: The Philosophy of 'Harm Reduction.'" *Health/PAC Bulletin*, Fall, 4–10. Clipping, Box 32, folder 11, ACT UP/NY Records, NYPL.

Stallybrass, Peter. 1990. "Marx and Heterogeneity: Thinking the Lumpenproletariat." *Representations* 31: 69–95.

Sullivan, Ronald. 1991. "Needle Exchangers Had Right to Break Law, Judge Rules." *New York Times*, June 26.

————. 1993. "Yolanda Serrano, 45, Organizer of Anti-AIDS Needle Exchanges." *New York Times*, October 22.

Thoburn, Nicholas. 2003. *Deleuze, Marx and Politics*. London: Routledge.

Vazquez-Pacheco, Robert. 2002. Sarah Schulman interview, December 14. ACT UP Oral History Project. www.actuporalhistory.org/interviews/images/vazquez.pdf.

White Lightning. 1974. "Two Hundred Demonstrate against Bronx VA Methadone: The Government Is a Dope Pusher!" In *White Lighting: A Revolutionary Organization Dedicated to Serving the People*, August–September. Author's possession.

Williams, Dan Keith. 2004. Jim Hubbard interview, March 26. ACT UP Oral History Project. www.actuporalhistory.org/interviews/images/williams.pdf.

"WAGES FOR HOUSEWORK MEANS WAGES *AGAINST* HETEROSEXUALITY":

On the Archives of Black Women for Wages for Housework and Wages Due Lesbians

Beth Capper and Arlen Austin

$\mathcal{I}$n "Capitalism and the Struggle against Sexual Work," the Marxist feminist theorist Silvia Federici (2017a: 144) asserts an analogous relation between lesbian visibility and the strike on reproductive labor, contending that "coming out is like going on strike." Delivered at a Wages for Housework conference in Toronto in 1975, Federici's comments emerged alongside her better-known essay "On Sexuality as Work" (2017b), which explores heterosexuality as a form of socially necessary labor inclusive of sex, care work, and emotional management.[1] "Capitalism and the Struggle against Sexual Work," by contrast, positions lesbian sexuality as simultaneously "a direct attack on the work-sexual discipline imposed on women in capitalist society" and a placeholder for "a redefinition of what our sexuality should be" (Federici 2017a: 146). Federici's celebration of lesbianism as a form of work refusal might, then, seem to call for a politics of lesbian separatism as an antidote to the sexual division of labor. Such a reading, however, misses how in this text the homo/hetero binary is recast as both an instrument and an effect of capitalist divisions of labor—divisions that lesbian separatism only serves to reconsolidate. Moreover, Federici is clear that lesbianism does not signal "the end of work"; rather, it is a historically specific strategy of refusal under present conditions of sexual labor and sexual relation. By approaching "coming out" in terms of a strike on (hetero)sexual labor, Federici therefore reconfigures lesbian struggle

GLQ 24:4
DOI 10.1215/10642684-6957772
© 2018 by Duke University Press

as a starting point for an anticapitalist commoning project that *all* women have an interest in defending.

Federici's anticapitalist treatment of lesbian sexuality broaches the relation we chart in this article between the politics of housework and the provocation of a "queer commons" that this special issue foregrounds. Most directly, her assertion that lesbianism could be understood as a form of housework refusal situates reproductive labor both as the *common ground* of feminist struggle and as a pivotal terrain that must be collectivized through this struggle. This is a position she later echoed in her contention that any vision of the commons must recognize "reproductive labor as an important sphere of human activity . . . to be revolutionized . . . revisited and revalorised" in order to understand how anticapitalist movements and social forms might sustain themselves (Federici 2012b: 145). At the same time, "Capitalism and the Struggle against Sexual Work" and its emphasis on lesbianism as a *means* towards this collective vision of reproduction illuminates the less remarked upon importance of queer sexualities to the Wages for Housework (WfH) movement's broader conception of social reproduction struggles. Instead of seeking to further entrench the housewife in the heteronormative household by rewarding her with a wage (a common misconception about the movement), WfH instead sought to refuse and destroy this household as a central unit of capitalism's social reproduction, and along with it the figure of the housewife.[2] Indeed, while the WfH movement broadly retained the "housewife" as a figure of negative identification, Federici (2012a: 9) emphasizes that "we fought for wages for *housework* not for housewives." Rather than a stable location, the house was understood, on the one hand, as a political-economic modality that regulated racialized, gendered, and sexual labor across multiple sites that included, but was not confined to, the heteronormative familial household and, on the other, as a mutable and contested form that, if imagined collectively, might yield an altogether different organization of sexuality and social reproduction.

This effort to revalorize reproductive labor as the ground of anticapitalist struggle under the banner of a "reproductive commons," however, has also come under scrutiny from theorists and activists who argue that such discourses inevitably reinvest in a normative reproductive order. Melinda Cooper (quoted in Marble 2018), for example, has voiced concerns about "a revalorization of women's caring role as distributed nurturers of the left and mothers of the common." Likewise, Angela Mitropoulos (2016: 178) has suggested that any conception of the household, even a revitalized or radicalized one, threatens to remain entangled with "the reproduction of family, race, and nation" that has long structured the organization of the household and its constitutive boundaries. These concerns signal potential tensions between certain discourses of the commons and queer critique, given that queer critique is arguably one name for a mode of theorizing that interrogates the differential forms of incorporation and exclusion that produce *any* commons. According to Mitropoulos (quoted in O'Brien 2017: 89), one aim of queer critique is to make space for "uncommon forms" of life and "unconditional (rather than universal) reasons for care or welfare." Similarly, Kevin Floyd (2009: 9) has argued that in recent years queer studies has been increasingly motivated by a maneuver of "simultaneous expansion and internal complexification," refusing to "isolate sexuality from other horizons of knowledge" while acknowledging the limits of the critical imperatives that undergird its own theory of the social. In other words, even as queer studies has expanded the terms and figures of queer political struggle, this "generalizing impulse" (indeed, what we perhaps might call a commoning impulse) has often been paired with a necessarily vigilant attention to those forms of life that fall away from—and constitute an irreducible remainder to—articulations of the general or the common (ibid.).[3] As such, historical and contemporary arguments for a figure of the common potentially sit in tension with queer critique's interrogation of the violence of "common measure" (Mitropoulos, quoted in O'Brien 2017: 85).

Returning to the archives of the WfH movement, we explore the tensions between the common and the uncommon that come to the fore when nonheteronormative sexualities and socialities are centered in struggles over reproduction and when struggles over social reproduction are centered in demands for sexual liberation. In particular, we consider the activist histories of two autonomous factions within the WfH campaign: the Canadian/UK group Wages Due Lesbians (WDL) and the US/UK-based Black Women for Wages for Housework (BWfWfH). Reconsidering the WfH movement from the vantage point of these groups and their intellectual production is, perhaps, already to register the internal conflicts and divisions that contoured the WfH movement in ways that pressure the call for a commons grounded in housework as a unified and unifying site of struggle. Yet we also contend that positioning these groups as mere correctives to the broader WfH campaign has the effect of asserting a clear origin story of the movement, stabilizing the meaning of WfH in a particular geographic and historical context rather than as a perspective that shifted and evolved over time. Through a critical reorientation of the texts and figures placed at the center of the movement's analysis, we hope to reorient the theoretical claims and questions derived from a reading of this archive.

These groups can be situated in a broader history of feminist, gay and lesbian, and left activism from the late 1960s to the 1980s that articulated the demand for an entwined vision of redistributive justice and sexual liberation. These demands were confronted by a coalition of neoliberal and neoconservative forces that reconfigured the state's regulation of social reproduction by further entrenching the racialized, gendered, and sexual form of the nuclear household as "the foundation of social and economic order" (Cooper 2017: 49). Crucially, at this same moment, movements for welfare rights and reproductive justice were also mobilized as ciphers for what the ecologist Garrett Hardin described in 1968 as "the tragedy of the commons." While the discourse of the commons as a form of collective property under threat of enclosure has a multipronged history, Hardin's account of a tragic commons linked the welfare state's imagined support of "unmanaged" (nonwhite) reproduction to a neo-Malthusian discourse of "overpopulation." This argument was pivotal to the articulation of what Rob Nixon (2012: 593) calls "a neoliberal rescue narrative, whereby privatization . . . is deemed necessary for averting tragedy." Within this historical conjuncture, BWfWfH and WDL's vision of a "reproductive commons" issued the demand for an alternative, collective, organization of reproduction that would not replicate existing sexual and racial divisions of labor and initiated a praxis of forming alliances among reproductive workers against neoliberal enclosures.

BWfWfH and WDL advanced a political theory of housework in which the broad-based mobilizing capacities of this rubric were shown to require an analytic centering of those divisions and incommensurabilities that the house and housework also named. These articulations resonate with contemporary queer (of color) critiques that do not assume the normative home as a given terrain to be struggled within (and against) but instead foreground the positions of those constitutively expelled from *and* unevenly incorporated into its architectures and imaginaries (Reddy 1998; Shah 2003; Ferguson 2004).[4] By re-visioning the demand for WfH as pivotal to the fight against forms of what BWfWfH cofounder Wilmette Brown (1976a: 8) called the racialized "heterosexual work discipline" that mandated women perform low-waged and unwaged reproductive labor (whether in their own homes, in the homes of white and wealthy families, as sex workers, or as mothers on welfare), BWfWfH and WDL impressed that "the home" disciplines the sexualities and labors of even those seemingly excluded from its domain. Both groups emphasized that heteronormativity, as a modality of a work-discipline, especially targeted women of color (and) lesbians who were refused by, or who refused, the regulatory ideals of (white) femininity associated with the housewife, and who faced criminalization, sexual violence, forced sterilization, welfare austerity, and the loss of child custody for their transgressions.

As WDL (1976) put it in an op-ed for the Canadian gay liberation journal the *Body Politic*, "wages for housework are wages *against* heterosexuality." Rather than assert strict divisions between "straight" and "queer" women, WDL framed heterosexuality in a manner far closer to Cathy J. Cohen's (1997) use of the concept of heteronormativity to describe how normative heterosexuality's state-sanctioned and institutional organization regulates and immiserates a range of social subjects (including those who may nevertheless engage in hetero-sex). Such a position is reiterated in the potential alliances that Brown argues might be forged among black lesbians and "straight" mothers on welfare: "Black women with ten children who are on welfare are struggling against their heterosexual work as I am struggling against my heterosexual work [as a lesbian]." While this "heterosexual work" was often performed directly for men, BWfWfH underscored that such labors were ultimately required by "the Man," an idiom of black vernacular political critique that BWfWfH redeployed, following welfare rights activist Johnnie Tillmon (1972), to conceptualize the pervasive effects of capitalist state power as they manifested in "the very ways that domestic space is constituted and the heteropatriarchal family normalized" (Kandaswamy 2010: 254). Activists in the WfH movement thus asserted that neither lesbian nor straight sexual relations existed outside of the framework of capitalist work relations. It is in this sense that Federici (2012c: 20) defined the movement's intellectual and activist project as that of demarcating the intimate and sexual relations that must be understood as work "so that eventually we might rediscover what is love and create what will be our sexuality which we have never known."

As a contribution to the theory and practice of a queer commons, we are especially interested in foregrounding the strategy of collective autonomy advanced by these groups. Autonomy, which was explicitly opposed to both separatism and left-vanguardism, was activated as an organizational tactic to mobilize across and beyond existing racial, gender, sexual, and class configurations while recognizing the irreducible differences between reproductive laborers. This strategy informed BWfWfH and WDL's efforts to interrogate the housewife as a site of negative identification at the center of WfH's coalitional politics. Attending to "the tension between autonomy and commonalities" (Mitropoulos 2016: 170) or between their own demands and the broader WfH movement, these groups centered those reproductive workers often rendered disposable or superfluous to white heteronormative reproductive imaginaries. Nevertheless, even as these groups destabilized the terms through which their own visions of a reproductive commons took shape, to the extent that they focused exclusively on cisgender women, their analyses are necessarily incomplete. We therefore position this article as a partial contribution to a wider discourse and history of queer social reproduction.[5]

The insights of BWfWfH and WDL toward an articulation of a queer commons reside in their twinned understanding of reproduction as a terrain of collective maintenance and insurrection, or what Stefano Harney and Fred Moten (2013: 76) term "militant preservation." They struggled, first, for an autonomous nonheteronormative mode of social reproduction, and second, for an insurgent mode of common world-building. Here, we echo Peter Linebaugh's (2013) preference for the verb-form "commoning" over the characterization of the commons as a set of resources available for value extraction. Likewise, we build on Massimo de Angelis's stance against conceptions of the commons as a preformulated telos of collective struggle. As de Angelis (2006: 238) emphasizes, "The problematic of overcoming division is one with the problematic of the production of the commons." This problematic cannot be set aside through calls for unity but must be actively (re)produced and constantly critiqued. We find "commoning" as a process of communitarian resistance to enclosure, including the enclosures of liberal forms of identity politics, to be resonant with imaginations of queer world-building. Yet since one strength of queer critique lies in its interrogation of the regimes of common sense, we understand it as a central task of a theory of the queer commons to probe the common sense of the commons itself. If there is such a thing as a "queer" commons, it will have been one that refuses fidelity to many of the founding assumptions of commons discourse.

Black Feminist Refusal and the Reproductive Commons

BWfWfH officially declared itself an autonomous group within the WfH campaign in a 1976 press release titled "Birth Announcement," illustrated with a hand-rendered stork carrying a basket of dollar bills. "Our group is a rainbow of black women," wrote Brown (2017: 116). "Some of us are married, some of us are single; some of us have children, some don't; some of us are straight, some are lesbian; most of us have second jobs, some of us are on welfare; some of us are older, some younger. ALL OF US WANT WAGES FOR HOUSEWORK." Under the banner of the WfH perspective, BWfWfH was involved in struggles for sex workers' rights, fights against welfare austerity, efforts to create sanctuaries for political and economic refugees, and advocacy work on behalf of black women victims of serial murder. The group had aspirations of becoming an international organization of black and Third World women, with members across the United States, the UK, and Trinidad and Tobago; their involvement in US and UK black (and) queer feminist struggles, however, has been archived in greater detail.

The record of this explicitly black feminist demand for WfH stands in complex relation to conceptions of the WfH perspective as irreconcilable with black women's freedom struggles. "The Approaching Obsolescence of House-work" (1983), by Angela Y. Davis, remains the most well-known and comprehensive of such statements. In this essay, Davis argues that the WfH strategy fails to account both for black women's differential relation to the domestic and for the racial divisions of reproductive labor internationally that have forced black women to leave home to work for others. Similar critiques were leveraged from collectives such as the Brixton Black Women's Group, whose 1984 statement "Black Feminism" rebuked WfH's campaigns as "middle class deviations from the real issues of women's liberation" (quoted in Sudbury 1998: 164). For these activist-intellectuals, to recenter the house and the houseworker as unproblematic categories of analysis was to resediment the racial-sexual determinations of the domestic as a gendered spatial arrangement.

In the activist and intellectual production of BWfWfH, however, black women's housework is positioned in a nonidentical, and at times antagonistic, relation to the labors of the (white) housewife. Drawing on the history of slavery and its afterlives as the basis for its analysis, the group emphasized the racialized "divisions of labor" between white and black women, and especially the labors black women had historically performed for white women, in ways that interrupted (but did not render impossible) alliances over the conditions of reproductive work (Brown 1976a: 5). At the same time, the group's approach to "housework" as an analytic was aimed at overwhelming this category from the inside in order to unbraid the moralistic, and ultimately ideological, distinctions between the work of the housewife and other reproductive workers (such as the mother on welfare, the paid domestic, and the sex worker). This perspective is encapsulated by Yolanda Jones of BWfWfH in a 1980 interview with WBAI (FM radio) in New York: "[BWfWfH is for] women in any kind of housework, it's for men who might be doing that housework, whether you're married or not has nothing to do with it, and whether you don't or do do the traditional idea of 'housework' in quotes is not the issue."

The conceptual impropriety of "housework" propagated by the WfH movement at times led contemporaneous feminist critics to argue that this analytic was incoherent. This is encapsulated in one review for the feminist magazine *Spare Rib* of the WfH film *About Time* (1976). Made in collaboration with the London Women's Film Group, the film subsumes under the umbrella of housework the labors of a (traditional) housewife with those of a nurse, a lesbian waitress, and other protagonists. "The waitress character complains that her pay is so low that she has to do the 'housework' of smiling and flirting with customers to get good tips," writes Zoe Fairbairns (1977: 43). Querying why these labors are understood by the movement as housework, Fairbairns continues: "But this isn't an argument for wages for smiling and flirting, it's an argument for better pay for waitresses" (ibid.: 43). What Fairbairns misses about this strategy, however, are the ways in which it illuminates how the affective and communicative modes characteristic of housework had always been diffuse across multiple sites and labors, even as WfH also presciently diagnosed the increasing hegemony of affect and communication to late capitalist service and caring economies.

For BWfWfH, the promiscuity of *housework* as a rubric was activated in order to relocate the constitutive (and constitutively sexual and racial) "outsides" of the domestic imaginary *inside* the figure of the housewife in ways that displaced her status as a privileged metonym of property, propriety, and protected interiority. This is a strategy employed by Margaret Prescod (1982: 33) in her 1977 speech "Bringing It All Back Home," later circulated as a BWfWfH pamphlet. In it, she articulates a capacious sense of the "emotional housework" of black domestic workers from the West Indies (specifically Barbados), from the housework involved in preparing to work abroad to the housework of assimilation in the United States or the UK, to the housework of managing everyday racism and racial violence. Linking these quotidian labors to movements for reparations and radical redistribution, Prescod foregrounds struggles to bring the massive wealth expropriated through slavery and colonialism back home. In a manner that recalls Davis's earlier "Reflections on the Black Woman's Role in the Community of Slaves" (1972), Prescod rearticulates the history of slavery and its destruction from the vantage point of its reproductive laborers, and reclaims "the Mammy" as a radical figure whose fugitive labors within the master's household enacted a refusal and corrosion of the slave regime. Her important addition to Davis's analysis is in announcing the black immigrant domestic worker as a resonant figure internal to the "master's house" of those nations who had most profited from slavery in the West Indies.

Like the broader WfH movement, BWfWfH framed the struggle for WfH as a struggle for sex workers' rights. In so doing, the group refused the contemporaneous state politics of propriety that sought to regulate black women's sexuality by tying welfare provisions to sexual abstention (Tillmon 1972; Smith 2007; Kandaswamy 2010). A 1977 BWfWfH manifesto, "Money for Prostitutes Is Money for Black Women," extended the Los Angeles and San Francisco WfH chapters' claim that "an attack on prostitutes is an attack on *all* women" (Los Angeles and San Francisco Wages for Housework Committees 1977: 1) and is most explicit in establishing alliances among sex workers and black women. This manifesto performs the terms of this alliance through the claim that money for prostitutes *is* money for black women. This is, of course, partly because *some* black women *are* sex workers. However, the basis for this potential alliance was understood to rest, more fundamentally, in a common relation to the criminalization and containment of sexual expressions and sexual labors:

> The terrorism that is practiced by the Man and by individual men against prostitute women is a terror we all know. . . . Whether it is the terror of being beaten in the bedroom or in a parked car, on the street or in the jail, or the terror of not being able to find a decent place to live where the police don't feel free to break down the door, it is terror rooted in our having to be at everyone's disposal because we don't have the money to be able to say NO. (Black Women for Wages for Housework [1977] 2012: 230)

Terrion Williamson (2016: 133, 105) explores the terrorism of state and extra-state violence wrought on black women "in the life." She considers how the descriptor "in the life"—often used by prostitutes and sex workers as well as black people who "act on same-sexual desire" to refer to themselves—is itself a way to establish "a space of vitality, a space for living, that is primarily inhabited by those who engage in activities that put them in close proximity to death and whose existence is externally conditioned by their supposed nonexistence." Exploring black female victims of serial murder, many of whom are sex workers, Williamson (2016: 134) considers how the lives of these women disarrange the maldistribution of value and nonvalue, "acknowledging the absolute violence of value" through an insistence on a space for living in and on their own terms. Prefiguring Williamson's analysis, in the mid-1980s Prescod and Brown connected the fight for WfH to justice for black female victims of serial murder in Los Angeles, many of whom were also sex workers, to illuminate the imbrication between the state-sanctioned femicide of black women, the violence of economic value, and discourses of sexual propriety. BWfWfH therefore outlined its own refusals of the structures of value through which black women's social and sexual lives and labors were expropriated, regulated, and met with murderous violence.[6]

As we have suggested, BWfWfH responded to a renewed mobilization of the figure of the commons during this period, one that targeted the social and sexual reproductions of women of color. This was a discourse exemplified by Hardin's "Tragedy of the Commons." Written on the occasion of the 1967 United Nations Universal Declaration of Human Rights proclamation that named the family as a "fundamental unit of human society" with the right to determine its own size, Hardin's (1968: 1246) argument was largely a polemic against what he terms the "commons in breeding." At the heart of Hardin's diatribe lay fears about the excesses of racialized and gendered reproductions that are, in turn, posited as the central locus of all the other problems that assail the commons in general, spelling ruination for putatively "common lands" and the distribution of state resources.[7] The racialist underpinnings of his reproductive politics are further corroborated by Nixon's (2012: 596) observation that Hardin had "no hesitation in siring four children" himself.[8] Hardin's elegy for the commons can be read as continuous with his staunch anti-immigration politics. Indeed, his article coincided with a historical restructuring of global capital that demanded the intensified recruitment of (gendered) immigrant labor to the United States (Lowe 1996) as well as the passage of the 1965 Immigration and Nationality Act, which administered eligibility for migration under the doctrine of family reunification (Parreñas 2008: 129). His claims, additionally, were in tune with a host of contemporaneous attacks on the US welfare state that emerged as a result of its perceived "abuse" by poor black women. Hardin (1968: 1244) begins his essay with an allegorical tragic theater in which a "pasture open to all" is laid to waste by the unbridled self-interest of cattle herdsman.[9] The most immediate target of his ire, however, comes directly into view at the article's midpoint: "In a welfare state, how shall we deal with the family, the religion, the race, or the class . . . that adopts overbreeding as a policy to secure its own aggrandizement? To couple the concept of freedom to breed with the belief that everyone born has an equal right to the commons is to lock the world into a tragic course of action" (ibid.: 1245).

Prefiguring the narrative invention of the "welfare queen," Hardin's critique of the "commons in breeding" is contoured by a racialized and sexualized image of black women's hyperfertility sedimented in chattel slavery (Hancock 2004), one disarticulated from the ascriptions of normative gender, domesticity, and kinship through a metonymic "proximity to . . . breeding livestock" (Morgan 2004: 80).[10] In "The Tragedy of the Commons," the commons thus signals the threat of racialized reproductivity in ways that illuminate how the reproductions of people of color are prominently figured as perverse, destructive, nonproprietary, and queer. In this vein, Andil Gosine (2010) has situated Hardin's article in a broader environmental discourse where nonwhite sex and reproduction as well as ostensibly "nonreproductive" gay sex were cast as queer threats to nature.

Against Hardin's white supremacist discourse of a "tragic commons," BWf-WfH articulated a vision of the commons transformed by black women's sexual freedom and redistributive justice. In a paper she wrote for a course at the New School taught by Rayna Reiter and Heidi Hartmann, Brown (1976b: 10) charts a host of "counterattack[s]" against black women's social and political power, from

Hardin's calls for "forced sterilization" to Daniel Patrick Moynihan's 1965 report on the "pathologies" of the black family. Refusing to assuage this animus against black "hyper-reproductivity" and "pathology" through recourse to an alternative discourse of the "respectable" family, Brown instead refracts white supremacist fears and anxieties about black kinship as a cultural figure of "nonheteronormative perversions" (Ferguson 2004: 87). Linking the language of sexual liberation to demands for reproductive justice, she claims the success of black's women's "refusal to limit the expression of their sexuality to producing only the number of children capital requires" and black women's "persistence in fucking when and whom they please regardless of the consequences for the state" (Brown 1976b: 9).[11] As a response to the state's regulation of black reproduction, she also recalibrates the meaning of reproductive refusal, often understood within WfH discourse as the refusal to have children for the labor force. In so doing, she prefigures contemporary articulations of the relation between black (social and biological) reproduction and queer futurity, showing how black reproductive futures serve as a negation of white heteronormative reproductive futures (such as Hardin's) that require the nonexistence or destruction of blackness (Keeling 2009; Bliss 2015).[12]

In her later essay and pamphlet *Black Ghetto Ecology* (1986), Brown takes up the black feminist struggle for welfare rights as an ecological issue. She explores the environmental degradation of the "ghetto," where high rates of cancer evidence the "malignant kinship" between racism, sexism, and economic exploitation. "I grew up in Newark, New Jersey, one of the cancer centres of the US. My sister calls it 'Cancer Alley,' because the petrochemical plants reek for miles around" (Brown 1986: 7). Showing the entanglements between the destruction of the racialized poor and the destruction of the broader environment, she argues that the demand for economic redistribution through welfare is a means of black women "reclaiming the earth" toward their own survival and self-care—that is, toward an organization of the commons that would support black women's social reproductions and that might, in turn, transform all our ecological relations (ibid.: 14). Placing black women's redistributive justice at the center of environmental struggles, Brown suggests, would galvanize an alternative relation to the earth and the environment as such.

"Coming Out Is Like Going on Strike"

The same year that BWfWfH formed, WDL (1975a) "came out" as an autonomous collective at a WfH conference in Montreal, where a group of lesbian-identified women authored a manifesto titled "Fucking Is Work." WDL were influenced by

Mariarosa Dalla Costa's (1972: 31–32) argument that contradictions within the division of labor meant that capitalism presented a "homosexual framework for living." Building on and extending this provocation, WDL argued that lesbians were uniquely placed within these contradictory relations, subject to the sexual labor that heterosexual women perform (whether through marriage to a man, through their work in prostitution, or through child rearing) while threatening the stability of capitalism through their sexual desire for women. Selma James had reached similar conclusions in her earlier unpublished essay "When the Mute Speaks" (1971). James names lesbians as the "enemy within" capitalist relations, referencing and upending the anti-immigration rhetoric deployed in 1970 by British Tory MP Enoch Powell. Her appropriation of this rhetoric posited lesbian relationality as an anticapitalist potential immanent to the structure of existing work relations: "They [female workers] are more intimate with the woman they work next to . . . and that is a lesbian relationship. Capital undermines heterosexuality even while it is fundamental to its structure" (ibid.: 13). Similarly, for WDL, capital disciplined lesbians because their sexuality figured as a potential rupture within the domain of the house and its worker. In the words of WDL London cofounder Ruth Hall (1975: 3), capital disciplines lesbianism "in every way because it threatens an explosion."[13]

WDL advanced a radically expanded portrait of the lesbian, where lesbian sexuality appears as at once a particular form of housework and as a structural contradiction internal to capitalism that might herald housework's refusal and eventual abolition. Although WDL positioned lesbianism as an attack on work, they argued that lesbian sexuality was still reproductive of capitalist relations. Such an analysis, written well before the widespread legalization of gay and lesbian marriage, is prescient in its articulation of lesbian sex as a form of reproductive labor as opposed to common ascriptions of lesbian sexuality as "non-reproductive."[14] As the authors of a collectively written essay "Lesbian and Straight" argue: "In lesbian relationships we still take care of ourselves and other women (other workers) so it is not an escape from our work" (Wages Due Lesbians 1975b: 22). At the same time, the authors of "Lesbian and Straight" elucidate that lesbian sexuality is dual in nature, simultaneously reproducing capitalism *and* reproducing the struggle that might augur the end of work: "When we sleep with a woman we are still serving the state—she too must be kept happy enough to keep working. But at least when we spend our time and sexual energy on women we are also maintaining her for her struggle against our work" (ibid.: 23). The wage demand, far from occluding this possibility of work refusal, is its necessary and enabling condition—

a claim to "wages due" through which the lesbian as houseworker found the material means of organizing toward collective resistance.

Nevertheless, WDL was clear that lesbian sexuality should not be separated from other social determinations. This is where the group irrevocably breaks with a politics of lesbian separatism, which was understood by WDL as "a strategy based on defeat, based on an acceptance of the divisions by which capital rules us; it is capital's strategy" (Hall 1975: 4). Against separatist politics, they argued that "only the revolution destroying all productive relationships will destroy the *hell hole* of our sexual relations, lesbian and heterosexual" (ibid.). In contrast to what Annamarie Jagose (1994: 2) nominates as a lesbian utopics that announces the "ontological priority of the lesbian body before the repressive mechanisms of power," for WDL, lesbianism was not external to the "hell hole" of capital's sexual relations; it was inscribed within them. Since WDL never advanced lesbianism as liberatory in itself, the group has in recent years renamed itself "Queer Strike" to advocate for economic justice for lesbian, gay, bisexual, transgender, and queer people.

The oscillation between lesbianism as a structural position within the sexual division of labor and as a queer horizon that might yield a futural transformation of sexual and social relations undergirds the claims of a collectively written speech "Lesbianism and Power" delivered by Hall at a 1975 WfH conference in London. Hall's speech explores the radicality of lesbianism through the lesbian's refusal of those forms of reproductive labor that support the heteronormative household. The relation between the refusal of housework and lesbianism operates in both directions, so that just as coming out as a lesbian was, in Federici's terms, likened to "going on strike" against housework, refusing to do housework was itself a simultaneous provocation for being read as a lesbian. As Hall (1975: 3) elaborates, "Women are told that if they step out of line, if they are not submissive enough to men, or refuse their housework—any part of it from laundry to the smiles in the street—they will be taken for a lesbian, ostracized as a lesbian, may even, horror of horrors, become a lesbian."[15]

That said, Hall emphasizes that the strategy of lesbian refusal brings into being a host of regulatory mechanisms that respond to this refusal, alternatively, by disciplining lesbianism and by seeking to reincorporate those designated as lesbians back into the relations of heterosexual production and reproduction.[16] Thus, even as the lesbian is positioned as a point of exit from the heterosexual work-discipline of housework, she is still inscribed in (and produced out of) the heart of the household as a hidden abode of social reproduction. Consequently,

many of the group's activist campaigns were articulated to the concerns of lesbians who were or had been in heterosexual relationships. In 1976, for example, the
Toronto WDL group campaigned against government cutbacks to a women's shelter
called Nellie's that provided refuge to homeless women fleeing domestic violence,
arguing that these cutbacks were an assault on the exodus of women from the
violence of heteropatriarchal family structures. "To support Nellie's is to support
lesbians" became the slogan for the campaign supported by WDL groups throughout the network (Toupin 2014: 266–69). Similarly, in "Child Custody, Motherhood,
Lesbianism" (1976), one of the most widely distributed WDL pamphlets, Francie
Wyland underscores the heightened vulnerability of lesbian women to policing by
the Canadian child welfare system. In this text, the legal judgment of lesbians as
"unfit mothers" stands metonymically as a broader warning of the violence wielded
by the state against nonheteronormative formations. Strikingly, though, Wyland
(1976: 29) does not defend lesbianism as a category commensurate with "proper"
mothering but instead affirms lesbianism as mothering's improper horizon: "We
are demanding not only the power to choose to be lesbian without losing our children. . . . We are demanding the power to be with those children *in a way that is
not work*. We will no longer accept . . . the guilt of being a 'bad mother' if we take
time away from them."

Wyland affirms the impropriety of the lesbian mother in ways that posit
her as external to both heteronormative motherhood and, perhaps, to the contemporary homonormative family unit.[17] At the same time, by confirming a collective
practice of (lesbian) mothering that could exit the disciplinary and exploitative
machinations of "work," she firmly embeds lesbianism in the WfH demand and
suggests that anyone might be—or, at least, could be—a lesbian mother. This is
not simply a matter of (object) "choice." Rather, lesbian mothering comes to signal
a fundamental material rearrangement in the organization of labor such that the
lesbian demand forwards a common call that implicates the entire field of social
reproduction. Additionally, pamphlets like Wyland's underscored that the demand
for welfare rights was and is a queer issue, in much the same way that Johnnie
Tillmon had proclaimed in the pages of *Ms. Magazine* in 1972 that "welfare is a
women's issue."

The strategy of autonomy advanced by WDL and BWfWfH was mobilized
in relation to the intersections of sexuality, race, and gender that contoured wom-
en's uneven relations to the labor of social reproduction. This is encapsulated in
the speech "The Autonomy of Black Lesbian Women" delivered by Brown (1976a)
in Toronto. Brown's arguments combine an intersectional analysis with a Marxist feminist account of social reproduction in ways that pressure contemporary

arguments that pit social reproduction feminism against intersectionality (Ferguson 2016). In the speech, Brown unbraids the overdetermined oppressions faced by black lesbian women in ways that mirrored the Combahee River Collective's ([1977] 1979: 368) contemporaneous "A Black Feminist Statement," particularly the collective's oft-cited line: "If black women were free, it would mean that everyone else would have to be free since our freedom would necessitate the destruction of all the systems of oppression." Similarly, Brown (1976a: 9) claims black lesbian autonomy as a perspective that "makes it possible for us to connect with all Black women and to connect finally with all women."

Combahee member Barbara Smith makes Brown's speech central to her argument for the future-oriented creation of a black lesbian-feminist criticism. Smith (1978: 26) draws on Brown's contention that "I have searched through Black history, black literature, whatever, looking for some women that I could see were somehow lesbian. Now I know that in a certain sense they were all lesbian," arguing that lesbianism, understood as a commons among black women, might break the silence that had separated them from one another. Black lesbianism stands in Smith's text as a resource to encourage all black women to refuse the discipline of sexual and social propriety, to renunciate "the crumbs of 'tolerance' that non-threatening 'lady-like' black women are sometimes fed" (ibid.). In this vein, Brown's strategy of black lesbian women's autonomy is deployed in recognition of the violence that targeted black lesbian women, while providing an analytic ground for a coalitional queer feminist sexual politics.

Even as Brown's analysis of black lesbian autonomy impresses the coalitional or commoning possibilities of lesbianism, it equally impresses the specific material constraints placed on lesbian-identified women (and particularly lesbians of color) by capitalism. Beyond all the labors that lesbians performed for capital, WDL worked to foreground the myriad and particular "labors of lesbianism" that contoured the lived experiences of lesbian, bisexual, and queer women. As Hall (1976: 7) put it in her testimony for the International Tribunal on Crimes against Women in Brussels in 1976, for lesbian women "there's the emotional housework—which in some ways is less than it is with a man, but in some ways is more, because there's so much pressure all the time on all of us that we are continually having to struggle to hold each other together and keep sane. We're all mothers, all the time mothering each other and trying to keep a grip on ourselves." Lesbians, Hall makes plain, were mothers not only to their own (biological) children but to the broader queer community fighting for survival.

In *Counter-planning from the Kitchen* (1975), Federici and Nicole Cox stress that WfH must be understood as a perspective, rather than one demand among other demands, with the power and potential to radically recalibrate the terms of political struggle. This perspective simultaneously targeted the regulatory enclosures of capitalist, heteromasculinist, and Marxist common senses in order to register all the invisible labors of what James and Dalla Costa elucidated as the community that subtends capitalist production, the erasure of which has heretofore divided and distorted conceptions of the commons and the common good. As Maria Mies (2014) contends, *there is no commons without this community.* By organizing autonomously under the banner of the WfH movement, BWfWfH and WDL, in turn, transformed the meaning of the WfH perspective, elucidating the uncommon remainders that fissured (feminist) community, even as they simultaneously advanced a politics of what Cohen (1997: 438, 452) calls "progressive transformative coalition work" through a practical-theoretical centering of the entanglements between housework and (sexual) nonnormativity. These groups therefore imagined commoning precisely as the refusal to seek a communitarian horizon entirely free of the divisions, antagonisms, or, in Lauren Berlant's (2016) parlance, ambivalences about being, working, and struggling together. As we collectively produce and reproduce theories and histories of a queer commons, BWfWfH and WDL offer us urgent political imaginaries and theoretical idioms. These imaginaries invite us to remain vigilant that any queer commons will be located in the horizon of a persistent queer critique that interminably unfixes the common ground on which any commons rests from the critical perspective of the un(der)commons.

Notes

The authors would like to thank Nadja Millner-Larsen, Gavin Butt, Jennifer DeVere Brody, Michael Litwack, and the anonymous peer reviewers.

1. The Toronto conference was one of four major international conferences organized by the Wages for Housework movement between 1974 and 1977, with others in Brooklyn, Montreal, and London.

2. WfH is adamant that the movement be understood as a "perspective" so as not to "detach the end result of the struggle from the struggle itself and to miss its significance in demystifying . . . the role to which women have been confined" (Federici 2012c: 15).

3. This similarly includes those lives rendered unthinkable within the common parameters of "queerness" when this term has been used as a measurement of transgressive subjectivity and practice. See Puar 2007.

4. Following Roderick Ferguson (2004), queer of color designates not only LGBT people of color but all those for whom processes of gendered and sexualized racialization

have foreclosed access to the privileges that accrue to normatively gendered/sexed bodies.

5. We highlight here (some) scholars who have already been doing crucial theoretical, archival, and activist work on trans* and queer social reproduction. See, for example, Nat Raha's (2017) research on the social reproduction of trans* and queer communities in the activism of the New York Street Transvestite Action Revolutionaries (STAR) and WDL, Martin Manalansan's (2008) call to "queer the chain of care paradigm," and Aren Aizura's (2011, 2014) explorations of affective labor and transfeminine value within transnational divisions of reproductive labor.

6. For a detailed analysis of BWfWfH in relation to broader activism around black women's serial murder, see Anne Gray Fischer's (2018) dissertation, "Arrestable Behavior: Women, Police Power, and the Making of Law-and-Order America, 1930s-1980s."

7. As J. Kēhaulani Kauanui (2013) has argued, there is "nothing common about the 'commons'" insofar as recent mobilizations of this concept have reproduced the logics of settler colonialism.

8. Hardin was more explicit about his white supremacist commitments in his writing for white nationalist forums, claiming that "passive genocide" was under way in North America and northern Europe with the growth of nonwhite populations. See Southern Poverty Law Center 2017.

9. Nixon (2012: 596) has also argued that the herdsman in Hardin's allegory equally indexed the threat of Third World struggles for decolonization and self-determination.

10. Ange-Marie Hancock (2004: 6) elucidates how the "public identity" of the US "welfare queen" is grounded in "two discursive themes about black women traceable to slavery: their laziness and their fecundity."

11. Thanks are due Aren Aizura for pointing out the connection between discourses of sexual liberation and reproductive justice in Brown's essay.

12. Alternatively, as Jennifer DeVere Brody (2003) has argued, Angelina Weld Grimké's story "The Closing Door" (1919) for Margaret Sanger's *Birth Control Review* articulated a form of queer black maternal reproductive withdrawal (in this instance, infanticide) in order to critique white supremacist violence and terror. As Brody notes, such withdrawals draw on the history of enslaved women's refusal to reproduce progeny for the slave mode of production.

13. Here, WDL echoes the Radicalesbians manifesto "The Woman Identified Woman" (1970). However, WDL departed from the separatist agenda advanced by such groups.

14. Lynda Hart (1994: 116), for example, notes that the lesbian has been made to bear "the onus of the nonreproductive woman and her threat to the future of the species."

15. Victoria Hesford (2013) has explored how the 1970s saw the cultural production of the "feminist-as-lesbian," a repository figure for anxieties provoked by women's liberation.

16. Our interpretation here bears the imprint of Harney and Moten 2013.

17. The term *homonormativity* was coined by Lisa Duggan (2002).

References

Aizura, Aren Z. 2011. "The Romance of the Amazing Scalpel: 'Race,' Labor, and Affect in Thai Gender Reassignment Clinics." In *Queer Bangkok: Twenty-First Century Markets, Media, and Rights*, edited by Peter A. Jackson, 143–62. Hong Kong: Hong Kong University Press.

———. 2014. "Trans Feminine Value, Racialized Others, and the Limits of Necropolitics." In *Queer Necropolitics*, edited by Jin Haritaworn, Adi Kuntsman, and Silvia Posocco, 129–48. New York: Routledge.

Berlant, Lauren. 2016. "The Commons: Infrastructures for Troubling Times." *Environment and Planning D: Society and Space* 34, no. 3: 393–419.

Black Women for Wages for Housework. [1977] 2012. "Money for Prostitutes Is Money for Black Women." *LIES: A Journal of Materialist Feminism* 1: 229–34.

Bliss, James. 2015. "Hope against Hope: Queer Negativity, Black Feminist Theorizing, and Reproduction without Futurity." *Mosaic: a journal for the interdisciplinary study of literature* 48, no. 1: 83–98.

Brody, Jennifer DeVere. 2003. "Queering Racial Reproduction: 'Unnatural Acts' in Angelina Weld Grimké's 'The Closing Door.'" *Text and Performance Quarterly* 22, no. 2: 205–23.

Brown, Wilmette. 1976a. "The Autonomy of Black Lesbian Women." Box 1, Wages for Housework Special Collections, Lesbian Herstory Archive, Brooklyn, NY.

———. 1976b. "Black Women's Struggle against Sterilization." Box 1, Wages for Housework Special Collections, Lesbian Herstory Archive, Brooklyn, NY.

———. 1986. *Black Ghetto Ecology*. London: Housewives in Dialogue.

———. 2017. "Birth Announcement (1976)." In *The New York Wages for Housework Committee, 1972–1976: History, Theory, and Documents*, edited by Silvia Federici and Arlen Austin, 116–18. Brooklyn, NY: Autonomedia.

Cohen, Cathy J. 1997. "Punks, Bulldaggers, and Welfare Queens: The Radical Potential of Queer Politics?" *GLQ* 3, no. 4: 437–65.

Combahee River Collective. [1977] 1979. "A Black Feminist Statement." In *Capitalist Patriarchy and the Case for Socialist Feminism*, edited by Zillah R. Eisenstein, 362–72. New York: Monthly Review Press.

Cooper, Melinda. 2017. *Family Values: Between Neoliberalism and the New Social Conservatism*. New York: Zone Books.

Dalla Costa, Mariarosa. 1972. "Women and the Subversion of Community." In *The Power of Women and the Subversion of the Community*, by Selma James and Mariarosa Dalla Costa. Bristol, UK: Falling Wall.

Davis, Angela Y. 1972. "Reflections on the Black Women's Role in the Community of Slaves." *Massachusetts Review* 13, nos. 1–2: 81–100.

———. 1983. "The Approaching Obsolescence of Housework: A Working-Class Perspective." In *Women, Race, and Class*, 222–44. New York: Random House.

De Angelis, Massimo. 2006. *The Beginning of History: Value Struggles and Global Capital*. London: Pluto.

De La Cruz, Iris, Yolanda Jones, and Karen Green. 1980. "P.O.N.Y. (Prostitutes of New York): Decriminalization of Prostitution." Pacifica Radio, April 9. North Hollywood, CA. archive.org/details/pacifica_radio_archives-IZ0440.01.

Duggan, Lisa. 2002. "The New Homonormativity: The Sexual Politics of Neoliberalism." In *Materializing Democracy: Towards a Revitalized Cultural Politics*, edited by Dana D. Nelson and Russ Castronovo, 175–94. Durham, NC: Duke University Press.

Fairbairns, Zoe. 1977. "About Time by The London Women's Film Group." *Spare Rib* 58: 42–43. journalarchives.jisc.ac.uk/britishlibrary/sparerib.

Federici, Silvia. 2012a. Introduction to *Revolution at Point Zero: Housework, Reproduction, and Feminist Struggle*, 5–14. Oakland, CA: PM / Common Notions.

———. 2012b. "Feminism and the Politics of the Commons in an Era of Primitive Accumulation (2010)." In *Revolution at Point Zero: Housework, Reproduction, and Feminist Struggle*, 138–49. Oakland, CA: PM / Common Notions.

———. 2012c. "Wages against Housework (1975)." In *Revolution at Point Zero: Housework, Reproduction, and Feminist Struggle*, 17–22. Oakland, CA: PM / Common Notions.

———. 2017a. "Capitalism and the Struggle against Sexual Work (1975)." In *The New York Wages for Housework Committee, 1972–1976: History, Theory, and Documents*, edited by Silvia Federici and Arlen Austin, 144–46. Brooklyn, NY: Autonomedia.

———. 2017b. "On Sexuality as Work (1976)." In *The New York Wages for Housework Committee, 1972–1976: History, Theory, and Documents*, edited by Silvia Federici and Arlen Austin, 149–51. Brooklyn, NY: Autonomedia.

Federici, Silvia, and Nicole Cox. 1975. *Counter-Planning from the Kitchen*. Bristol, UK: Falling Wall.

Ferguson, Roderick A. 2004. *Aberrations in Black: Toward a Queer of Color Critique*. Minneapolis: University of Minnesota Press.

Ferguson, Sue. 2016. "Intersectionality and Social-Reproduction Feminisms: Toward an Integrative Ontology." *Historical Materialism* 24, no. 2: 38–60.

Fischer, Anne Gray. 2018. "Arrestable Behavior: Women, Police Power, and the Making of Law-and-Order America, 1930s-1980s." PhD diss., Brown University.

Floyd, Kevin. 2009. *The Reification of Desire: Towards a Queer Marxism*. Minneapolis: University of Minnesota Press.

Gosine, Andil. 2010. "Non-White Reproduction and Same Sex Eroticism: Queer Acts against Nature." In *Queer Ecologies: Sex, Nature, Politics, Desire*, edited by Catriona Mortimer-Sandilands and Bruce Erickson, 149–72. Bloomington: Indiana University Press.

Hall, Ruth. 1975. "Lesbianism and Power." July 20. Box 2, Wages for Housework Special Collections, Lesbian Herstory Archive, Brooklyn, NY.

———. 1976. "Lesbian Testimony Presented at the International Tribunal on Crimes Against Women in Brussels, Winter '76." In Wages Due Lesbians, *Lesbians Organize*. Box 2, Wages for Housework Special Collections, Lesbian Herstory Archive, Brooklyn, NY.

Hancock, Ange-Marie. 2004. *The Politics of Disgust: The Public Identity of the Welfare Queen*. New York: New York University Press.

Hardin, Garrett. 1968. "The Tragedy of the Commons." *Science* 162: 1243–48.

Harney, Stefano, and Fred Moten. 2013. *The Undercommons: Fugitive Planning and Black Study*. Brooklyn, NY: Minor Compositions / Autonomedia.

Hart, Lynda. 1994. *Fatal Women: Lesbian Sexuality and the Mark of Aggression*. Princeton, NJ: Princeton University Press.

Hesford, Victoria. 2013. *Feeling Women's Liberation*. Durham, NC: Duke University Press.

Jagose, Annamarie. 1994. *Lesbian Utopics*. New York: Routledge.

James, Selma. 1971. "When the Mute Speaks." July 28. Box 2, Wages for Housework Special Collections, Lesbian Herstory Archive, Brooklyn, NY.

Kandaswamy, Priya. 2010. "'You Trade in a Man for The Man': Domestic Violence and the U.S. Welfare State." *American Quarterly* 62, no. 2: 253–77.

Kauanui, J. Kēhaulani. 2013. "Nothing Common about 'the Commons': Settler Colonialism and the Politics of Indigenous Land Dispossession." Paper presented at Brown University, Providence, RI, October 9.

Keeling, Kara. 2009. "Looking for M—Queer Temporality, Black Political Possibility, and Poetry from the Future." *GLQ* 15, no. 4: 565–82.

Linebaugh, Peter. 2013. *Stop, Thief! The Commons, Enclosures, and Resistance*. Oakland, CA: PM.

Los Angeles and San Francisco Wages for Housework Committees. 1977. "An Attack on Prostitutes Is an Attack on All Women." Box 1, Wages for Housework Special Collections, Lesbian Herstory Archive, Brooklyn, NY.

Lowe, Lisa. 1996. *Immigrant Acts: On Asian American Cultural Politics*. Durham, NC: Duke University Press.

Marble, Ben and Melinda Cooper. 2018. "Family Matters." *Viewpoint Magazine*. March 19. viewpointmag.com/2018/03/19/family-matters/

Manalansan, Martin F., IV. 2008. "Queering the Chain of Care Paradigm." *Scholar and Feminist Online* 6, no. 3. sfonline.barnard.edu/immigration/manalansan_01.htm.

Mies, Maria. 2014. "No Commons without a Community." *Community Development Journal* 49, no. 1: 106–17.

Mitropoulos, Angela. 2012. *Contract and Contagion: From Biopolitics to Oikonomia*. Brooklyn, NY: Minor Compositions / Autonomedia.

———. 2016. "The Commons." In *Gender, v2: Nature*, edited by Iris van der Tuin, 165–81. London: Macmillan.

Morgan, Jennifer. 2004. *Laboring Women: Reproduction and Gender in New World Slavery*. Philadelphia: University of Pennsylvania Press.

Nixon, Rob. 2012. "Neoliberalism, Genre, and the 'Tragedy of the Commons.'" *PMLA* 127, no. 3: 593–99.

O'Brien, Sean. 2017. "Border, Theory, Contract: An Interview with Angela Mitropoulos." "Demos." Special issue, *PUBLIC Journal: Art Culture Ideas*, no. 55: 84–92.

Parreñas, Rhacel Salazar. 2008. *The Force of Domesticity: Filipina Migrants and Globalization*. New York: New York University Press.

Prescod, Margaret. 1982. *Black Women: Bringing It All Back Home*. Bristol, UK: Falling Wall.

Puar, Jasbir. 2007. *Terrorist Assemblages: Homonationalism in Queer Times*. Durham, NC: Duke University Press.

Raha, Nat. 2017. "Queering Marxist [Trans]Feminism: Queer and Trans Social Reproduction." Paper presented at "Marxism in Culture," Sussex University, Brighton, UK, February 11. www.history.ac.uk/podcasts/marxism-culture/queering-marxist-transfeminism-queer-and-trans-social-reproduction#.WSXv5mWcVAE.twitter.

Reddy, Chandan. 1998. "Home, Houses, Nonidentity: *Paris Is Burning*." In *Burning Down the House: Recycling Domesticity*, edited by Rosemary Marangoly George, 355–79. Boulder, CO: Westview.

Shah, Nayan. 2003. "Perversity, Contamination, and the Dangers of Queer Domesticity." In *Queer Studies: An Interdisciplinary Reader*, edited by Robert J. Corber and Stephen Valocchi, 121–41. Oxford, UK: Blackwell.

Smith, Anna Marie. 2007. *Welfare Reform and Sexual Regulation*. New York: Cambridge University Press.

Smith, Barbara. 1978. "Toward a Black Feminist Criticism." *Radical Teacher* 7: 20–27.

Southern Poverty Law Center. 2017. Extremist Files. "Garrett Hardin." www.splcenter.org/fighting-hate/extremist-files/individual/garrett-hardin/.

Sudbury, Julia. 1998. *"Other Kinds of Dreams": Black Women's Organisations and the Politics of Transformation*. London: Routledge.

Tillmon, Johnnie. 1972. "Welfare Is a Women's Issue." *Ms. Magazine*, Spring, 111–16.

Toupin, Louise. 2014. *Le salaire au travail ménager: Chronique d'une lutte féministe internationale (1972–1977)*. Montreal: Les éditions du remue-ménage.

Wages Due Lesbians. 1975a. "Fucking Is Work." *Activist: A Student Journal of Politics and Opinion* 15, nos. 1–2: 25–26.

———. 1975b. "Lesbian and Straight." In *All Work and No Pay: Women, Housework, and the Wages Due*, edited by Wendy Edmond and Suzie Fleming, 21–25. London: Falling Wall.

———. 1976. "Lesbian Autonomy and the Gay Movement." *Body Politic: Gay Liberation Journal* 25: 8.

Williamson, Terrion L. 2016. *Scandalize My Name: Black Feminist Practice and the Making of Black Social Life*. New York: Fordham University Press.

Wyland, Francie. 1976. "Child Custody, Motherhood, Lesbianism." Box 1, Philadelphia Wages Due Lesbians Wages for Housework Action Group, Wages for Housework Special Collections, Lesbian Herstory Archive, Brooklyn, NY.

THE SUM OF ALL QUESTIONS:

Returning to the Clit Club

Julie Tolentino, Vivian A. Crockett, Tara Hart, Amira Khusro, Leeroy Kun Young Kang, Dragon Mansion

The Clit Club was in the Meatpacking District on the West Side of Manhattan, just blocks from the Hudson River and the decaying piers at what, in the early 1990s, felt like "the edge of the city" (Hernandez 2016). Meat carcasses hung from hooks underneath warehouse awnings, and the industrial neighborhood smelled of the previous day's detritus of intestines, blood, and fat. The district had two- and three-story brick warehouses that held meatpackers during the day and transient inhabitants at night. At night, Clit Club staff, dancers, and patrons navigated wide and winding Belgian block streets, making their way to the corner of Fourteenth Street and Washington, guided by the illumination of the occasional street lamp. Patrons would hear about the club through word of mouth, and they knew that they were in its vicinity from the long queue of women stretching down the block, with dykes and gay men working the door.

Upon entering, one was immediately propelled onto a wooden dance floor, a dark space illuminated by strobe lights that stilled the many bodies in motion. Shigeru "Shigi" McPherson (2016)—a Clit Club aficionado-turned-staffer—recalled a dance space suffused by "soft, hard, *deliberate* movements" mingling with the scent of cigarette smoke, Drakkar cologne and sweat. The dance floor was driven by the DJ spinning records and "accented" by dancers who did not strip but "engaged in their own pleasure of movement," their bodies charged by the crowd (Tolentino 2017).[1] The Clit Club was known for this rare concurrence of women dancing specifically for women on the dance floor, with a variety of porn playing on the floor below. Breaking expectations of desire, the Clit Club hired dancers whose embodiment included expressions and experiences of femininity, femme power, and butch and transgender masculinity. While the club was open to manifold ways

GLQ 24:4
DOI 10.1215/10642684-6957786
© 2018 by Duke University Press

to understand the experiences and expressions of women, it also provided space for what today is sometimes described as "gender-queer" and "gender-nonconformity" that was then named by such terms as *androgyny* or *gender-bending*.

As patrons moved through the densely packed bodies, a door off the dance floor led them through a narrow hallway into a smaller room with a different vibe that often included performances and art installations.[2] In the early years, a dark room downstairs was available for kink, play, and exhibitionism, and for strict and exploratory S&M, though sex was palpable and explicit throughout the space. Rooms had dark corners and bright centers, and encompassed cooler areas and hot, sweaty ones, places to hang out and talk, places to smoke, and other areas offering relief from smoking. Every single place in the club was for sex. "Sex in fact looked like many things," Julie Tolentino (2017), an artist and Clit Club cofounder, recalls. "Couples cruised. Sex happened on the pool table, the bathroom, and on the dance floor. People were turned on and sometimes, turned out."

The different sensory environments inside the club were intentionally affective, emphasizing somatic and haptic experience. This was upheld through the explicit prohibition of photography, which released attendees from having to defend themselves as an image, and encouraged club-goers to concentrate on their co-presence with one another, on physical interplay, and on the pleasures of open, embodied acts of voyeurism. Instead of being "captured" on film, this refusal of photography also resisted the rhetoric of identity-based visibility politics that embraced legibility and commodification. Lesbian identity flourished at the Clit Club because attention was directed inward, toward the communities it served.

Though it remains legendary in many New York subcultures, the Clit Club is an underacknowledged part of the city's queer history, which is so often canonized to privilege white, cisgender, gay male culture. The club was cofounded by Tolentino and another artist, Jaguar Mary, in the summer of 1990 and was sustained by Tolentino with the support of a deeply dedicated staff that ran the party every Friday night in the Meatpacking District until 2000, sometimes operating below the radar of New York City law enforcement. After this, the party continued in various downtown venues until the final club night was held in 2002. Though its name referenced a body part, the Clit Club did not seek to claim or put forward notions of sexual experience, identity, or relationality based on gynocentric or essentialist notions of biological sex. Tolentino coined the name as a direct, audacious unearthing of pleasure, at a time when mainstream gay politics valued monogamy as a symbol of heteronormative respectability.

The Clit Club: A Sexual Undercommons

The Clit Club kept the company of many, and we keep company with it here by approaching it as a sexual *undercommons*, drawing on Stefano Harney and Fred Moten's use of the term. The undercommons appears inside yet also surrounds, and exceeds, the forces that would privatize and prevent social bonds. For Harney and Moten, the social gathering of people in study—inside or outside the university—is an undercommons, that consists of "recursive and recessive activity," that evades recognition and hides from forces of privatization (MPA 2016; Harney and Moten 2013: 3). The general intellectuality of the undercommons might include scholarly work, but also informal publics in putatively private spaces—Harney and Moten mention, for instance, the barbershop on campus or the nurses' coffee room (ibid.: 65). While sex and sexuality are not explicitly theorized by Harney and Moten, the present article riffs on their concept of the undercommons, and the improvisational and renegade space it opens up. We posit the Clit Club as a sexual undercommons that refused the misery and moralizing enclosures of spaces, sexual practices, and social being of 1990s New York City, by creating a place for sexual play and social intimacy in its tiny, hot, crowded spaces of intense proximity.

This queer, sex-positive women's club night brought together communities that were largely underserved by the surrounding gay nightlife of the time. In comparison with the clubs, bars, bathhouses, and cruising areas offered to gay men, there was a pronounced scarcity of available spaces for lesbian and queer women, and gender-nonconforming people of color. Inspired by and responding to the unabashed culture of sexual desire found in gay men's nightlife, the Clit Club also offered an alternative to lesbian nightlife that was largely segregated along race, sex, gender, and class lines, and dogmatic about lesbian identities and social formations in New York City. Clit Club attendees have recalled instances of discrimination in New York City nightlife, where black women were singled out and double-carded (asked to show two forms of identification) upon entry, leading to physical and relational forms of separation between black and white lesbians (Schulman 2008: 26). Such borders between people were actively crossed by those at the Clit Club, whose organizers assiduously sought to welcome and feature the images, lives, and talents of women of color (ibid.: 24–25). A flyer for a Clit Club party on June 27, 1997, advertised the event as for "women of all descents ages colors sexually deviant exhibitionists," in addition to promising "three rooms, interactive altars; sex-positive; gorgeous women . . . fierce party" (Clit Club c. 1997).

Figure 1. *Unite '93/Clit Club Meat/DYKEFAG Experience* poster, Clit Club, 1993

FROM THE QUEERS WHO RE-INVENTED NEW YORK NIGHTLIFE.

THE SEX-POSITIVE
DYKE & FAG PRIDE PARTY
SUNDAY JUNE 27
1993
432 WEST 14 ST.

The Clit Club was also a space flowing into others. In addition to its primary location at 432 West Fourteenth Street, which became known as "Mother" after the Clit Club opened, the party was also held at other venues over the years, such as Bowery Bar, King, and Pyramid Club in the East Village. It operated in affinity with other activist and artist-led parties, such as Meat (organized by Aldo Hernandez) and PORK (directed by the artist John Lovett), that were similarly club nights working with failing bars to host events with a greater sense of permissiveness in their policies. Though mostly gay men attended Meat and PORK, the organizers included and admitted dykes, who also performed, bartended, and worked the door. The histories of these parties are threaded by friendship: the artist Alessandro Codagnone, for instance, worked the door at PORK and was a dancer at the Clit Club. While especially attuned to women, the staff of the Clit Club also sought to welcome gay men and people with varying presentations of gender, queerness, and trans-ness beyond the gender binary.

Through its permissiveness, the Clit Club made available for queer women what Samuel Delany (1999: 170) called "contact venues, from the social to the sexual." Writing in the 1990s amid the shuttering of massage parlors and sex shows in Times Square, and the "violent suppression of urban social structures, economic, social and sexual" in the name of "family values," Delany defended multiform and variegated social levels and cross-class interactions against their erasure, which, for him constituted a crucial constituent of "a positive and pleasant democratic urban atmosphere" (ibid.: 153, 170). The Clit Club's multiplicity attracted its non-white, transgressively sexed, working-class, and multigendered community while resisting the norms that upheld racial separatism, classism, or elitism. Attendees bore scars of violence or exclusion, yet many felt unburdened to experiment with public sex, explore their own bodies, or merely experience the heat of unhinged sexuality on the Clit Club dance floor.

We might understand the Clit Club by way of what Laam Hae (2012: 41) has called the value of "social dancing" as an important avenue of collective pleasure, ritual, and politics. For Hae, social dancing is a mode of expression constituting a "right to the city" (ibid.: 39). Rights to the city—especially for those evicted from housing, resources, and participation in the common transformation of urban life—were called for because of increasing regulation by the city's expanding police department and Mayor Ed Koch's (1978–89) urban "revitalization," which targeted and restricted the sociality and informal economies of queer women, trans and gender-nonconforming people of color, and immigrant communities (ibid.: 74). The Koch administration regulations privatized and policed public and underground spaces, including venues of queer nightlife. The Clit Club's years of operation negotiated the longer effects of Koch's administration, as well as Rudy Giuliani's tenure as mayor (1994–2001). Giuliani's privatization of the city was conducted through quality-of-life initiatives notable for aggressive law enforcement that pursued broken windows policing (preemptive prosecution of minor offenses such as jumping subway turnstiles) and stop-and-frisk (the searching of civilians for weapons or contraband) as anticrime measures.[3] At this time, police aggressively targeted New York nightlife and queer sociality through the select enforcement of the city's Cabaret (No Dancing) Law. What Neil Smith (1998) has called a mayoralty enacting "a vendetta against the most oppressed" saw its counterpoint in the Clit Club, whose organizers refused New York nightlife's "velvet rope" preferential policies so prevalent at other venues, in which certain patrons were privileged because of their celebrity status, perceived wealth and access, and conventional standards of beauty (Tolentino 2017).

Working at the Clit Club

The Clit Club endured for more than a decade at its home space in the Meatpacking District, through the micro-socialities of organization, logistics, and planning, through which forms of desire, difference, and dependency coexisted in friction and exuberance. The relationships, meeting points, and links between the Clit Club and caregiving and support systems for friends with HIV and AIDS might be understood as webs of care, by which people and methods traveled in and out of many sites and spaces. Many friends of the Clit Club were AIDS activists trained in passive resistance, as well as registered nurses, emergency responders, people working on the front lines of providing support to LGBTQ youth, and people involved with harm reduction approaches to drug use and safer-sex organizing. The Clit Club was a space where such different lines of experience moved, and their struggles were acknowledged and supported. Attendees often began their evenings at meetings, memorials, and direct actions prior to arriving at Clit Club. Many were active in ACT UP, as well as its affinity groups such as House of Color, Art Positive, DIVA TV, or affiliated with other groups such as Lesbian Avengers, Kilawin Kolektibo, Prostitutes of New York (PONY), or Gabriela Network. Over the years the Clit Club also showed and generated many forms of art, and invited a number of artists to present work.[4]

Safer-sex materials were readily available at the Clit Club throughout the venue, and Clit Club staff themselves were pivotal in developing the safe-sex practices formulated by ACT UP.[5] Notably, the "Guide to Safer Sex for Lesbians," produced by the Lesbian AIDS Project of Gay Men's Health Crisis, was coauthored by the artist/activists Cynthia Madansky and Tolentino and featured images of Clit Club staff members. The club's irreverent, tongue-in-cheek approach to sex and self-representation was a welcome counterweight to, and extension of, the Clit Club's equally serious, audacious approach to propagating safer-sex practices.[6] The Clit Club spearheaded the original grassroots outreach and distribution program featuring the handbook packaged with gloves, dental dams, and condoms. These safer-sex kits were prominently displayed around the party, and in other New York nightclubs and bars. Safer sex was also stealthily encouraged in colloquial and entertaining language on Clit Club fliers, situating these practices within promises of festivity, sustenance, ritual, and promiscuity. For instance, a 1993 New Year's Eve party flyer promised

> 2 floors of Delicious Dyke Rituals * Ceremonious Dancing and Female Worship till 8am . . . Finger-licking edibles all night long * Continental breakfast to bring in the dawn * Dancers and Drummers to bring us to a

rhythmic frenzy * Safe sex gift giveaway packets for your pleasure * Party Hats, Dyke Crowns and Party Favors provided: Toys, Tricks, Fear and Exhibition Rewarded!*

The expansiveness of the Clit Club's project sought to embrace people—as they were and as they could be—in all their awkwardness and uncertainty. By holding open the possibilities of experimentation within a sexual culture of closeted moralism, the party traded invisibility and shame for the audacity of (re)living a queer, uninhibited life. Clit Club offered, for some, first-time voyeurism into (and participation in) sex practices like flogging, tattooing, piercing, and blood sports in a club environment, particularly among lesbians.[7]

The Clit Club was built on practices of care that pervaded the perspectives and shared and practical knowledge of its staff. In organizing the space as a mixed party, Clit Club staff did not operate through a stringent set of rules or policing, even as door and management staff were open about and mindful of the ratio of men to women in the room and often prioritized entry for female-identified people. Door staff often conversed with young queers who approached the door with potentially fake IDs, and subtly signaled bartenders and others to not serve them alcohol. In negotiating the scope of law enforcement, the Clit Club navigated how its attendees included people more affected by the policing in the area, particularly women of color, trans and gender-nonconforming people, sex workers, street youth, and the homeless. And, as opposed to other clubs or bars where a door person might abandon his or her post with the arrival of cops, at the Clit Club the safety, cover, and exit of club attendees was paramount.

Throughout its twelve-year existence, the Clit Club was necessarily a changing, mutable entity.[8] While organizers were mindful of public-private intimacies, its underground character evolved, becoming increasingly discussed and recognized in the media concurrent with the heightened attention and adoption of tropes of lesbian sexuality by the media in the latter half of the 1990s. The Clit Club, established prior to the increased commodification of lesbian and gay sexualities in the mid-1990s in New York City, responded critically to the new incorporation of lesbians and gays as consumer-citizens rather than homosexual menaces. One notable Clit Club flyer by McPherson wittily responded to a wide-reaching Absolut Vodka advertising campaign that targeted gay and lesbian bars and clubs. Appropriating this ad, McPherson swapped the vodka's brand-name with "Clit Club" and changed the slogan to read "Absolut Lesbian," with the word *Lesbian* boldly crossed out in orange scrawl and replaced with the word *Dyke* (McPherson n.d.a). In another appropriation of a well-known slogan, McPherson altered

Figure 2. *Dove Soap* flyer, Clit Club. Attributed to Shigeru McPherson

the wrapper for Dove™ soap bars to include the tagline: "She floats" (McPherson n.d.b). This doubled as an invitation and a keepsake that was distributed at the club, thus transforming a product used for "cleaning up" and marketed to women of all sizes, to promote "dancing, sweating, getting dirty . . . the finer things in life" (ibid.).

Recollecting the Clit Club

Recollecting and returning to the Clit Club happens here in the context of ongoing mourning, both for lives lost in the 1990s whose voices haunt the history of the Clit Club, and for those lost in the present. This return to the Clit Club takes place in a moment in which the state physically and legally threatens women, the undocumented, immigrants, Muslims, trans people, and queers of color in the United States, and in which the gentrification and militarization of public space is all the more palpable. It is also a return to an ongoing AIDS crisis that was exacerbated by active negligence, prohibitively expensive health care, and other forms of enclosure. We also return in the wake of 9/11, which occurred a year before the end of the Clit Club, and the neo-imperial global War on Terror that continues to mobilize a liberal rights discourse to locate the bodies of women and gay people in predominantly Muslim countries such as Afghanistan, among many others, as objects of liberation in their "civilizing missions." [9] Lastly, we return to a moment of hypervisibility for narrow forms of LGBT life and now state-sanctioned homosexuality in the United States that is violently disassociated with the transgressively sexed and raced bodies that refuse its liberal politics of representation.

Returning to the Clit Club today entails naming the structures contributing to its absence from queer history while recognizing the nuanced ways in which the club resisted the glare of visibility and capture. The present article is shaped by reckoning with the vicissitudes of people acting as one another's archives, within relations striated by poverty, racialized and sexualized death, struggle and coping in the context of HIV/AIDS, through which many lives of the Clit Club recede from being known. But this is also a project of holding on to life: by way of those who survived and whose relationships to the Clit Club have been fundamental to materializing its existence and endurance, whose voices we turn to today.

The writers of this article—with the exception of Tolentino—did not attend the Clit Club and feel called to name what makes us motion toward it or, inversely, pulls us away from it. We have asked ourselves what invites or denies us permission to access these past formations of queerness that we seek to hold in common yet approach so differently because of intergenerational and cross-cultural understandings of language, culture, and sexual and gender identifications. Returning to the Clit Club has been a process fraught with difficulty. Some of this may be traced to the elisions of mainstream historical texts and capitalism, the contestation of women's spaces, and the historical violence of separatism across gendered, raced, and classed lines. Further challenges arise from the coerced shame attached to the sexualities and bodies of women, and the biological essentialism connoted merely by the club's name. In gathering around the Clit Club, we neither ignore nor deny these issues but instead aim to position ourselves in closer proximity to those who have lived in these times and who continue to find their place in the present.

For José Esteban Muñoz (2013), as described in his last work on what he called the "brown commons," "the commons is never placid. Life in the commons is and should be turbulent, not only because of the various enclosures that attempt to overwhelm a commons, but because disagreements within the commons . . . are of vital importance to the augmentation of the insurrectionist promise of the commons." In the months spent thinking through and writing this piece, we engaged in our own uncertain process of convening through this collective text, as six people with divergent interests, modes of being and perceiving, and entry points into the Clit Club. In this coming together, we exposed our varying desires and investments and discovered that our process mirrored many of the modes of creation and negotiation employed by the Clit Club staff, of trying new things, of mapping new methods and new forms of connection. This has also required us to embrace the commitment of those at the Clit Club who returned weekly to activate the space anew and critically engage with both personal and collective desire, knowing that the act of showing up is necessary and itself a commitment of difficulty and labor.

As we decided to return to the Clit Club of the early 1990s, we wondered if there was a way to write one history of it without smoothing its edges, without contributing to the continued erasure and amnesia of transgressive queer of color histories, while not forcing its history to fit the nomenclature that defines sociality, politics, and sexual practices in contemporary queer life. We have contended with the task of creating an access point to the club's history without rendering it legible to the very institutional and state-sanctioned forces that would criminalize and thereby threaten the livelihood of people so fundamental to the spaces of the Clit Club. Yet how might we also return without refusing the possibility of joy, vitality, and excess that can still exist despite the enhanced state violence and contemporary repressions of queer life today? How to remain with the club's unabashed love for sexuality, for gender-nonconforming women of color, for interclass conviviality, for the working poor, and for strangers who did not fall under today's rubric of "queer" recognition or of what is now a calcified rubrics of inclusion associated with homonationalism and gay imperialism? How might we make space for the regulars, the newbies and one-timers, the activists who came in late night or early morning before wheat-pasting flyers around the city, the trans-masculine partner taking a break to have a drink, the folks working the street? How to understand the resistance embodied by the attendees, as Tolentino (2017) puts it: "To be matter of fact, to be plain, to be wildly plainly oneself, actually—that was a weapon that was worth wielding."

While Tolentino maintains an invaluable collection of print ephemera, the Clit Club also persists and lives on in the subterranean memories, perspectives, sexual lives, and embodied practices of the staff who worked there, and in the innumerable attendees over the years, some who came repeatedly and others perhaps just once.[10] We make little claim on the actual experience of the Clit Club for all its attendees—these experiences are necessarily multiple, conflicting, and deserving of a broader accounting that exceeds the scope of this text. Knowing that the Clit Club meant a lot of different things to a lot of different people, we devel-

oped a set of questions in an attempt to gain a sense of individual interests alongside varying commonalities, and begin with multiple rather than singular narratives. We asked our Clit Club friends to meet us initially in words, to learn about
how they suffered and strived together in search of models resistant to neoliberal
late capitalism. It then was up to us as authors to negotiate and parse out the areas
that they brought forward.

The process of working collaboratively on this questionnaire served to connect those who have never attended the Clit Club with those who have. Through the
survey responses, we glimpsed the forms of pleasure found at the Clit Club, and
these are quoted here not as evidence but as a gathering of feelings by which the
legacies of the Clit Club might be sensed. Our focus here is on how it felt to create
and maintain the Clit Club and how it mattered in hindsight, from the perspectives
of key former staff (known as the Clit Club "crew") who were the most consistent
in running it, operating it, and constructing the force of its sexual undercommons.
The responses we gathered serve as points of entry into the Clit Club's expansive
histories, beginning with taking in the voices of those who lived it then and live it
still. In this way we hope to instigate others to write, participate, contribute, and
widen our understanding of the marks that this past leaves on our present. What
follows are excerpts compiled from the responses to the questionnaire that was
sent out to Shigeru "Shigi" McPherson, Lola Flash, Cinnamon, Pam L, Aldo Hernandez, Michele Hill, Pamela Sneed, dM, Jet Clark, and Dez in December 2016.

1. What was the Clit Club known for—and not sufficiently known for? How did you
understand or perceive the Clit Club during the time you attended?

Shigi (Graphic design, Door): The Clit Club was not sufficiently known for the
sociopolitical ramifications of its existence, why it was conceived, how it was conceived and run, and the sometimes subtle and sometimes not-so-subtle manifes-
tations of its concept. Nor for when people were clearly there to just have a good
time, but there were safe-sex pamphlets, condoms, dental dams, and exposure to
subversive art, including palm-sized golden vagina sculpture giveaways.

Lola Flash (Bartender): The club was known for the music and the mix of people.
There were so many beauties of all genders wrapped in skins of all colors, especially melanin-filled.

Cinnamon (Dancer): The creativity, the vibe, the mixture of all roles and ethnicities, the amazing sexual freedom you felt when you were there. For someone like

me who was experiencing my first time at a lesbian club, I felt a true connection to my sexuality.

2. How would you describe the crowd at the Clit Club?

Pam L (Door/Inside): I remember women being in their element and the palpable feeling of camaraderie in the air.

Aldo Hernandez (Clit Club DJ, also proprietor of Meat): Dyke diaspora. A spectrum of the femalia. Mixed ages, races, ethnicities, sexual identities, and genders (though not necessarily all in the same room at one time). My guess is that 80 percent of club-goers were between twenty and forty years old who identified as lesbian. There was dancing, cruising, love, competition, sparks, jags (at times, bruising), and lots of fire.

3. What attitudes toward sex and sexuality were experienced and/or encouraged at the Clit Club?

Dez (Door/Outside): Sexuality was an open book.

Shigi: I learned that being a *sexual* being is not just OK, it's good. This resonated for me even before I learned that being a *lesbian* is not just OK, it's good. This is part of the freedom I felt in the club that allowed anyone to be who/whatever they wanted to be. The club encouraged exploration, freer expression, and it allowed us to move forward with a proper head because it came with an "education" and "awareness" of what was at stake.

Lola Flash: It was no-holds-barred. A couple of times, I remember that we tied a young lady up nearby in a staff member's artists' loft down the block, went to Clit Club, and came back for her later.

4. When and how did you first hear about the Clit Club?

Michele Hill (Door/Outside): Through word-of-mouth while working at another club in the West Village called the Duchess.

Pamela Sneed (Bartender): At a House of Color video collective meeting.

dM (Clit Club DJ, Manager): Hmmm, I must have heard about the club in the *Village Voice*. No maybe *HX* zine.

Cinnamon: I heard about the Clit Club from my first girlfriend, who was several years older than me. Clit Club was the first lesbian club I ever went to.

Shigi: It was my senior year of college, and it was quite by accident. I ended up there with a few of my Columbia friends and acquaintances who were already out and taking up the AIDS movement in one way or another.

5. What were your impressions or experiences of Clit Club staff members (bartenders, organizers, DJs, those working the door, performers, events, etc.?). Did any interactions or aspects stand out in your memory?

Michele: The door staff was AMAZING. Our staff was all about making people aware of the sexuality of the space and how to enjoy it in a safe atmosphere. I know from being a part of the security team that we were very conscious of the neighborhood we were in, and it was imperative that our customers were safe coming and going home from the club. Inside, the club was also taken care of by the club-goers, who were often inside being our eyes and ears because they saw how important it was for women to feel safe. They would tell us what was going on, if someone needed to leave or if some guy was being a bit too creepy.

Aldo: As the DJ, you want to get in a groove with your dancers, working together to "jack the room" so to speak. The key for me was to not let any occasional tense moments or hiccups override or obstruct my mission of serving the party with the best tunes I could pull up. Wanting to deal with "palm trees"—tall men who somehow plant themselves in the middle of a jumpin' dance floor—was a challenge when I would see and feel it from the DJ booth, but there would be a crush of twenty feet of people dancing between us. Sometimes the staff interjected and moved them aside. These "frozen" guys occasionally ended up blocking someone's view of the stage performers too. Gawkers and grabbers were also off-putting, and they were usually dressed down, or booted from the club.

6. What were some of your best and worst experiences of working at the Clit Club, and why?

Lola Flash: One of my favorite experiences was setting up the club. Before opening or after closing the club, I used to get up on the stage, totally uninhibited, and would dance to DJ Aldo's tunes when it was just the staff. I also loved the "women workers of the night," who used to come in for a quick drink before their night-time work began. I can still see them spinning around with their handbags on their arms. What was memorable is that the club always had a lovely mixture of die-hard regulars and a continuous flow of newbies.

Jet Clark (Door, Manager): There was a night when a pack of drunk, off-duty cops barged in through the back door. I held my ground between them and the main room, but it was a helpless feeling. . . . They were disgusting pigs.

Aldo: I loved the camaraderie with girlfriends and sister soldiers. I loved seeing them happy, finding a hookup, that love, living for the fling, and grooving in sync, while discussing our all and all each week, like for the first time. I also miss the "way out" stage performances, the dirty dancing on the bar, and the howling at the night with a devil-may-care black-booted spark.

Shigi: The best thing was working with everyone there because we were all nuts and loved every bit of it together. The worst were candy shoppers a.k.a. "couples" (straight men?) masquerading as gay in order to seek out lesbians for sex.

7. What specific night, incident, event, performance, or action stands out in your memory?

Cinnamon: Honestly all. Every night was a different theme, at certain points of the night the crowd would go completely topless. In the downstairs area and the side room, there would be art installations, some S&M happening in the dark corners, and I felt the love of the crowd every time we performed.

Michele: A night that will always stand out is the night a Russian basketball team was partying around the corner at Hogs and Heifers and heard that women were around the corner at a place called Clit Club. Pam Willis and I were at the door. I remember we both looked at each other and said, "This is not good." All of a sudden, the door of the club opened and it seemed like every butch came outside and had our back. It was so amazing that all these women came out to protect their spot. It was so funny seeing these bad-ass men just walk (well, run) away. They knew they weren't getting into the club no matter what they did.

Jet Clark: There was the memorable night that we held a benefit dedicated to the memory of our dear friend Dee Finley. A few hours after we opened the club, she came walking in the door. (Obviously, we had bad information.) The conversations that we had before and after she showed up, the mortality-check, and the many unsaid acknowledgments it provoked us to say to reflect and voice to each other, stick with me. It ended up being an amazing night.

8. What forms of gathering, process, activity, social interaction, and/or culture did you think of as overlapping or associated with the Clit Club, influencing it, or extending out of it?

Aldo Hernandez: Some of us were involved in ACT UP and its subgroups, like Art+Positive. The activism of those groups was an integral part of our parties, and was reflected in the safe-sex posters we pinned up, and the prophylactics and reading material we distributed. Our explicit, self-made sexual imagery was projected across the walls of the club, becoming a dominant visual language at our parties. The Clit Club, Meat, and Art+Positive (which Julie Tolentino, Lola Flash, Leon "Tracy" Mostovoy, Diviana Ingravallo, and Catherine Gund participated in) espoused and practiced what I call "Militant Eroticism."

Michele: The Clit Club encouraged women to be aware of their bodies, HIV, and STDs. We spoke openly and handed out literature to make sure safety was a key in sexual health.

9. How did cultural/social/political/economic circumstances affect the Clit Club—and did the Clit Club change? If so, what were the conditions surrounding these shifts?

Michele: Well, socially things changed 'cause before Clit Club I don't think black women and white women really partied together. Back then, there were bars with predominantly white clientele like Crazy Nannies, the Cubby Hole and "Hens" (a.k.a. Henrietta Hudson), as well as long-running spaces like the Duchess, which attracted mostly black women, and Hatfield's, a bar for Latinas. Clit Club brought everyone together and that was amazing. There were other places, of course, but the scene was separated either by color or money. Clit Club took that all away. We just wanted women to have a good time.

Shigi: One of the best things at the time was that our community was becoming more and more visible and was hot on the heels of gaining basic human rights because of the gay movement that was already in place by the time I showed up. The feeling of urgency in our movement was the most painful part because we were losing so many people to HIV/AIDS, including many of our leaders. The resilience of our community despite those losses was so inspiring.

It sucks that I feel this way, but one of the unfortunate things that inadvertently happened is that the movement became too granular. I think we kind of wound up separating ourselves by becoming very specific about what "kind" of queer existed. This, coupled with the Giuliani era, devastated us, and one by one we started to lose the places where we gathered not just to party but to exchange real ideas and ideals concerning our community.

One of my favorite things was that while the Clit Club changed as a result of changing times, the club also upheld the idea of change as something that could be a necessary catalyst.

Aldo: In the 1990s women—particularly women of color—earned much less than men. Clit Club organizers wanted to make the club as cheap as possible for women to be able to afford admission and a drink, especially women coming in from Brooklyn, the Bronx, Queens, or Staten Island. From the first nights, the club's core concepts were expressed—if somewhat innocently—through its visuals, performers, and staff. I think Clit Club & Meat directly and creatively responded to oppressive social/political/cultural/economic circumstances through the shared use of quick and accessible formats like slide photography and copy machine graphics. The club's provocative weekly invites, flyers, and posters encouraged and reinforced individuality while also recognizing shared community. There was a charged confidence that initiated innovative and unchartered ways of celebrating together or even living openly as a queer within our society.

10. Who held political office during these years (e.g., as governor, mayor, and/or president), and did this affect your understanding of your experience at the time, or now?

Michele: Did politics affect me? Hell no. Politics never played a part in my development from Baby Butch to now. My Elders had that influence on my life. They were the ones that gave us guidance back then.

Aldo: Mayors Ed Koch and David Dinkins come to mind, and we preferred the latter. Andrew Cuomo was governor during the first few years, followed by the noncharismatic Republican, George Pataki. Bill Clinton was elected president a few months after the Clit Club's opening. I think the NYC mayors, along with the Westside Neighborhood Community Board No. 2 had the most impact on how local laws were enforced by city police, fire and health departments, and the all-important State Liquor Authority.

The Clit Club was a nontraditional, sex-positive, queer women's club, in a space that also presented its male equivalent, Meat, and shared space with a weekly themed, pan-sexual performance and dance party Jackie 60. New York City's Cabaret Laws (enacted in 1926), which forbade dancing or musical groups in any nightclub or space without a license, was a massive headache then and is enacted as a form of crowd enforcement, even today. It deeply influenced how the Clit Club was run, and it was a constant cautionary effort to evade being unfairly fined and/or shut down. It was also equally important that all the weekly parties not jeopardize the bar owner's liquor license. The Clit Club was harassed the most out of all the weekly parties that were hosted at Mother, period.

11. What was it like outside (the door, the streets, social scenes in NYC)?

Cinnamon: The Meatpacking District was gritty, raw, transient, and dark. It had a feel of old New York and was known for its predominantly gay male scene. The Clit Club was embedded in the surrounding warehouses. You saw all types of people—including the queens and the working girls of the night—on Ninth and Washington making their living.

Pamela Sneed: It was vibrant and gritty. This was when there were a number of trans sex workers, before too much gentrification came.

dM: The outside scenes near the club were very "raw" and much in need of help/ guidance/education. It was not the same as inside the Clit Club, where help guidance/education, etc., was poured out and available. The city needed the Clit Club organizers to assist on many levels.

Aldo: The Meat Market blocks were a sort of dark, menacing no-man's-land at night, so it was wise to stay alert to potential danger. The persistent stench of dead livestock entrails, the sight of thick pools of blood around dumpsters filled with pork trimmings, was prevalent from Fourteenth Street and Ninth Avenue to our spot at the corner of Washington Street. There were artist's lofts, dilapidated buildings, and not much else on the block. With the expanse of the Hudson River and the rotting piers two blocks west, we were on our own at the edge of the city.

12. What sounds do you remember from the Clit Club?

Lola Flash: Crystal Waters: "Gypsy Woman (She's Homeless)"; Black Box: "Everybody, Everybody"; Robin S.: "Show Me Love."

Michele: Moaning and heavy breathing when folks came outside for air and the MUSIC 'cause you never heard those sounds on the radio at the time.

Shigi: Thumping bass and the muffled audio of porn under the music. The sound of the person you were dancing with breathing in your ears while you were "going down" on the dance floor. Queen's "Bohemian Rhapsody" after all was done, and it was just staff at the end of the night. The song that Michele, Dez, and Pam would sing at the end of every Clit Club night: "YOU DON'T HAVE TO GO HOME, *but you just can't stay here . . ."*

Pamela Sneed: House music.

13. What scents or smells do you associate with the Clit Club?

Michele: Drakkar cologne wore by the butches and the *meat meat meat* being delivered up and down the street. When we closed at 4 a.m. and walked to the train, we passed the bagel shop Dizzy Izzy's midblock. The fresh bagels smelled amazing.

Cinnamon: Sweat, fog lights, and sexual energy.

Pam L: Incense.

Julie Tolentino (Clit Club proprietor, Design, Manager): Mix of Nag Champa, Vetiver, and Aquaphor—the lube of choice for new tattoos.

Shigi: Sweat, Nag Champa, candle wax, cigarette smoke (pre-Giuliani), and occasionally burning hair.

14. How did you get ready to go to the Clit Club?

Dez: There was no getting ready . . . you came as you were, because there were no judgments.

Lola Flash: Leather attire or overalls.

Pam L: Braided my hair and smoked a joint.

Michele: Back then the "Boys" always "Dressed to Impress." When I was working, I was always in black.

Aldo Hernandez: I would usually shower, shave, and slip into my Clit Club fishnet briefs to spin in. I'd throw on a slinky tank top, or "activist" tee and a pair of jeans or black/green/silver parachute fabric pants. I often wore caps backward then. Converse or short boots protected my toes. I would add a jean or leather jacket, scarf and a beanie for cold nights.

In extending and invoking the Clit Club, we are also cognizant of the historical recovery and examination that has taken place since its years of operation. Recent and burgeoning exhibitions, public programs, and archival explorations of the Clit Club have guided us to the publication of this collective document.[11] Drawing from Tolentino's citation of Stuart Hall and her long-standing enactment of a living archive in her art practice at large, we recall that "the most important things an archive can do is to ask or allow us to interrogate those moments of transition, because they are often also the moments of high creativity and we cannot see from our privileged position where those ruptures are most likely to occur or in what direction they are likely to lead" (Hall 2001: 92).[12] In approaching the Clit Club as a "living archive," one "whose construction must be seen as an on-going, never-completed project" (ibid.: 89), we are also compelled to reckon with what the Clit Club is insufficiently known for, what McPherson (2016) identifies as the "socio-political ramifications of its existence: why it was conceived, how it was conceived and run." Rather than insist that the Clit Club be brought to us only through our current vocabularies and political persuasions, we resist the normalizing effects of progressive or inclusionary ambitions to encounter the Clit Club where it currently resides—as a collection of fragments and filtered tangled recollections, whose gathering generates an eroticized corporal materiality to the gaps and imperfect weavings between past and present. We persist in this space of study to dwell with what remains uncategorizable and concealed in the shadows; the unseen labors of the many women, gender-nonconforming individuals, and men who shaped much of what we now partake in within the realms of queer scholarship, cultural production, and sex.

Notes

In support of the Clit Club archive and future events, Tolentino wishes to acknowledge the core Clit Club staff contributors: Michele, Shigi, DM, Lola, Aldo, Pamela, Dez, Jet, Cinnamon, dM; co-writers: Amira, Leeroy, Tara, Dragon, and Vivian; Art Matters and Sacha Yanow. Additionally, my contribution is made legible by my long-term collaboration with Clit Club book editor, writer, dramaturg, and scholar, Josh Lubin-Levy.

1. Many of the historical details in this article have been drawn from multiple interviews with Julie Tolentino, conducted during 2016–17 by Kang, Hart, Crockett, Khusro, and Mansion.
2. Many Clit Club staff members were artists with performance, video, dance, or poetry practices. The club produced and generated performance, text, and video art.
3. See Harcourt 2001; Podair 2011: 210; Traub 2001. Giuliani's "Quality of Life" pilot program was launched in the West Village in 1994 by the city's Sixth Precinct, which was a few blocks from the piers. The Sixth Precinct went on to issue more quality-of-

life summonses than the whole borough of Manhattan combined. See Andrea McArdle and Tanya Erzen, quoted in Hanhardt 2013: 199.

4. Artists invited to show at the Clit Club included Ron Athey, Tolentino / Jet Clark, the Gauntlet Staff, Annie Sprinkle, LSM exhibitionists, Lovechild, Cheryl Dunye, Pamela Sneed, Trash, Lola Flash, and others. House of Color (Robert Garcia, Wellington Love, Idris Mignott, Jeff Nunokawa, Pamela Sneed, Jocelyn Taylor/Jaguar Mary, Julie Tolentino) was an affinity group of ACT UP made up of queer people of color, whose efforts challenged the representation and exclusion of people of color in the media.

5. The forms of sexual care and education may be understood as equally vital forms of activism alongside the demonstrations or slogans more typically associated with ACT UP's activities. See Sharkey 2015, an interview with Emily Colucci and Osman Can Yerebakan.

6. See Catherine Gund and Julie Tolentino's *B.U.C.K.L.E.*, "a humorous fast-paced parody of women dancing, cruising and picking up women at New York City's legendary Clit Club (www.cinenova.org/filmdetail.php?filmId=91).

7. This ran parallel to the emergence of underground tattooing communities, play piercing, water sports, and cutting, and the Clit Club afforded a site for advancing and developing practices for working with movement and bodily fluids. These practices were also developed in performance works devised by artists such as Tolentino, Athey, Sheree Rose and Bob Flanagan, Realyn Galin, and others, who conceived aesthetically challenging and complex ways of working with blood and the body.

8. See event description for Participant Inc., New York, *Clit Club Reactivated*, as part of *Dirty Looks: On Location*, July 30, 2015 (www.facebook.com/events/1626959910903819/).

9. For more on the global War on Terror's production of a "Muslim" enemy, see Shirazi 2016. For a critique of the "Gay International" and the US discourse of gay rights, see Massad 2002. On homonationalism, see Puar 2007. For a debate on the limits of academic critique in relation to queer lived experience and activism that examines Massad's text as well as the limits of homonationalism, see Schotten and Maikey 2012.

10. Portions of what documentation did exist have been misplaced and lost over the years by even those lesbian and queer archives that would shelter the Clit Club's remains. Tolentino maintains a small collection of print ephemera and other material that she has gathered for safekeeping. For a discussion of the role of ephemera as evidence, and the methodological importance of following its "traces, glimmers, residues and specks of things," as anchored in the social and including "traces of lived experience and performances of lived experience," see Muñoz 1996: 10.

11. See the following programs, exhibitions, and talks: La MaMa Galleria 2014; Participant Inc. 2015. For film screening, public program, and a display of ephemera from the Clit Club archive held by Julie Tolentino, see La Mama Galleria 2015; Tolentino, Hernandez, and Lubin-Levy 2015; Tolentino 2016.

12. While it exceeds the scope of this article, much of Tolentino's creative practice considers the body a living archive, as demonstrated in projects that highlight artist-to-artist relationships such as "The Sky Remains the Same (2008–ongoing)." See Hart 2015; and Crockett 2015.

References

Clit Club. c. 1997. "Clit Club flyer." Collection of Julie Tolentino.

Crockett, Vivian A. 2015. "evidence induces a strong sense of longing, unfulfilled desire: a taunting, a haunting, a wanting." *Visual AIDS Blog.* www.visualaids.org/blog /detail/vivian-crockett-evidence.

Delaney, Samuel. 1999. *Times Square Red, Times Square Blue.* New York: New York University Press.

Hae, Lam. 2012. *The Gentrification of Nightlife and the Right to the City: Regulating Spaces of Social Dancing in New York.* New York: Taylor and Francis.

Hall, Stuart. 2001. "Constituting an Archive." *Third Text* 15, no. 54: 89–92.

Hanhardt, Christina. 2013. *Safe Space: Gay Neighborhood History and the Politics of Violence.* Durham, NC: Duke University Press.

Harcourt, Bernard E. 2001. *Illusion of Order: The False Promise of Broken Windows Policing.* Cambridge, MA: Harvard University Press.

Harney, Stefano, and Fred Moten. 2013. *The Undercommons: Fugitive Planning and Black Study.* New York: Minor Compositions.

Hart, Tara. 2015. "How Do You Archive the Sky?" *Archive Journal.* www.archivejournal .net/essays/how-do-you-archive-the-sky/.

Hernandez, Aldo. 2016. Questionnaire responses to authors, December.

La MaMa Galleria. 2014. *Ephemera as Evidence*, curated by Joshua Lubin-Levy and Ricardo Montez, New York, June 5–29.

La Mama Galleria. 2015. *Party Out of Bounds: Nightlife as Activism since 1980*, curated by Emily Colucci and Osman Can Yerebakan, New York, September 18–October 10.

Massad, Joseph Andoni. 2002. "Re-Orienting Desire: The Gay International and the Arab World." *Public Culture* 14, no. 2: 361–85.

McPherson, Shigeru. n.d.a. Ephemera A, New York. Collection of Julie Tolentino.

———. n.d.b. Ephemera B, New York. Collection of Julie Tolentino.

McPherson, Shigeru "Shigi," and Michele H. 2016. Questionnaire responses to authors, December.

MPA. 2016."Dear S/F: Scribes of *The Undercommons: Fugitive Planning and Black Study.*" In *MPA: The Interview: Red, Red Future*, 1–7. Houston, TX: Contemporary Arts Museum.

Muñoz, José Esteban. 1996. "Ephemera as Evidence: Introductory Notes to Queer Acts." *Women and Performance* 8, no. 2: 5–16.

———. 2013. "The Brown Commons: The Sense of Wildness." INT Dialogue 2013: The Queer Commons Lecture. Eastern Michigan University, Ypsilanti, March 25.

Participant Inc. 2015. *Clit Club Reactivated*, curated by Leeroy Kun Young Kang and Vivian Crockett, New York, July 30.

Podair, Jerald. 2011. "'One City, One Standard': Civil Rights in Giuliani's New York." In *Civil Rights in New York City: From World War II to the Giuliani Era*. New York: Fordham University Press.

Puar, Jasbir K. 2007. *Terrorist Assemblages: Homonationalism in Queer Times*. Durham, NC: Duke University Press.

Schotten, Heike, and Haneen Maikey. 2012. "Queers Resisting Zionism: On Authority and Accountability beyond Homonationalism." *Jadaliyya*, October 12. www .jadaliyya.com/pages/index/7738/queers-resisting-zionism_on-authority-and -accounta.

Schulman, Sarah. 2008. "Interview 091: Lola Flash," July 8, 1–47. ACT UP Oral History Project. www.actuporalhistory.org/interviews/images/flash.pdf.

Sharkey, M. 2015. "The Politics of Partying: Nightlife as Activism." *Out*, September 18. www.out.com/art-books/2015/9/18/politics-partying-nightlife-activism.

Shirazi, Sadia. 2016. "Muslim Futurism." Paper presented at King's College, Cambridge University, Cambridge, England, February 3.

Smith, Neil. 1998. "Giuliani Time: The Revanchist 1990s." *Social Text*, no. 57: 1–20.

Tolentino, Julie. 2016. "Making the Queer Scene." Panel, Museum of the City of New York, December 6.

Tolentino, Julie. 2017. Interview with fellow authors, Brooklyn, NY, May.

Tolentino, Julie, Aldo Hernandez, and Joshua Lubin-Levy. 2015. "The HARD CORPS: Clubs, Sex, Activism, Bodies." Panel, New York, October 1.

Traub, James. 2001. "Giuliani Internalized." *New York Times*, February 11. partners .nytimes.com/library/magazine/home/20010211mag-giuliani.html.

THE AFFECTIVE COMMONS:

Gay Shame, Queer Hate, and Other Collective Feelings

Eric Stanley

Love Trumps Hate
—Human Rights Campaign

Queers Hate Techies
—Gay Shame

$\mathcal{T}$he commons has reemerged in left organizing and study to name ways of coming together that disrupt racial capitalism's technologies of accumulation, extraction, and alienation. From mass resistance to austerity policies in the streets of London, and antituition book blocs in Montreal to insurgent mapping projects in Rio de Janeiro—the commons offers radical collectivity as a mode of living against the bounded present. As a place, a structure of feeling, and an idea, the commons provides refuge in the ruins of capital's totality, yet its liberatory promise is betrayed by the abstraction of indigenous land, which is to say the imposition of settler-sovereignty, that allows it to be imagined in the first instance. What, then, remains of the commons if we abandon it as an innocent object immune to the force of capital's colonial violence?[1]

As an experiment in common, Occupy Wall Street gathered at Zuccotti Park in New York City with the aim of expropriating land from the lethal machines of enclosure and its transformation into the commodity form. Through its encampments in US cities and beyond, Occupy provided material-semiotic zones where the economic order was rendered suspect by left critique. It was also an occasion for the speculative work of fashioning anti-authoritarian group infrastructure from below liberal democracy's mandates of privatization or state control (Mitropoulos 2012). However, the sign that assembled them, "We are the 99 percent," captured the trouble with the commons and the tensions that exceed the banality of

GLQ 24:4
DOI 10.1215/10642684-6957800
© 2018 by Duke University Press

the slogan. This movement of scale from the singular subject to the multiple "we" collapses difference through the quake of equivalence. Or put another way, this consolidation demands a repetitious flattening that unequally disappears those already on the edges of the "we." For example, during my short time at Occupy Wall Street, I witnessed transphobic and antiblack violence that was confronted by a political education session on gender self-determination and trans liberation led by Reina Gossett of the Sylvia Rivera Law Project. Furthermore, at Occupy Oakland there was an attempt to rename the encampment "Decolonize Oakland"—an effort initiated by Indigenous organizers who argued that *occupation*, rather than a strategy of decolonization, is the methodology of the settler state.

I make this point not to rehearse the tragedy of the commons thesis (Hardin 1968), which argues collectivity comes undone because individuals will inevitably sacrifice the multitude in the service of their own interest.[2] To be clear, it was the state that choreographed paramilitary assaults against Occupy Wall Street and Occupy/Decolonize Oakland, and not internal turbulence that caused them to fall. Further, it is not that the commons must adhere to a cohesive, if not totalizing, inhabitance because difference is what animates its radical potential. However, the struggle to claim *Occupy* versus *Decolonize* Oakland exposed how forcing the incoherence of relationality into representation, or at least a language in common, while preserving the political order, traps us in a loop. Here the scene of Occupy dramatizes the incommensurability of a common desire when the possessed individual, the subject of liberal democracy, remains intact. This brutal figure, the universalizing author of settler-sovereignty, persists in its ability to claim the commons as object while negating the anticolonial praxis that is collective-determination. Or, when the commons is thought and lived through settler epistemologies, and not a world ending, which is to say world-making struggle, "the commons" like *Occupy* sutures the very disruption it claims to enact. Figuring decolonization as the end of the world—"a program of complete disorder," as Frantz Fanon (2005: 36, 2) reminds us, "infuses a new rhythm, specific to a new generation of men, with a new language and new humanity." Here, then, the destruction of settler-sovereignty—the end of the world—is not generativity's conclusion but its anticolonial precondition (Gould et al. 2011).[3]

From Occupy/Decolonize to the differently intensified yet ongoing time of pressure for those held against the wall of white cisnormativity, the drive that finds form in the idea of the commons remains seductive. Following the True Levellers' "Common Treasury" (Winstanley 1649), Karl Marx (1992: 877) wrote that "common land" offered peasants "pasture to their cattle, furnished them with timber, fire-wood, turf," a pre- or para-capitalist resource outside the law of individual possession held for communal use.[4] This "common land" is now the psychic and material reserve from which both a mythic past and a utopian future is forged in much anticapitalist analysis. Yet, thinking with Decolonize Oakland in the settler context, the commons endures through a repudiation of indigenous sovereignty in order to render "common land," whether Zuccotti Park or Oscar Grant Plaza, anachronistic—a space outside relational time. This is to say that the forced removal of Native peoples, the theft of land and language—the ongoingness of settler colonialism—is what allows the commons to appear empty and available (Goeman 2009; Wolfe 2006; Coulthard 2014: 12).[5] As J. Kēhaulani Kauanui (2015) argues, "The concept of the commons is itself a historically racialized and gendered concept, as well as one implicated in colonial structures."

Staying with the troubled concept, I am concerned with how affect, in particular disgust and hate, structures relation, even as nonrelation, in and through space. Specifically, I am interested in how negative affect, or bad feelings, produce psychic bonds and collective energies in the practice of queer worlding (Haraway 2008; Muñoz 2013)—an affective commons. I read these entanglements via the still-unfolding archive of Gay Shame, a trans/queer collective that instigates through its posters, stencils, and zines, as well as by staging theatrical direct actions. Working explicitly against the nonprofit model, the group holds open meetings, and it does not fund-raise or have an operating budget—supplies are scavenged or stolen—and whoever is present constitutes the group. In other words, there is no formalized membership structure; rather, a core number of people continue to show up each week, as some participants have been there from its inception and others come and go. This shifting terrain has transformed the composition of those active in the group from predominantly, but not exclusively, white to mostly trans/queer people of color.

In 2001 Gay Shame started organizing in San Francisco, a city that has been so radically transformed by capital's upward consolidation of life chances that the term *hypergentrification* fails to capture the speed and scale of change (Tiku 2013). Since the early 1990s the accelerator of San Francisco's transformation, evidenced by the massive accumulation for some, and ruthless dispossession for others, is the tech industry, with its newly settled ruling class of young, mostly white, cisgendered and male, millionaires and billionaires.[6]

Along with this sustained ambivalence toward the idea of the commons, here I am interested in how a city is "known viscerally" through the echo of geography's affective registers (Tuan 2001: 162). Gentrification is imagined by both New Urbanists and antidisplacement activists as spatially and architecturally organized, felt indeed, but not constituted or attacked through the affective. Yet the sensorium of displacement, or that which interrupts the idea of *home*, expands from the pronounced violence of mass houselessness—to the quotidian ways one's connections are worn down by the closing of bookstores, evictions of neighbors, and policing of streets—the white noise of white return. The commons, then, is a limit and a door leading to both the irreducible friction of togetherness, the constriction of the "we," and its transformative potentiality to open to another world.[7]

The affective commons for Lauren Berlant (2012: 77) tells us something about the "formation of structures of feelings" as the "unstated residue of collective life." In particular, the residue of Gay Shame's collectivity is evident in, which is to say lives beyond, the ephemera of their direct actions. For the group, the affective commons—a cosmology of feelings, a resource in common—names the methodology through which they hold the joined questions of space, difference, and conjuncture. Attention to the affective work of Gay Shame, and not simply its expressed critique, opens an analysis of the devastation of racial capitalism's modes of extraction, which might better apprehend what slides alongside the properly political. To this end, if the political is constituted as the domain of settler-sovereignty—the world of the human—then centering the affective commons might help chart a politics after the political, or a way to survive the unsurvivable present, and remain beyond the end of the world.

Runway as a Weapon

A wheat-pasted flyer on a light pole in the Tenderloin neighborhood asked us to "Prepare for the Exploitation Runway." In 2002 Gavin Newsom was a San Francisco supervisor in the midst of a mayoral campaign that articulated a "clean up the city" ethic intended to return white capital, and its people, to San Francisco, much like similar programs across the United States. Central to his platform was Proposition N, "Care Not Cash," which promised to reduce General Assistance checks from $359 a month to $59, the difference to be replaced with social services. However, this increased "care" was legislatively undefined and unfunded; the proposition functioned as a semiotic attack and punitive gesture that ensured poor people remained structured as phantom wards of normative civil society (see Coalition on Homelessness 2002).

Gay Shame's response, "Prop N Stands for Nightmare," called for people to directly confront Newsom in his Marina neighborhood, which is among the wealthiest and whitest districts in San Francisco. A flyer for the event read,

> October 25th 5:30 pm at Webster and Chestnut Streets, San Francisco Gay
> Shame plans to take on Gavin Newsom's Proposition N, misnamed "Care

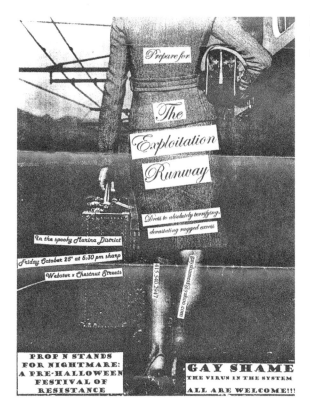

Figure 1. *Exploitation Runway* poster, Gay Shame, 2002

Not Cash," in his home turf with a pre-Halloween Festival of Resistance in the Marina District. Events include an Exploitation Runway, a Gavin Newsom Look-Alike Contest, and food and music will be provided. Dress to ragged, stultifying, terrifying excess and join us in the Marina to defeat Prop N! (Gay Shame 2002)

Activists constructed a haunted city out of cardboard and found objects in order to block the entrance of his campaign headquarters as well as provide a backdrop for their festival of resistance. Along with the Gavin Newsom Look-Alike Contest promised on the flyer, the action ended with the Exploitation Runway, where "exploiters of the past, present, and future," including Christopher Columbus and Senator Dianne Feinstein, walked the bloody runway in categories like Gentrification Realness (Old School and New School), Displacement Divas, and Eviction Couture. M. Lamar and Mattilda Bernstein Sycamore emceed as house music filled the streets from a PA system hitched to the back of a bike. Through camp sensibilities, the theatrics of humor, and duct tape, the runway—a motor of commodity fetishism—was temporarily repurposed as a barricade against Newsom's claim to the city.[8]

After the energetic pulse of the event, Gay Shame continued targeting Newsom, and while the group did not endorse candidates or engage with electoral politics in an affirmative sense, it was clear in its opposition. Shortly after "Prop N stands for Nightmare," a $150-a-head "Hot Pink" fund-raiser for the newly constructed and already challenged San Francisco LGBT Community Center was announced, with Gavin Newson and his wife, Kimberly Guilfoyle Newsom, as its guests of honor.[9]

Protesters gathered outside the center to greet attendees by handing them hot-pink bags of trash. These agitprops refracted the negative use-value of those unpropertied who are reduced into debris through the equation "Care Not Cash." In an aesthetic assault, the trash bags dulled the shimmer of San Francisco liberalism, exposing the collaboration between antihomeless policy, capital investments, and mainstream LGBT politics. Many of the gala's attendees had recently fought, and successfully blocked, the construction of a permanent trans/queer youth shelter in the Castro, citing the fear of stalled property appreciation as their reason for opposition.[10]

Gay Shame's actions, like the Exploitation Runway, use the performativity of protest to incite cooperation—resistance in common. They break the circuits of spectatorship and audience that tend to divest those who show up from feeling connected to the event. Shortly after Gay Shame assembled, about two dozen cops suited in riot gear and state power formed a blue wall of revenge in front of the center's glass doors. Newsom and his wife arrived and were smuggled in under armed guard, which signaled the locking of doors behind them by the center's staff. Moments later, the police advanced toward those still assembled on the sidewalk and began beating people with batons, tackling others to the concrete, including myself, and leaving at least one person bleeding from head wounds with multiple missing teeth. While the attack raged, the center's staff, straight politicians, and their gay best friends cheered the police on in celebration from the building's rooftop bar and behind the safety of locked glass doors.

The night ended on the pavement with protesters receiving medical treatment and at least four arrests, including a Black Gay Shame protester who was held under felony lynching charges for breaking the fall of a victim of police violence. Here, the polemics of their analysis crashed into the absurd force of the real. Or put another way, Gay Shame's critiques, specifically those targeting the constitution of LGBT politics as, and in service of, white normativity, manifested in incarceration and spilled blood for trans/queer people who were denied entrance to "gay space" (Read 2003).

The SF LGBT Center (2016) produces itself as the "heart, home and hands of the San Francisco LGBT community." Although it is owned and operated by a nonprofit and its board of directors, its affective appeal to "community" animates this imagined and shared vision, articulated through the historical and present exclusions of LGBT people from public and intuitional space. This is to say, it mobilizes the fantasy of a safe space—a common space in name—yet on the night of "Hot Pink," it was both the place where, and the mechanism through which, a straight politician was protected and trans/queer activists were locked outside, beaten, and arrested. Rather than an anomaly, this bloody scene brings into relief the geometry of contemporary power that maintain its consistency under the twinned practices of liberal inclusion and brutal force.[11]

Complaining Is Not a Luxury

Gay Shame formed in the late 1990s in Brooklyn in opposition to the corporatization and otherwise assimilatory grounding of mainstream LGBT politics. Its first events there, and a few years later in San Francisco, were offered as a DIY "alternative" to the massively commercialized Pride parade, where speakers, workshops, bands, and DJs assembled in an attempt to fuse partying with a radical queer analysis. Many of the early organizers were alienated by the austerity of left politics, which attended to sexuality, gender, disability, race, and aesthetics as an inconvenience (at best) to class struggle. While drawn to the collective potential of nightlife, they also wanted to confront the racism, classism, and transmisogyny of the gay party scene.[12]

Because Gay Shame is not legally or economically tied to legitimate and legitimating institutions, or perhaps because of the group's bad attitudes, it continues to produce incendiary interventions that disturb across the political range. This nonalignment to a controlled platform, or the political as such, planned through an anarchist consensus model, has found the collective being charged as *divisive*, *negative*, and *disruptive*. In their 2017 zine, "Is there room for direct action divas?," a how-to guide for horizontal organizing, between sections on building takeovers and wheat pasting is the "complaining is not a luxury" subheading that states,

> People are often confused by the name "GAY SHAME." The more people hate on our name the more we realize it's working. People think that sarcasm is for people who are too scared to speak truth to power. But Bayard doesn't know how bad it is now. No matter how outrageous the messaging of our actions is, it pales in comparison to the genocidal realities that

we're up against. Actually, our jokes are always about 8,000 steps behind how bad things actually are. We don't feel it's worth starting a conversation with Power™. We don't want to work within a shitty system that is already stacked against us. We complain. After all, our purpose is not to propose policy. We find community through expressing resistance. ALL ARE WELCOME. (Gay Shame 2017)

For Gay Shame complaining names forms of disruption made by those outside, which is to say those captured inside, the properly recognized, might include trolling politicians like Gavin Newsom, critiquing gay marriage, reading the ableism of much direct action organizing, and more. Complaining is the lower frequency of objection that vibrates in the same field and might be the method of expressing anger for those at the borders of the properly human. Rather than situate complaining as that which inhibits direct action, for Gay Shame it is a form of struggle in a long practice of interruption. Complaining reorders the political logic that demands the affective be exchanged for the pragmatism of legislative maturity and parliamentary participation. A politics against the political—they weaponize the negativity of critique in and against a world where the respectable modes of operation catch participants in the ruse of democracy. Yet this negativity is not aimed toward self-obliteration or a decomposition into the nihilism of finitude. By scavenging the remnants of the social, Gay Shame finds, or more precisely fashions, collectivity through the commons of hate.[13]

Brogrammers off the Block

The question of space and the sense of displacement have mobilized many of Gay Shame's interventions for the last decade. Although the history of Silicon Valley as a site of technocapital (Suarez-Villa 2009) is much longer, the recent past has seen its massive expansion, with the headquarters of Google, Facebook, Uber, AirBnB, Salesforce, Twitter, and countless others erected in San Francisco or within a forty-mile radius. Those struggling to survive the city use the cutting terms *brogrammer* or *techie* to name the mostly young, white, cisgender male employee-owners of these massive corporations. Adorned with the casual confidence of their historical experience and uniform in logoed hoodies and suburban fear, techies sleep in the city and are driven to work on "Google buses," the private buses that shuttle employees to work, ensuring that they are not inconvenienced by the *public* of transportation.

While the city actively supports these techies and the corporations for which they work through tax incentives and the legalization of their illegal use of public bus stops, and countless other "private public partnerships," many low-income residents, especially Latinx and Black communities, now find their own streets unrecognizable and increasingly hostile. The nightmare for those living under constant threat of displacement is scandalously inverted through the calculus of individuated risk and American ingenuity, which locates the gentrifier, and not the victim, in need of care. Justin Keller, a tech entrepreneur, in his open letter to Mayor Ed Lee proclaimed, "The wealthy working people have earned their right to live in the city. They went out, got an education, work hard, and earned it. I shouldn't have to worry about being accosted. I shouldn't have to see the pain, struggle, and despair of homeless people to and from my way to work every day" (quoted in Miller 2016).

The trespass, for Keller, is articulated at the level of the scopic, but he also offers a nonphenomenology, a theory of antirelationality against a practice of worlding. His treatise mobilizes a sterile individualism to argue cross-class contact is the symptom of a state that is failing to shield him from the very conditions he has created. For him, the offense is not that the unequal structuring of racial capitalism produces abject precarity but that he is subjected to observing "the pain," which disturbs his ability to "not know." As a proper subject of settler sovereignty, his analysis, by way of a counterreading, brings into view the secret betrayal that is liberal democracy—the anticommons. In contrast to Gay Shame's commons of hate, which works to destroy the logics of civil society, Keller's revulsion confirms the subjugation of those banished by private property—normativities structuring drive. Keller's recent arrival is mirrored by the closing of Esta Noche, the last queer Latinx bar in the city, and Marcus Books, the oldest Black-owned bookstore in the United States, along with countless other spaces, as luxury condos crowd the sky. Keller's attack, which finds as its target homeless people, demands and is rewarded with increased policing, unmitigated condo development, and drip coffee (Crucchiola 2016).

While resistance to gentrification, including much of the organizing in San Francisco, rightfully narrates the most recent generation of those under threat of removal as having a claim to where they live, Gay Shame's flyer from 2014 links the current gentrification of Latinx residents from the Mission to the longer and ongoing displacement of indigenous Ohlone people. Through a nonmimetic juxtaposition, the image places Spanish colonization in the field of vision with the Google buses turned Armada. This nonlinear image of "a new old course" arranges gentrification as a practice of spatial and temporal reordering, for both recent and older projects of de- and repeopling, while "innovation," the promise of technol-

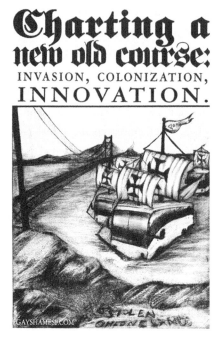

Figure 2. *Gentrification and Colonization in the Mission* poster, Gay Shame, 2014

ogy from Marx to contemporary tech empires, is announced as the justification for occupation and exploitation, and not its remedy.

Without guarantees, Gay Shame's poster asks how we might apprehend the porous contours of gentrification, in perhaps its deadliest form—as a low-intensity battle waged in the affective materiality of the everyday, and not a single and always knowable moment in time and space. Here, the left orthodoxy that assumes "innovation" self-evidently builds toward horizontally distributed relief is necessarily jeopardized by reinserting San Francisco as Ohlone land. It also situates displacement as protracted, immanent, and nonteleological, which pushes against a settled story and the romance of the commons as its antidote. Or, the image asks how might we inhabit collective action against gentrification that does not reproduce the inevitability of settler colonization, or collapse the two?[14]

To further entrench the antagonism between displacement and its champions, for the past few years Gay Shame has stenciled "QUEERS HATE TECHIES" in pink and purple paint on sidewalks around the city. The text lays bare the resentment many of its organizers experience, and the critique, by way of opposition, affirms hate as the idiom through which queers, and many others, might organize collective life. The stencil also provokes the city to proclaim, through the cunning silence of policy, how it hates queers and all those who struggle against urban renewal as social cleaning. In the tradition of class warfare, the incivility of the

Figure 3. *Queers Hate Techies* sticker, Gay Shame

"Queers Hate Techies" message is rigorous and strategic.[15] Rather than a call for *dialogue*—the liberal technic of liquidation by other means—it is the desperate tonality of existing in a world where estrangement and dislocation are the condition of being. For Gay Shame, this sensorium of fear, anger, rage, and hate, felt in common, provides, at least momentarily, a respite from the isolation and exhaustion of living on in a vanishing city.

Against hate, everywhere in liberal and leftist rhetoric love is mobilized as the proper defense for marginalized people under threat. From Che Guevara's (2003: 225) often-cited "the true revolutionary is guided by great feelings of love," and the anarchist call to arms, "love and rage," to the proclamation "Love Trumps Hate" currently dotting manicured lawns and city windows alike, love becomes tautologically cemented as the primary if not singular affect in which liberatory action might live. Put plainly, this instrumentalization of love is a liberal lockdown that wages an already lost war of maneuvers for recognition against what seeks nothing other than its elimination.[16]

Love is revolutionary, especially for those whose access to it has always been under siege, yet it is also the site of mass mobilization against trans/queer people of color in various forms. White nationalists, and their liberal simulacra, also cite love as their motivation, here for racist action, which clarifies its nonidenticality. If the prohibition against hate maintains its strength, even in otherwise critical thought, then perhaps it is there, in the negative, that a queer affective commons builds, as much against bad objects as it does through bad feeling. On Gay Shame's antitech stencils, a reporter echoed popular opinion, "And, the irony of a queer activist group promoting hate of any kind, or violence against an undesired group, is clearly lost on them" (Pershan 2015). The "irony" that this writer misnames is not that oppressed people hate their oppressors: it is that they do not always. This sentiment, which exists as gospel, renders the never-ending violence of displacement as inevitable, and its resistance unbearable. Here, then, it might be precisely through trans/queer hate that possibilities in the form of collectivity are organized against these normative mandates when love means self-annihilation.[17]

Recalling this deconstructive potentiality, Audre Lorde (2007: 127) exhumes, with demanding clarity, how anger is instrumentalized as a felt analytic of Black feminism in and against an antiblack and misogynist world. "Everything can be used / except what is wasteful / (you will need / to remember this when you are accused of destruction)." She anticipates the charge of being labeled destructive, which, like complaining, is gendered in a racist syntax that leaves the *real* work of objection to the rationality of the human—the proxies of white cis heteronormativity. Resisting the ways anger is argued to only destroy those who hold or express it, she states "that anger has eaten clefts into my living only when it remained unspoken, useless to anyone" (ibid.: 131). For Lorde, like in Gay Shame's zine, anger, and even hate, is a way to "find community through expressing resistance," an affective commons, built in part through negativity, but whose antisocial orientation is orchestrated toward ante-social life.[18]

Decenter the Center

In the shadow of San Francisco's LGBT Center is a dead-end street, obscured by the wall of an adjacent building. Because of its relative shelter from moving traffic, houseless people have made their lives on the sidewalks and pavement of the cul-de-sac. Its proximity to a freeway underpass has defended it, to some degree, from the real estate speculation swallowing everything around it. Yet in an attempt to empty out those who find some protection there, it was turned into an "off the grid" food truck corral, where commerce and artisan tacos crowded out the tent homes of its residents. However, the food trucks disappeared each night and the street was reoccupied, intensifying the harassment experienced by those sleeping there from neighborhood groups intent on increasing the value of their newly purchased property. As remedy for the *problem* of people using public space outside, or perhaps beside legal exchange, the city turned the dead end into a public park. The people were removed, and the sloping hill was terraced, up-lit, and planted with drought-tolerant succulents—markers of revitalization for some, signifier of life's end for others (Wenus 2015).

McCoppin Hub remained a public park for three years and was still used primarily by houseless and marginally housed people as a place to gather. Still, this use of the park by those placed under the sign of homelessness, most of whom were of color, was so intolerable to the owning class who now called this stretch of Valencia Street theirs, propertied residents demanded that Supervisor Jane Kim build a permanent fence around the park to ensure that it could only be used for official purposes under the keyed administration of the city.[19]

In contrast to the commonly held land that Marx narrates, here making the land "common" was the durational mechanism that allowed it to no longer be accessed by specific publics, namely, those assumed to be homeless. This is of course a sustained practice of state land acquisition from settler accumulation to the forced removal of Native people from national parks (Burnham 2000) and the deracination of Black communities from what became New York's Central Park, in order to produce them as "natural"—that is to say, *unspoiled* by human inhabitance.[20]

The twelve-foot fence now circling the Hub is a form of "defensive architecture," a cruel theory and practice in urban design that anticipates the way space might be reclaimed by, or used in opposition to, the intentions of its owners. The fence was erected the same week as the massive "No Ban No Wall" protests at San Francisco International and airports across the United States in protest of Trump's order to further restrict travel to the United States by people from Iran, Iraq, Syria, Sudan, Libya, Yemen, and Somalia, which was deployed alongside his plan to build a wall between the United States and Mexico. Gay Shame dropped a banner on the new fence that read "NO WALLS NO FENCES NOT KIM'S NOR PENCE'S" to tie together the ways the atrocities of state violence are, under neoliberal common sense, imagined to be elsewhere. Or, the banner as pedagogy reads its viewers that might justifiably express outrage at Trump's Islamophobic and xenophobic policies but support antihomeless actions, like the building of fences, in their own neighborhoods.[21]

Ten years after the original scene of police brutality at the "Hot-Pink" riot, Gay Shame returned to the LGBT Center. Resisting the illusion of possible redress from an institution it understood to be foundationally dangerous, the group's demand was for the end of demands, by way of repurposing the center itself. Fearing that squatting the building would continue the ways it is already enclosed, after much debate the group took a different approach. Along with citing the violence of the action a decade earlier, Gay Shame diagnosed the center as a "non-profit vor-

Figure 4. *No Walls No Fence Not Kim's Nor Pence's* banner, Gay Shame, 2017

tex." The center has no open, or even semipublic, space, and trans/queer youth of color are regularly removed from the property by force. One of the few times I have been inside the building, a uniformed and armed police officer who was acting as a receptionist confronted a friend and me, demanding that we leave the building because this was "the lobby of a business and not a meeting place."

Gay Shame's high-concept, low-resolution action included the clandestine hanging of a tarp from the building's fourth floor that read, "the center sucks our . . . inspiration, potential, dreams, money, time, imagination." Wrestling matches raged out front between recognizable and less recognizable nonprofiteers, including Human Rights Campaign canvassers, AIDS service organization executive directors, and gala attendees, all emceed by Sir Isaac Newton. The same glass doors that were, ten years earlier, locked tight to prevent trans/queer escape from police brutality were bolted open with bike U-locks. Under a forty-foot banner, protesters forced—to the point of collapse—the center's affective scaffolding that allowed it to remain both an LGBT home and an antiqueer fortress.

The commons here serves as a limit concept through which we might better understand the conditions of space and its affective tempo as contingent and disjointed. Or, it operates as a reading practice that charts the structuring parameters of the social while inciting us to dream against the hard pragmatism of the present. The doors to the center, now locked open, were one such imagining, a revolt against neoliberal spacialization—the distance between the organization of common space and the materiality of enclosure, including national parks, dead-end streets, and LGBT centers.[22]

With ambivalence, the commons remains useful even as an object of critique, because it approximates the drive for, and the impossibility of, being together in difference, when these asymmetries disaggregate as much as they collect. What I have been calling the affective commons might more accurately be named the affective commune, following Marx's (1993: 483) distinction: "The commune thus appears as a coming-together [Vereinigung], not as a being-together [Verein]." Here, the commune, or perhaps more precisely, communing, is a process of coming-together, and not instantiated as arrival or absolute being. On the obligation of coming-together, Jean-Luc Nancy (2010: 149) suggests that "communism, therefore, means the common condition of all the singularities of subjects, that is of all the exceptions, all the uncommon points whose network makes a world (a possibility of sense)." I take this to mean that communism, here again as an activity and not a location, is the placeholder for a communing that might bear, or perhaps account for, singularities and exceptions. Communing, then, serves as antidote, at least in aim, to the deadly individualism of Justin Keller's fantasy while sustaining the difference necessary to defend against the majoritarian weight of common rule.

Following Nancy, the affective commons, as commune, is the coming together of singularities and exceptions, toward a queer future, and against what disciplines us to love our oppressors while awaiting a freedom that never comes. This communing through affect gathers a nonidentity forged in joyful negation, a motley assemblage of outsiders, freaks, and queers, those disposed of and made disposable by latest capitalism. The affective commons, through the provocation of Gay Shame, builds not toward a reincorporation of the social but toward the total destruction of a world constituted through the vertically distributed violence of modernity. Under the banner of the affective commons, revolutionary love might set us free, but perhaps hate, too, grows freedom.[23]

Notes

This article is indebted to all those who have organized and continue to organize with Gay Shame in an attempt to build cultures of resistance in hostile worlds.

1. I am here thinking with Cedric Robinson (2000) on the production of race as the precondition for capitalist modes production. Book blocs are a form of black-bloc organizing where shields are made out of large pieces of wood and painted as book covers. For an account, see Wojtek 2012.
2. For a critique of "The Tragedy of the Commons," see Harvey 2011.
3. Here I am suggesting that without destroying the fantasy and practice of modernity's possessed individual, which serves as a scaffolding of settler colonialism, "the commons" will reproduce the same violence it attempts to escape. Further, if taken seriously, this demands an end of the world as it currently exists, which is also an occasion to imagine alternative forms of sociality.

4. Here I am referencing John Locke's (1993) theory of possessive individualism as a settler epistemology.

5. See also Indian Country Today 2011.

6. I am referencing Donna Haraway's (2016) idea of "staying with the trouble" as a way to inhabit the contradictions of the political. For more on how queer worlding operates in the rub of political feelings, see Muñoz 2009. Also, much of my thinking here has been sharpened by his work and our many conversations about the queer and brown commons. A recent study (Nested 2017) found that San Francisco has the highest residential rents per square foot in the world. For an ethnographic account of space of affect, see Stewart 2007; Tiku 2013.

7. I am here also thinking with Delany 2001 on the question of the "affective registers" of gentrification, sex, and place. See also Muñoz 2013.

8. For a more detailed account of this action, and the early history of Gay Shame, see Bernstein Sycamore 2004 and Weiss 2008. Other insights into the structure and history of the group are from my experiences organizing with them.

9. Rather than endorse candidates, Gay Shame ran "Mary for Mayor," a performative candidacy whose platform included "compost the SFPD."

10. An example of how LGBT mainstream politics reproduces antihomeless violence was dramatized in the fight led by the Castro Business District association against a trans/queer homeless shelter proposed for the Castro; see Avicolli-Mecca 2015.

11. For an excellent account of how "safe spaces" have and continue to be mobilized in the service of gentrification, see Hanhardt 2013.

12. Gay Shame continued to organize, meeting every Saturday for sixteen years in the back of Modern Times Bookstore in San Francisco's Mission District, until its eviction in 2016.

13. Here the queerness of negativity and the negativity of queerness are functioning as a kind of melancholic utopianism. In other words, I am not suggesting that Gay Shame is invested in an antisocial lockdown that forecloses pleasure. I see it creating a space for, or at least a mode of, joyful persistence that does not hinge on liberal enactments of hope. I am here thinking about how "the human" as a disciplinary category is deployed and withheld. For more on how Black feminist thought, trans theory, and some formations of posthumanism understands "the human" as a situated concept, see Weheliye 2014.

14. We could look at the recent prison abolitionists' pushback against police unions and antigentrification activists' critiques of white communal houses in neighborhoods of color for two other examples that point to the limit of collectivization. For more on the critique, see Remle 2017.

15. At least two of Gay Shame's organizers, both of whom are of color, have been recently evicted from their long-term homes in San Francisco.

16. Michael Hardt and Antonio Negri (2011: 181) on the productivity of love affirm,

"To say love is ontologically constitutive, then, simply means that it produces the common."

17. On love and white nationalism, see Ahmed 2014. For more on the ways queers have used hate, see Anonymous 1990. See also Cobb 2005.For another example, see the ways love is mobilized through the discourse of "protecting women and children" (whom are always assumed, thus produced, as nontrans) in the most recent iteration of antitrans bathroom laws. Ngai's (2007: 339) attentiveness to the uses of disgust as a self-preserving tactic is vital.

18. I am using "ante-social life" as a way to point toward a melancholic utopian longing for complex relationality.

19. For another example (in New York City) of how space is turned "public" in order to police it toward the goal of gentrification, see Manalansan 2005.

20. Harney and Moten (2013: 65–t6) point us, in different terms, to the way "public and private" are reassembled.

21. For more on Trump's travel ban, see Merica 2017. For coverage of the "No Ban No Wall" protests, see Swartz 2017.

22. Here I am thinking with Berlant (2016: 395) where she suggests, "the better power of the commons is to point to a way to view what's broken in sociality, the difficulty of convening a world conjointly, although it is inconvenient and hard, and to offer incitements to imagining a livable provisional life."

23. Queerness is working as an assembly of the dispossessed, not unlike the formation that Cohen 1997 offers. *Latest capitalism* was a term Angela Davis used when I was a student in her Critical Theory Seminar in 2004 at the University of California, Santa Cruz. I read her use of the phrase as a kind of serious joke to show how "late capitalism" is ever transforming.

References

Ahmed, Sara. 2014. *The Cultural Politics of Emotion*. Edinburgh: Edinburgh University Press.

Anonymous. 1990. "Queers Read This." *Queer Resources Directory*, June. www.qrd.org /qrd/misc/text/queers.read.this.

Avicolli-Mecca, Tommi. 2015. "The End of the Dream." www.avicollimecca.com/the-end -of-the-dream/.

Berlant, Lauren. 2012. "Affect in the End Times: A Conversation with Lauren Berlant." *Qui Parle* 20, no. 2: 71–90.

———. 2016. "The Commons: Infrastructures for Troubling Times." *Environment and Planning D: Society and Space* 34, no. 3: 393–419.

Bernstein Sycamore, Mattilda. 2004. "Gay Shame: From Queer Autonomous Space to Direct Action Extravaganza." In *That's Revolting! Queer Strategies for Resisting*

Assimilation, edited by Mattilda Bernstein Sycamore, 237–62. Brooklyn: Soft Skull.

Burnham, Philip. 2000. *Indian Country, God's Country: Native Americans and the National Parks*. Washington, DC: Island.

Coalition on Homelessness. 2002. "The Thirteen Biggest Lies Prop. N Backers Are Telling San Francisco Voters." *Street Sheet Online*, September 1. www.streetsheetsf.wordpress.com/2002/09/01/the-13–biggest-lies-prop-n-backers-are-telling-san-francisco-voters/.

Cobb, Michael. 2005. "Uncivil Wrongs: Race, Religion, Hate and Incest in Queer Politics." *Social Text*, nos. 84–85: 251–74.

Cohen, Cathy J. 1997. "Punks, Bulldaggers, and Welfare Queens: The Radical Potential of Queer Politics?" *GLQ* 3, no. 4: 437–65.

Coulthard, Glen Sean. 2014. *Red Skin, White Masks: Rejecting the Colonial Politics of Recognition*. Minneapolis: University of Minnesota Press.

Crucchiola, Jordan. 2016. "SF's Tech Bus Problem Isn't about Buses. It's about Housing." *WIRED*, February 17. www.wired.com/2016/02/sfs-tech-bus-problem-isnt-about-buses-its-about-housing/.

Delany, Samuel R. 2001. *Times Square Red, Times Square Blue*. New York: New York University Press.

Gay Shame. 2002. "Proposition N Stands for Nightmare, a Pre-Halloween Festival of Resistance." *Indybay*, October 7. www.indybay.org/newsitems/2002/10/07/15346391.php?show_comments=1.

———. 2017. "Is There Room for Direct Action Divas?" www.bigdoorbrigade.com/wp-content/uploads/2017/02/GayShame-DirectAction-Zine.pdf.

Goeman, Mishuana R. 2009. "Note towards a Native Feminism's Spatial Practice." *Wicazo Sa Review* 24, no. 2: 169–87.

Gould, Corrina, Morning Star Gali, Krea Gomez, and Anita DeAsis. 2011. "Decolonize Oakland: Creating a More Radical Movement." *Decolonize Oakland*, December 3. www.occupyoakland.org/2011/12/decolonize-oakland/.

Guevara, Ernesto Che. 2003. In *The Che Guevara Reader: Writings on Politics and Revolution*, edited by David Deutschmann. Havana: Ocean.

Hanhardt, Christina B. 2013. *Safe Space: Gay Neighborhood History and the Politics of Violence*. Durham, NC: Duke University Press.

Haraway, Donna J. 2008. "Forward: Companion Species, Mis-recognition, and Queer Worlding." In *Queering the Non/Human*, edited by Myra J. Hird and Noreen Giffney. London: Routledge.

———. 2016. *Staying with the Trouble: Making Kin in the Chthulucene*. Durham, NC: Duke University Press.

Hardin, Garrett. 1968. "The Tragedy of the Commons." *Science* 162: 1243–48.

Hardt, Michael, and Antonio Negri. 2011. *Commonwealth*. Cambridge, MA: Belknap Press of Harvard University Press.

Harney, Stefano, and Fred Moten. 2013. *The Undercommons: Fugitive Planning and Black Study*. Wivenhoe: Minor Compositions.

Harvey, David. 2011. "The Future of the Commons." *Radical History Review* 109: 101–7.

Indian Country Today. 2011. "Indians Counter Occupy Wall Street Movement with Decolonize Wall Street." *Indian Country Media Network*, October 7. www .indiancountrymedianetwork.com/news/indians-counter-occupy-wall-street -movement-with-decolonize-wall-street/.

Kauanui, J. Kēhaulani. 2015. "Nothing Common about 'the Commons': Settler Colonialism and Indigenous Difference." Paper presented at the annual meeting of the American Studies Association, Toronto, October 10.

Locke, John. 1993. *Two Treatises of Government*. London: Everyman Paperback.

Lorde, Audre. 2007. *Sister Outsider: Essays and Speeches*. Reprint, Berkeley, CA: Crossing.

Manalansan, Martin F. 2005. "Race, Violence, and Neoliberal Spatial Politics in the Global City." *Social Text*, nos. 84–85: 141–55.

Marx, Karl. 1992. *Capital: Volume 1: A Critique of Political Economy*. London: Penguin Classics.

———. 1993. *Grundrisse: Foundations of the Critique of Political Economy*. London: Penguin Classics.

Merica, Dan. 2017. "Trump Signs Executive Order to Keep Out 'Radical Islamic Terrorists.'" *CNN*, January 27. www.cnn.com/2017/01/27/politics/trump-plans-to-sign-executive-action-on-refugees-extreme-vetting/index.html.

Miller, Michael E. 2016. "S.F. 'Tech Bro' Writes Open Letter to Mayor: 'I Shouldn't Have to See the Pain, Struggle, and Despair of Homeless People,' 'Riff Raff.'" *Washington Post*, February 18. www.washingtonpost.com/news/morning-mix/wp/2016/02/18/s-f -tech-bro-writes-open-letter-to-mayor-i-shouldnt-have-to-see-the-pain-struggle-and -despair-of-homeless-people/.

Mitropoulos, Angela. 2012. *Contract and Contagion: From Biopolitics to Oikonomia*. Brooklyn: Minor Compositions.

Muñoz, José Esteban. 2009. *Cruising Utopia: The Then and There of Queer Futurity*. New York: New York University Press.

———. 2013. "The Brown Commons: The Sense of Wildness." Feminist Theory Workshop, May 8. www.youtube.com/watch?v=huGN866GnZE.

Nested. 2017. "Rental Affordability Index (2017)." Nextday Property Ltd. www.nested .com/research/rental/2017/global/all.

Nancy, Jean-Luc. 2010. "Communism the Word." In *The Idea of Communism*, edited by Slavoj Žižek and Costas Douzinas, 145–54. London: Verso.

Ngai, Sianne. 2007. *Ugly Feelings*. Cambridge, MA: Harvard University Press.

Pershan, Caleb. 2015. "Nihilist Gay Group Adds Threatening Anti-Tech Fliers to Divis, Was behind Last Crop in Mission." *SFist*, November 23. www.sfist.com/2015/11/23 /nihilist_protestors_add_anti-tech_f.php.

Read, Kirk. 2003. "SF Street Theater: The Hot Pink Police Riot." *GayToday.com*, March 10. www.gaytoday.com/viewpoint/031003vp.asp.

Remle, Matt (Wakíŋyaŋ Waánataŋ). 2017. "Gentrification Is NOT the New Colonialism." *Last Real Indians*, December 5. lastrealindians.com/gentrification-is-not-the-new -colonialism/.

Robinson, Cedric J. 2000. *Black Marxism: The Making of the Black Radical Tradition.* Chapel Hill: University of North Carolina Press.

SF LGBT Center. 2016. "About | SF Center." www.sfcenter.org/the-center/about.

Stewart, Kathleen. 2007. *Ordinary Affects.* Durham, NC: Duke University Press.

Suarez-Villa, Luis. 2009. *Technocapitalism: A Critical Perspective on Technological Inno- vation and Corporatism.* Philadelphia: Temple University Press.

Swartz, Jon. 2017. "About One Thousand Flood SFO to Protest Immigration Ban." *USA Today*, January 28. www.usatoday.com/story/news/2017/01/28/1000–flood -sfo-protest-immigration-ban/97200022/.

Tiku, Nitasha. 2013. "Twitter Will Cause So Much Gentrification, They Invented a New Word." *Valleywag*, October 17. www.valleywag.gawker.com/twitter-will-cause -so-much-gentrification-they-invente-1447346147.

Tuan, Yi-Fu. 2001. *Space and Place: The Perspective of Experience.* Minneapolis: Univer- sity of Minnesota Press.

Weheliye, Alexander. 2014. *Habeas Viscus: Racializing Assemblages, Biopolitics, and Black Feminist Theories of the Human.* Durham, NC: Duke University Press.

Weiss, Margot D. 2008. "Gay Shame and BDSM Pride: Neoliberalism, Privacy, and Sex- ual Politics." *Radical History Review* 100: 87–101.

Wenus, Laura. 2015. "McCoppin Hub Will Be Fenced to Keep Out Homeless." *MissionLocal*, September 16. www.missionlocal.org/2015/09/mccoppin-hub-will -be-fenced-to-keep-out-homeless/.

Winstanley, Gerrard. 1649. "The True Levellers Standard Advanced by Gerrard Win- stanley." *Marxists.org*. www.marxists.org/reference/archive/winstanley/1649 /levellers-standard.htm.

Wojtek. 2012. "A Book Bloc's Genealogy." *Libcom.org*, November 21. libcom.org/library /book-bloc's-genealogy.

Wolfe, Patrick. 2006. "Settler Colonialism and the Elimination of the Native." *Journal of Genocide Research* 8, no. 4: 387–409.

SECOND NATURE / 2ND NATURE:

On Ultra-red, TLC, and Dependency

Amalle Dublon

On July 5, 1998, the Los Angeles Police Department swarmed Griffith Park, a rugged, sprawling city park abutting the Santa Monica Mountains. Arriving in squad cars, on horseback, and by helicopter, officers arrested or expelled hundreds of mostly black and Latinx queers. Members of the "audio-activist" art group Ultra-red had been visiting Griffith Park for a while, making field recordings at cruising sites and conducting actions in response to raids and arrests. These commingled recordings of police activity, fuzzy megaphone yelling, didactic recitation, casual conversation, flirtation, "sighs and slurps," insects, and swelling and receding music from passing speakers became the material for their 1999 album *Second nature: an electro-acoustic pastoral.*

      The question of second nature (in the title of Ultra-red's album), and its relation to a queer commons is the subject of this article. The term has two familiar senses, which Ultra-red submits to a perhaps equally familiar critique. Nature appears, on the one hand, as internal law or logic that directs form's growth and decay, and, on the other hand, as spatialized living terrain. This latter sense tends to give rise both to a set-theoretic problem of ecosystem, field, cosmology, or world, and to questions of ecological wealth or common resource, or in other words, of social reproduction and accumulation. *Second nature* is, among other things, a critique of the idea of nature in the interlocking contexts of sex and the garden. Part of a broader queer and feminist interest in "public sex" amid urban gentrification and rezoning in the 1990s, Ultra-red's album title mediates between these senses of "nature": the notion of immanent need and enjoyment implied by the idea of sexual nature, and the spatialized sense of terrain, ecosystem, or unsheltered, undomestic publicity.

      In the early 1990s, as Ultra-red was forming, another group temporarily gathered under the name 2nd Nature. By 1992, when they released their first

GLQ 24:4

album, *Oooooh… On the TLC Tip,* 2nd Nature changed its name to TLC, after members T-boz, Lisa "Left Eye" Lopes, and Chilli (who replaced the original "C," Crystal Jones). As on Ultra-red's *Second nature,* TLC's debut album critiques "naturalized" codes of sexual comportment alongside commentary on sex as a quasi-ecological common resource. The slide from second nature to tender loving care could also describe the sexual and gendered trajectory the album takes up on songs such as "Hat 2 da Back," "Das da Way We Like 'Em," and "Ain't 2 Proud 2 Beg." Tender loving care, and its relation to a sexual commons, ecological wealth, and social reproduction, emerges on the album as a question concerning dependency on and enjoyment of such care. This commingled dependency and enjoyment, I would suggest, is the wealth that a queer commons distributes and multiplies.

By its own account, Ultra-red (1996)—a collective of shifting composition over the last two and a half decades—began "not as electronic musicians doing political music but as political activists accidentally acting as electronic musicians." Ultra-red grew out of Clean Needles Now (CNN), a Los Angeles syringe exchange network founded in 1992. Artists who were among CNN's founders made audio documents of its work, since participants in the needle exchanges sensibly declined to be videotaped. These recordings were sometimes cut up and incorporated into artworks or live sets at the venue Public Space. The methodologies that came to inform Ultra-red's subsequent work, including *Second nature,* thus developed from not only electronic music but also contemporary art and its protocols, as well as an organizational need for both documentation and the evasion of representation. The turn toward audio thus already begins to suggest how Ultra-red used sound recording and reproduction to preserve both a publicity, and a secrecy, that visual evidence would compromise.

These themes persisted in the Griffith Park recordings several years later, as did a general orientation toward the entanglement of enjoyment, need, and dependency that both drug use and park sex offer up: common enjoyment, common need, common dependency. On *Second nature,* amid a series of tracks called eclogues—the term referring to pastoral poetry—the liner notes for "Cruise Control" recount the arrest, in April 1998, of two men engaged in "flirtatious behavior . . . the sort of discrete conduct enjoyed by millions of paramours who retreat to this, the world's largest, urban public park," resulting in an eventual charge of disturbing the peace. They conclude: "Public sex is thus a transgression on the level of acoustics" (Ultra-red 1999).

We might turn here to José Esteban Muñoz's (2013: 98) elaboration of a brown queer "punk rock commons" as a site of contrarian noise against both musical harmony and notions of public good with which the commons as a site of resource management, distribution, and (aesthetic) proportion is generally imbued. For Muñoz, this commons arises in certain mosh pits, diners, motels, and apartment complexes where various forms of aleatory collision mark world-lines of possibility. On *Second nature*, the recorded traces of brushing up against one another are intercut with the more discretely articulated sounds of electronic beats, or a megaphone-amplified speech delivered at one of the park's abandoned zoo enclosures. Two tracks, both under the title "Lewd Conduct," layer electronic blips, scraps of music and speech, and the rustling of bodies and undergrowth too close to read or parse, brushing against and occluding one another. As in the needle exchanges, here a zone of sex and sociality resists representation, a difficulty that the album lingers in and takes up as an aesthetic resource. Skin, air, and fabric sweep across the microphone's awkwardly sensitive surface, yielding crackling and hissing over dilated breaths and crickets' steady throb. The resource here multiplied and shared is a "touching and being touched, heavy breathing with and alongside the other newest ones, as sweat mingles and hands linger"—a blurred proximity, and a blown-out, too-close sound (Muñoz 2013: 102).

Ultra-red's critique of pastoral music is about the garden, field, or park as a mode of containment, extraction, and governance under the rubric of natural order. For Ultra-red, the pastoral is a kind of exemplary scene, an encircled microcosmology. It must therefore be understood in the context of the field and the plantation as a site of production, extraction, and experimentation. Britt Rusert (2015) suggests that narratives of sustainability and preservation that became central to a certain pastoral ecological discourse arose in colonial monoculture, where "the strategic refusal of sustenance to, or un-sustaining of, slave populations was, in fact, internal to the disciplinary logic of the experimental plantation from its very beginnings in the New World" (372).[1]

But the album also records and partakes in the park as a geographic "erogenous zone"—terrain for barbeques, dalliances, and automotive as well as sexual cruising; Ultra-red (2006) itself was named after an auto-body shop in Silver Lake. The question of ecology, here inseparable from land use, invokes a dual understanding of enjoyment: both an aesthetic-erotic sense of the word and its legal dimension, which refers to the exercise or fruition of a right of use. The right of enjoyment, for example, might include cultivation or habitation, or the right to natural rainfall, sunlight, and so on, as part of land use.

Rooted in the ongoing practice and historical fact of shared ecological resource prior to—and under the pressure of—privatization and enclosure, the idea of the commons is both "wild and managed at the same time," as J. Kameron Carter and Sarah Jane Cervenak (Hartman et al. 2016) have said of the notion of the field. The productive and perhaps necessary entanglement with a pastoral imaginary has imprinted the commons with a set of erotic, political, and musical concerns. The pastoral thinks its central questions—sex, romance, reproduction, territory, governance, and (natural) law—through an aesthetic, and specifically musical, concern with proportion, harmony, distribution, and order. The idea of the commons conceives of social reproduction in terms of ecological management, an inheritance that has been the subject of Marxist feminist critique.

In *Caliban and the Witch*, Silvia Federici (2003: 97) argues that, as the European land enclosures of the fifteenth and sixteenth centuries accelerated, the enjoyment of women came to replace the enjoyment of the commons as a necessary means of social reproduction: "Proletarian women became for male workers the substitute for the land lost to the enclosures, their most basic means of reproduction, and a communal good anyone could appropriate at will. . . . in the new capitalist regime, *women themselves became the commons*, as their work was defined as a natural resource, lying outside the sphere of market relations." The common woman substituted for the commons, as the very figure of reproduction shifted from a spatialized field—an area of land—to an apparently measureless temporality, that is, lifetimes of reproductive labor. During processes of enclosure, Federici and others have demonstrated, feminized reproductive labor is made to bear and compensate for this loss; feminine labor is thus historically connected to capital's management of ecological nature and has perhaps consequently been "naturalized" as an attribute of women. Such feminized (in)exhaustibility, and its mensural rhythms and frequencies, describes a specifically ecological understanding of love and sex. Indeed, romance has been a fundamental condition of theories of and desire for the commons, perhaps especially within a US queer imaginary. The pastoral has been a persistent cipher for queer sociality and politics, from radical faerie sanctuaries, such as Ida, in rural Tennessee, to gay beaches and "women's land." In all these instances, a queer pastoral imaginary that is primarily aesthetic has posed questions of property, settlement, and communization, and how a queer commons may be constructed.[2]

A Marxist feminist critique of love and sex is introduced as a first step to conceptualizing caring labor as labor, and to struggling against it:

> We will fail in the struggle for the free laundromats unless we first struggle against the fact that we cannot love except at the price of endless work, which day after day cripples our bodies, our sexuality, our social relations, unless we first escape the blackmail whereby our need to give and receive affection is turned against us as a work duty for which we constantly feel

resentful against our husbands, children and friends, and guilty for that
resentment. (Federici 1975: 6)

There is much to say here about the question of crippled bodies, crippled sexuality, and crippled sociality—more directly, about the way that "crip" might signal
a privileged relationship to the dependency that is the very ground of embodiment, sex, and social life, rather than a diminishment of those capacities.[3] Such
dependency often emerges as the disavowed object of Marxist feminist critique,
for example, in discussions of the "man-baby," a figure whose oppressiveness is
implicitly attributed to his dependency, need, and "immaturity," rather than to
his more directly germane role as boss or manager. Thus Moira Weigel and Mal
Ahearn (2013) describe "the bourgeois Man-Child who refuses to 'grow up,' refuses
to mate, and refuses domestic labor" while remaining dependent on a figure they
approvingly call the "Grown Woman."

Despite this repudiation of dependency, the Federici passage above nonetheless contains a sidelong acknowledgment that not only labor power but also
dependency itself is an immanent capacity or power: "Our need to give and receive
affection" is the resource subject here to exploitation and extraction. This insight
echoes Karl Marx's (1993: 489) observation that, "when the limited bourgeois form
is stripped away, what is wealth other than the universality of individual needs,
capacities, pleasures, productive forces etc., created through universal exchange?"

How, then, is this wealth preserved and multiplied? One response is offered
by the apparent paradox in the bridge verse of TLC's "Ain't 2 Proud 2 Beg," in
which Chilli sings: "When I need 2 feel loved / Why wait 4 so long? / Cause I ain't
2 proud 2 beg / 4 something that I call my own." Declaring a readiness to beg for
something that one already has suggests that need, dependency, and (the need for)
love are here imagined not as lack but as surplus. I draw here on Fred Moten's
account in "An Ecology of (Eloquent) Things" (2011), in which he proposes a
"nonoppositional relation between wealth and poverty" that emerges through the
work of the artist Thornton Dial, liberation theology, and the passage from Marx's
Grundrisse that I cite above, to which Moten's talk directed me. He suggests an
alternative mode of accumulation structured by black life: "To say that we have
something, only insofar as we relinquish it, is to say that we come from somewhere,
only insofar as we leave that place behind." TLC conceptualizes the plenitude of
sexual need, and sexual care, as something that can be held only insofar as it is
released. In the next verse, T-boz sings, "Got to let it go while you can," in a kind
of looping back to the avowal of dependency in the Temptations' 1966 hit "Ain't
Too Proud to Beg," in which what is begged for slips away against a refusal to "let

you go." Here, however, relinquishment is the very site of getting together. Giving yourself away in order to receive what is already yours, but which nonetheless must always be given to you in order for you to have it, suggests an understanding of (sexual) dependency in which "giving" sex and "taking" it cannot be disentangled. This is an image of a queer commons of need, dependency, and enjoyment also assembled on Ultra-red's *Second nature*.

Here, dependency offers a form of surplus and accumulation that neither the home as a marketplace of reproductive and sexual labor nor the Marxist feminist critique of such exchange and extraction can account for or exhaust. TLC and Ultra-red describe a form of wealth and accumulation not fully governed by a logic of reciprocity and exchange, however violently it has been plundered. In other words, need is not a lack to be filled but a surplus accumulated in being spent. What we are offered is not an idealized "interdependent" reciprocity of give-and-take but a redoubled give-and-give or take-and-take.[4] The notion of a queer commons, as it emerges here and on Ultra-red's *Second nature*, poses the questions: what kind of resource and (or as) expenditure is sex, and, along with Muñoz, what in queer romance remains athwart to notions of public good?

Notes

I would like to thank the special issue editors, Nadja Milner-Larsen and Gavin Butt, as well as *GLQ* editor Jennifer DeVere Brody and the two anonymous peer reviewers, for their helpful suggestions. My gratitude is also due Jordan Lord, whose kindness and spooky genius has improved this and other writing.

1. See also Rusert 2010.
2. Elizabeth Povinelli's (2006) writing on the radical faeries, gay New Age aesthetics, and indigeneity is useful on this point. Scott Lauria Morgensen (2008: 68) has written on faerie sanctuaries and the notion of a "gay tribe" in relation to North American configurations of settlement, indigeneity, home, and ecology, and more broadly (2010) on how histories of colonization and settlement have shaped the idea of "queer land" in the United States. We might also consider the history of "women's land," in which music, sex, and small-scale agriculture are often irreducible components of a pastoral image of the commons, a configuration that did not shed its enmeshment with settlement and colonization, particularly in those instances in which it insisted on a narrowly genital notion of womanhood. Adrienne Rich's elegiac 1970s image of a depleted sexual commons—"the tragedy of sex," she writes, "lies around us, a woodlot / the axes are sharpened for"—may perhaps thus apply to "women's land" as well (2013: 18). The loss and depletion I refer to is not the ongoing closure of such spaces

but the enclosure that preceded it, an enclosure not only of land but also, impossibly, of a notion of womanhood as morphological corporeal boundary. In its rendering of queer affective entanglement as settlement and property, "women's land" foreclosed the desperately needed resource of that very entanglement.

3. On "crip" as a companion analytic to "queer," see McRuer 2006.

4. I am grateful to Constantina Zavitsanos for these two phrases and the whole way of thinking about dependency, enjoyment, need, and surplus that they imply.

References

Federici, Silvia. 1975. *Wages against Housework*. Bristol, UK: Power of Women Collective and Falling Wall Press.

———. 2003. *Caliban and the Witch: Women, the Body, and Primitive Accumulation*. New York: Autonomedia.

Hartman, Saidiya, Fred Moten, J. Kameron Carter and Sarah Jane Cervenak. 2016. "The Black Outdoors: Saidiya Hartman and Fred Moten in Conversation with J. Kameron Carter and Sarah Jane Cervenak." Duke University, Durham, NC, September 23.

Marx, Karl. 1993. *Grundrisse: Foundations of the Critique of Political Economy (Rough Draft)*. Translated by Martin Nicolaus. London: Penguin Books.

McRuer, Robert. 2006. *Crip Theory: Cultural Signs of Queerness and Disability*. New York: New York University Press.

Morgensen, Scott Lauria. 2008. "Arrival at Home: Radical Faerie Configurations of Sexuality and Place." *GLQ* 15, nos. 1–2: 67–96.

———. 2010. "Settler Homonationalism: Theorizing Settler Colonialism within Queer Modernities." *GLQ* 16, nos. 1–2: 105–31.

Moten, Fred. 2011. "An Ecology of (Eloquent) Things." Paper presented at "Hard Truths: A Forum on the Art and Politics of Difference." Indianapolis Museum of Art, Indianapolis, IN, April 8. www.youtube.com/watch?v=1oRKOhlMmKQ.

Muñoz, José Esteban. 2013. "'Gimme Gimme This . . . Gimme Gimme That': Annihilation and Innovation in the Punk Rock Commons." *Social Text*, no. 116: 95–110.

Povinelli, Elizabeth. 2006. *The Empire of Love: Toward a Theory of Intimacy, Genealogy, and Carnality*. Durham, NC: Duke University Press.

Rich, Adrienne. 2013. *Diving into the Wreck: Poems 1971–1972*. New York: Norton.

Rusert, Britt. 2010. "Black Nature: The Question of Race in the Age of Ecology." *Polygraph* no. 22: 149–66.

———. 2015. "Plantation Ecologies: The Experimental Plantation in and against James Grainger's *The Sugar-Cane*." *Early American Studies* 13, no. 2: 341–73.

Temptations. 1966. "Ain't Too Proud to Beg." *Gettin' Ready*. Gordy.

TLC. 1992. *Oooooooohhh . . . On the TLC Tip*. LaFace/Arista Records.

Ultra-red. 1996. Text for "Sound Tracks." "Without Alarm" exhibition, former Lincoln

Heights Division Los Angeles City Jail, curated by the Arroyo Arts Collective, April. www.ultrared.org/pso1a.html.

———. 1999. *Second nature: an electro-acoustic pastoral*. Mille Plateaux.

———. 2006. "encuentro los angeles." www.ultrared.org/pso6b.html.

Weigel, Moira, and Mal Ahearn. 2013. "Further Materials toward a Theory of the Man-Child." *New Inquiry*, July 9. www.thenewinquiry.com/essays/further -materials-toward-a-theory-of-the-man-child/.

DOI 10.1215/10642684-6957856

QUEERING COMMONS IN TURKEY

Cenk Özbay and Evren Savcı

If commons refer to spaces, knowledges, organizations, and services that are owned, controlled, and used publicly for the well-being and survival of all (Akbulut, Adaman, and Kocagöz 2017; Walljasper 2010), what might it mean to queer commons? We investigate queer commons as an emergent form in Turkey through the unfolding of the Gezi Park uprisings in the summer of 2013, which we argue help us think queer through commons, and think commons through queer. This investigation of queer commons as an "emergent" form might at first seem to historically erase older forms of what one might think of as queer commons in Turkey, such as certain bathhouses, parks, and fairly cheap adult movie theaters. While these spaces, along with numerous social services, have been disappearing under neoliberal assaults since the early 2000s (Özbay et al. 2016) and forms of sociability, including queer ones, have been increasingly privatized, we caution against a nostalgic romanticization of a preneoliberal, "old commons" for two reasons.[1] For one, while bathhouses and adult movie theaters have provided spaces for cross-class sexual contact, since they were open to all who could pay the very low admission fee, their operations have been nevertheless private and for-profit. Thus, it is impossible to argue that they have been accessible to the truly poor or the homeless. Further, most spaces one might consider "queer commons" in Turkey, such as the ones listed above, have historically been limited to masculine subjects.[2] If one of the important interventions of queer has been exposing and rejecting the gay male-centrism of "LGBT studies," then this project also requires we be attuned to which sexual subjects some of these old forms of commons were available to. The most recent public revolt against the neoliberal privatization of public spaces in Turkey featured all genders in the fight for a commons, from the perspective of both queer *and* feminist claims to public space.

The Gezi Park uprisings of June 2013 constituted the largest and most public performance of commons in the history of the country. People collectively organized to reclaim, repurpose, and reimagine the park's space as a venue that belonged to and was used by everyone who spent time there, engaging with each other outside capitalist, commercial, or state-led governance. This setting attracted many queers because of the park's history as part of the sexual commons of Istanbul. Starting from the late 1970s, Gezi Park has served as a cruising place for men and trans people and has been symbolically inscribed as a space for clandestine queer sexual encounters, commercial or otherwise (Özbay 2017). This historical significance mobilized many queer people to hold on to the "publicness" of the park in the face of the government's plans to demolish and replace it with a shopping mall built within restored Ottoman barracks. Istanbul residents occupied the park in order to resist its destruction by the government. The occupation lasted for days and publicly positioned queers as active urban citizens who fought against authoritarian oppression and violence alongside straight and cisgender compatriots.

During the resistance, other constituencies also made claims to Gezi. Armenian citizens pointed to the fact that those Ottoman barracks at the center of the conflict had originally been erected on the same land as an Armenian cemetery that was demolished in the process. The democratic space of the Gezi commons made room for various groups to make gendered, sexual, racial, and classed claims to a public space that nevertheless featured uneven histories of dispossession. In other words, the public assembly required to claim a commons also worked to intervene in the erasures that neoliberalism performs on collective memories of public space (Hong 2015).

As Gezi Park transformed into a commons under civilian occupation, queers and feminists organized to provide food and medical supplies, and to share in the cleaning of the park. In addition to their visible copresence, participants held workshops on how to avoid sexist and homophobic language.

Various goods and services, including food and water, medical supplies, books (via "Gezi library"), camping, concerts, and performances, remained free throughout the occupation. No monetary exchanges were permitted. This symbolic and exemplary case of "decommodified" communality (Esping-Andersen 1990;

Figure 1. A poster for the Twenty-First LGBT Pride Parade, 2013

Gibson-Graham [1996] 2006) triggered further questions about the lives made possible in the neoliberal city. It paved the way for money-free barter organizations and events, communal farming and guerrilla gardening, and cooperatives that linked the urbanites with "organic" farmers with no or minimum profit range in different places of Istanbul. Queers have taken an active role in all these forms of commoning since 2013.

Yet it was not simply the public participation of queer bodies in Gezi that queered this commons but also the collective rejection by those who constitute the "majority" of the respectability politics of the government (Savcı 2013, forthcoming). As the revolts and resistance continued, then Prime Minister Recep Tayyip Erdoğan's rhetoric increasingly positioned the protestors as a handful of "plunderers." Among other allegations, Erdoğan made the false claim that the protestors had entered a mosque with their shoes on to drink beer inside and assault his "sisters" with headscarves.[3] The protestors intervened in this rhetoric, refusing the divide between respectable pious (Sunni) Muslims and a "handful of drunkard

Figure 2. Photo from the LGBT Pride Parade, Taksim Square, 2013

plunderers." They demonstrated their solidarity with Muslim groups at the park by enacting the collective decision to refrain from alcohol consumption on the holy religious day Isra and Mi'raj (*Kandil Bayramı*). But they also refused to make rhetorical claims to respectability and instead identified themselves as "plunderers" and "drunkards" in slogans, banners, chants, and songs throughout the resistance. In addition to T-shirts and signs that simply read *çapulcu* (plunderer), a frequent slogan on banners declared "Neither am I left-wing, nor am I right, I am *çapulcu*, I am *çapulcu*." With this slogan, protestors distanced themselves from politics as usual and instead embraced the political potential of the disreputable subjectivity of the plunderer.

Gezi Park uprisings were certainly not the only performance of queer commons in Turkey, but they provide a promising model for how various bodies and sexual subjectivities can come together to resist the privatization of public goods as well as respectability politics that neoliberal governments impose on citizen subjects. For instance, in addition to the communal farming and guerrilla gardening practices we mentioned above, another exciting example of the Gezi-inspired commons has been the emergence of meetings and "health forums." Since 2013, queer and nonqueer volunteers, as well as doctors and medical professionals, have established these forums to discuss specific health-related issues of LGBT individuals and support the HIV-positive and AIDS patients. The "commons" performed

within these health forums and networks have inspired various Istanbul munici-
palities to launch specific clinics and collaborate with NGOs in order to provide
free health services and HIV tests for queer citizens.

Yet queer commons are not the only outcome of discontent with neoliberal
dispossession—reactionary ethno-nationalisms that seek to enforce borders prove
to be a much stronger and more widespread response to such conditions today.[4] We
believe that the distinction between these two results lay in the continual practice
of "the impossible politics of difference" that demands a radical rethinking of self
and community, and thus a radical rethinking of belonging and the concept of
commons itself (Hong 2015). Hong (2015: 15) theorizes "'difference' as a contradictory, *impossible* political and representational strategy that brings together and
holds in suspension the conflicting goals of the preservation or the protection of the
political subjects *and* the recognition of the others at whose expense that subject
is protected." The unrelenting recognition of whom our struggle for survival might
harm distinguishes queer commons from practices of self-preservation that readily
take racist, xenophobic, anti-immigrant, and otherwise exclusionary forms. If this
is the contribution of queer to commons, the contribution of commons to queer is
in its refusal to think respectability politics as divorced from material dispossession, and the increased securitization of peoples and borders. The execution of
the latter is increasingly justified with discourses that position immigrants and
refugees as morally suspect (Malkki 1992). These are the challenges the two terms
have to relentlessly pose to each other. This is necessary in order to have genu-
ine conversations about the uneven belonging and dispossession witnessed in all
"commons" historically so that we can imagine new ones.

Notes

We are equal co-authors of this piece.

1. While the introduction of neoliberal measures in Turkey dates back to 1980, there
    has been an intensification of them since the early 2000s. For more, see Özbay et al.
    2016.

2. Trans women have also occasionally occupied some of these spaces, but this has made
    them often subject to violence both by the police and by vigilantes. Therefore, it is
    unclear whether we can argue that they have had proper "access" to older forms of
    commons.

3. The allegation was subsequently denied by the mosque's imam (www.hurriyet.com.tr
    /dolmabahce-camii-imami-halil-necipoglu-cami-icerisinde-alkol-kullanan-gormedim
    -29264724).

4. While a detailed analysis of the current moment in Turkey is beyond the remit of the

present article, we would like to note that following the July 2016 coup attempt, and under the "de facto presidential rule without any checks and balances" (Arat 2016), the government has sacked and jailed tens of thousands in opposition and continues to promote patriarchal policies (Cindoglu and Unal 2016). While no other commons like Gezi has emerged since then, the resistance to the government continues. As the current authoritarian leadership labels any and all opposition "terrorism," this broad use inadvertently contributes to the public questioning of the very term *terrorism*, as well as the public questioning of both the current and historical forms of the Turkish security state and the Turkish nationalism it promoted.

References

Akbulut, Bengi, Fikret Adaman, and Umut Kocagöz, eds. 2017. *Herkesin Herkes İçin: Müşterekler Üzerine Eleştirel Bir Antoloji*. Istanbul: Metis.

Arat, Yesim. 2016. "Men's Coups, Women's Troubles." *Journal of Middle East Women's Studies* 13, no. 1: 175–77.

Cindoglu, Dilek, and Didem Unal. 2016. "Gender and Sexuality in the Authoritarian Discursive Strategies of New Turkey." *European Journal of Women's Studies* 24, no. 1: 39–54.

Esping-Andersen, Gosta. 1990. *The Three Worlds of Welfare Capitalism*. Princeton, NJ: Princeton University Press.

Gibson-Graham, J. K. [1996] 2006. *The End of Capitalism (As We Knew It): A Feminist Critique of Political Economy*. Minneapolis: University of Minnesota Press.

Hong, Grace. 2015. *Death without Disavowal: The Impossible Politics of Difference*. Minneapolis: University of Minnesota Press.

Malkki, Liisa. 1992. "National Geographic: The Rooting of Peoples and the Territorialization of National Identity among Scholars and Refugees." *Cultural Anthropology* 7, no. 1: 24–44.

Özbay, Cenk. 2017. *Queering Sexualities in Turkey: Gay Men, Male Prostitutes, and the City*. London: I. B. Tauris.

Özbay, Cenk, Maral Erol, Aysecan Terzioglu, and Z. Umut Turem, eds. 2016. *The Making of Neoliberal Turkey*. London: Routledge.

Savcı, Evren. 2013. "Why Every City Needs a Center Square: On the Turkish Uprisings, Coalition Building, and Coexistence." *The Feminist Wire* (blog), June 10. www .thefeministwire.com/2013/06/why-every-city-needs-a-center-square-on-the -turkish-uprisings-coalition-building-and-coexistence/.

Savcı, Evren. Forthcoming. *Queer in Translation: Sexual Politics under Neoliberal Islam*. Durham, NC: Duke University Press.

Walljasper, Jay. 2010. *All That We Share: How to Save the Economy, the Environment, the Internet, Democracy, Our Communities and Everything Else that Belongs to All of Us*. New York: The New Press.

DOI 10.1215/10642684-6957870

THE ANARCHO-QUEER COMMONS OF DENNIS COOPER'S BLOG, *THE WEAKLINGS*:

A Brief History

Diarmuid Hester

On June 27, 2016, the gay poet and novelist Dennis Cooper tried to log in to his popular blog *The Weaklings*, as he had almost every day for the previous decade, only to find that his account had been shut down and his blog removed. An automated message informed him that Google had revoked his access because he had violated Blogger's "terms of service." Cooper and his lawyer repeatedly asked Google for more information, but for over a month no response was forthcoming. The incident quickly caught the attention of the international media, with articles appearing in venues such as the *New Yorker*, the *Guardian*, *Le Figaro*, *Vox*, and the *New York Times*. An online petition was also launched, demanding that Google reinstate the blog, and was signed by over four and a half thousand people.

In the absence of any official word from Google, speculation was rife about the cause of the blog's removal. One guess that gained traction as the weeks went on was that Cooper posted "risqué material" deemed inappropriate by the tech behemoth, which has owned Blogger since 2003 (Cavalli 2016). The suggestion carried some weight: no stranger to controversy, Cooper's "risqué" novels have outraged readers as varied as the conservative *National Review*'s James Gardner (1996), who condemned Cooper's work as an odious attack on the status quo, and Queer Nation, a gay activist group that took umbrage at his depiction of at-risk gay teens and issued him a death threat in 1991. Why Google should suddenly become offended by his blog's content after ten years and about three thousand posts was anyone's guess, however. Regardless, most media pieces decried Google's apparent act of censorship, tapping into widespread fears about the increasing proportion of the Internet controlled by a tiny number of big tech firms with obscure links to three-letter government agencies.

Reports described *The Weaklings* as an "alternative Wikipedia"—"a prime destination for fans of experimental literature and avant-garde writing," where Cooper would post content six days a week on a variety of outré subjects (Romano 2016; Sidahmed 2016). Posts usually featured in-depth, eye-catching explorations of modern and contemporary writers, artists, filmmakers, and musicians, with a short introductory text written by Cooper and curated examples of the subject's work, including text, jpegs, gifs, hyperlinks, and YouTube clips. The expansive range of material ensured both relatively established and relatively unknown subjects received equal attention: a post on the work of the British writer Ivy Compton Burnett, for instance, might be sandwiched rather incongruously between posts devoted to, say, the American rock band Butthole Surfers and the German visual artist Susanne Hay.

Few of the many articles that followed in the wake of the Google incident peered very far past the blog's frontpage, however, and none reflected in any depth on the community that very much made Cooper's blog what it was. Content to portray Cooper as a wronged legislator of the world whose work had been shamefully desecrated, journalists overlooked the fact that for over ten years his blog was home to a dynamic and rapidly expanding network of queer subcultural producers and consumers. Since 2006, Cooper aficionados like me had logged on to his site in hopes of communing with a queer cult idol. In doing so, we unexpectedly became part of something multiple and cooperative, connected to other fans and friends by Cooper's tireless community building; Cooper's blog became for us an exemplary anarcho-queer commons.

Heir to José Esteban Muñoz's (2013: 96) "dark queer genealogy," which includes marginal figures like Rimbaud and Jack Spicer, Cooper has always occupied a dissident position when it comes to mainstream gay culture. In the past he has been thoroughly critical of conformity in the gay community, stating for instance that "my hope is that we stop buying so mindlessly into the notion of collective identity. Our attraction to members of our own sex gives us something in common but it doesn't make us inherently responsible to each other. We're not a family. We're not a religious sect" (Cooper n.d.). Relatively apprehensive about gay community in general, Cooper nonetheless readily identifies as an anarchist writer committed to anarchist forms of sociability. Speaking to Joyelle McSweeney, he characterizes "his form" of anarchism as an attentiveness to the multiplicity of ways in which power is wielded and an acknowledgment that hierarchies may insinuate themselves into every part of one's life. Anarchism, for Cooper, "is based on kind of really simple basic principles having mostly to do with a constant . . . gauging of power, my own and others', by which I guess I mean political, cultural, social, aesthetic, etc. power, and keeping a really close watch on the hierarchies that result whether inside me or all around me"—and he recognizes the effect on his life and work of anarchist ideas, encountered first through his collision with Queercore in the 1980s (Cooper and McSweeney 2015).

An anarchist-inflected DIY movement of queerish-punks and punkishqueers, Queercore, for Cooper (1996: 295), characterized "a new brand of queer defiance . . . where 'queer' defines not a specific sexuality, but the freedom to personalize anything you see or hear then shoot it back into the stupid world more distorted and amazing than it was before." Enthralled by the sexy improvised aesthetic of Queercore zines including Bruce LaBruce and G. B. Jones's *J.D.'s* and Vaginal Davis's *Fertile La Toyah Jackson*, Cooper was also fascinated by the vibrant anarchistic networks formed through Queercore writing and music— networks that Muñoz (2013: 96) might have likened to "circuits of being-with, in difference and discord, that are laden with potentiality and that manifest the desire to want something else." Years later, following the movement's demise, Cooper attempted to bring about the emergence of a similar network through the circuitry of his blog.

Comments were key to the whole endeavor. In the comments section beneath each day's post, a community began to come together made up of renowned artists, small-press authors, little-known photographers, up-and-coming musicians, film directors, and academics—all fans to some degree who initially came for Cooper: to praise his work, ask about the next project, or solicit reading recommendations. In the next day's post, Cooper responded to each commenter in turn—sometimes spending over five hours on his responses—and also distributed the discussion: a question asked of the blog's host could be relayed back to the rest of the group.

Fulfilling the utopian aspirations of technopositivists like Yochai Benkler, who argued for the democratizing potential of blogs that produced "a weighted conversation, rather than a finished good . . . because of the common practice of allowing and posting comments, as well as comments to these comments"—as a *Weaklings* commenter, one found oneself participating in a sustained, cacophonous conversation with Cooper and the other denizens of the comments section (Benkler 2006: 217). Here regulars traded important subcultural information: Kenneth Anger–quality gossip; literary rumors and speculation; delectable intrigues of little interest to outsiders ("Tim Dlugos slept with WHO?!"). Paul Curran (2015), a writer and commentator based in Tokyo, remembers, "My first comments were directed at Dennis and were related to my own writing and getting-to-know-you kind of things, or joining questions he asked to everyone, but then I started interacting with other [commenters] as we commented on each other's comments"; the comments section, he recalls, "became an extraordinarily vibrant and occasionally volatile virtual conversation or interactive text." This conversation continued beyond the virtual space of the blog, and commenters regularly made collaborative artworks, contributed to each other's zines and small presses—even created performance pieces together.[1]

On August 29, following immense public pressure, Google returned *The Weaklings* data to Cooper, and the blog relocated to a new web address.[2] It reappeared, however, shorn of its archives: although the data are now available, each post and its accompanying comments must be individually reinstated, an effort that will take months, if not years.

Considering the deletion of Cooper's blog according to the logic of the commons allows us to queerly intervene into contemporary debates about the status of the commons and illustrate how, in the words of Michael Hardt and Antonio Negri (2009: 282), "the common exists on a different plane from the private and the public, and is fundamentally autonomous to both." A commons denotes a set of resources shared by all the members of a community—resources that are generally considered in material terms: land, water, air, and so forth. Yet theorists like Hardt (2010: 348–49) have also argued for an immaterial twenty-first-century commons, made up of "ideas, information, images, knowledges, code, languages, social relationships, affects and the like." Where *The Weaklings* is concerned, this constitutes the entire body of discourse that made up the comments section and Cooper's posts: the knowledge, gossip, hints, tips, *information* shared through conversation and a history of interactions freely available to view online by past, present, and future members of the blog's community. By suppressing and withholding the blog's data, Google effected the enclosure of a commons, where enclosure designates the illegitimate withdrawal of common resources from circulation and the dispossession of the communities bound to them and, in this case, composed by them. George Caffentzis and Silvia Federici (2014: 93) insist that "history itself is a common": with total indifference, Google cut off access both to the community's refuge and to its *archive*—the discursive history that permitted it to develop, that sustained it, and that secured its continuity into the future.

Hardt and Negri (2009: 283) maintain that of late, "the common, which previously was cast as external, is becoming completely internalized": rather than exist outside it, the (immaterial) commons is increasingly a process that occurs from within capital itself. This observation addresses the apparently paradoxical idea that a commons such as that of *The Weaklings* could be made manifest on corporate servers via privately owned tech. Yet queer subcultures have a long history of founding precarious commons within enclosures controlled by both private and public interests that would ordinarily subdue them, which, pace Hardt and Negri, predates our era of biopolitical production. Bars on the bad side of town rented from unscrupulous landlords, bathhouses run by the Mob, polari composed through the *détournement* of straight speech, the intimate spaces of public restrooms—commons like these and their histories constitute a trans-temporal network of queer subcultural commons in which the anarcho-queer commons of *The Weaklings* participates. If the fate of these examples is a cause for sorrow (shut down, stamped out, scattered to the winds, and, most recently, deleted), the *persistence* of such queer commons even online, even under the constant threat of erasure, remains a source of joy; their histories (including this one) are an archive of hope and an invaluable resource for queer communities to come.

Notes

1. See *Weaklings*, by Chris Goode and Company, directed by Chris Goode, Warwick Arts Centre, Coventry, UK, October 7, 2015.
2. See Derk 2016.

References

Benkler, Yochai. 2006. *The Wealth of Networks: How Social Production Transforms Markets and Freedom.* New Haven, CT: Yale University Press.

Caffentzis, George, and Silvia Federici. 2014. "Commons against and beyond Capitalism." *Community Development Journal* 49, no. 1: i92–i105.

Cavalli, Lauren. 2016. "Google Deletes Dennis Cooper's Blog, Erasing Years of Artistic Output." *Artforum.com*, July 13. artforum.com/news/id=62177.

Cooper, Dennis. n.d. "Fax to Jessica Pegis." Dennis Cooper correspondence, Dennis Cooper papers, MSS 85, box 6, folder 274, Fales Library and Special Collections, New York University Libraries.

Cooper, Dennis. 1996. "Queercore." In *The Material Queer: A LesBiGay Cultural Studies Reader*, edited by Donald Morton, 292–96. Boulder, CO: Westview.

Cooper, Dennis, and Joyelle McSweeney. 2015. "In a State of Confusion and Being Lucid as I Can: Joyelle McSweeney Interviews Dennis Cooper." *Fanzine*, July 4. thefanzine .com/an-excitable-collaborator-joyelle-mcsweeney-interviews-dennis-cooper/.

Curran, Paul. 2015. "DC's Qs." Author correspondence, February 13.

Derk, Peter. 2016. "Dennis Cooper's Blog Returns!" *LitReactor*, August 26. litreactor.com /news/dennis-coopers-blog-returns.

Gardner, James. 1996. "Transgressive Fiction." *National Review*, June 17.

Hardt, Michael. 2010. "The Common in Communism." *Rethinking Marxism* 22, no. 3: 348–49.

Hardt, Michael, and Antonio Negri. 2009. *Commonwealth.* Cambridge, MA: Belknap Press of Harvard University Press.

Muñoz, José Esteban. 2013. "'Gimme Gimme This . . . Gimme Gimme That': Annihilation and Innovation in the Punk Rock Commons." *Social Text*, no. 116: 95–110.

Romano, Aja. 2016. "A Writer Kept a Blog for Ten Years. Google Deleted It. Why?" *Vox*,
    July 30. www.vox.com/2016/7/30/12303070/dennis-cooper-blog-deleted-google.
Sidahmed, Mazin. 2016. "Dennis Cooper Fears Censorship as Google Erases Blog
    without Warning." *Guardian*, July 14. www.theguardian.com/books/2016/jul/14
    /dennis-cooper-google-censorship-dc-blog.

DOI 10.1215/10642684-6957884

HOW TO BLOCK THE EXTRACTIVE VIEW

Macarena Gómez-Barris

As the ominous "final piece" of the Dakota XL oil pipeline presumably clicks into place for the transnational transfer of finite natural gas resources, the Standing Rock camp burns in our collective memory as a symbol of Indigenous-led transversal and multidirectional solidarities on Sioux and Cheyenne territories. At the same time, water and land protectors throughout the world proliferate and continue to challenge the presumed natural state of extractive capitalism (Gómez-Barris 2017). What Standing Rock protestors made transparent was how the valuation and conversion of land into a commodifiable resource in the Américas operates through *an extractive view*, the assumption that Indigenous territories are there for the taking. This view empties the land of Native peoples (terra nullius) to assert the legitimacy of dominant modes of seeing that divide nature from the human.

As J. Kēhaulani Kauanui (2013) asks us to consider, what are the contradictions and incommensurable tensions between Indigenous sovereignty, the settler state, and the idea of the commons? Specifically, Kauanui asks us to understand "the commons" as steeped in colonial structures and as perpetuating a framework of capitalist property that cannot escape its racial and gendered origins.[1] Does the concept of a queer commons go far enough to unsettle the pernicious history of the commons, or does it instead reinscribe an extractive viewpoint that blocks the possibility of Indigenous sovereignty, land use, and knowledge? Is it possible to queer the very idea of the commons by invoking the histories of occupation and genocide, and by engaging decolonial queer perspectives that invert the normalizing view of colonial extractivism in the Américas? What visual modes reroute, divert, and invert the straight progression of development that depends on colonial forms of viewing land and territories to produce the extractive zone? Can these approaches queer the commons in order to not participate in what Scott Morgenson (2011) refers to as settler homonationalism?

In the "Nature Self-Portraits" series (1999), created by the late Laura Aguilar, the queer Chicana, East Los Angeles–based photographer, dozens of photographs taken in the El Malpais and Gila Mountains of New Mexico and the Mojave Desert of California trouble the notion that either "the commons" or extractive capitalism is a natural state. By embedding herself in the smaller spaces of the Gila Mountains, a historical setting of intense confrontations between US white pioneers and Apache Indigenous defenders often over sacred lands, Aguilar also eschews the settler patriarchal gesture of owning the land with an investment in a grand scale of national representation. Through the self-imaging of her own body as standing in the foreground of the violent confrontations in the Southwest, the artist seems to luxuriate in the simple and profound relations of embodying rather than appropriating or commodifying the land. In this way, she eschews Aldous Huxley's (1932) past-oriented primitivism for a way to represent territory that perceives the porousness of the human's relation to earth matter, and thereby queering the dominant settler gaze.

By situating her queer mestiza body into the folds and amid the boulders of the Gila Mountains, Aguilar invokes the embodied historical memory of Spanish colonialism, US colonization, and settler violence during the expansionism of the American West in Southwest territories. The images disrupt normative sight lines by introducing her own body as imprinting the Gila Mountains and their micro-ecologies with her physical form as a collective trace. Unlike the landscape photography of Ansel Adams and Edward Weston, whose sweeping visuality monumentalize the timeless beauty of the Southwest environment, reinvesting in the commons as nationalism, Aguilar's portraits suggest an embodied and regional memory of US colonialism. Further, the singularity of the individual body melts into the trees, desert sand, boulders, and sky that surround her, challenging the boundaries that separate the human from the organic, or what Dana Luciano and Mel Y. Chen referred to in their analysis of Aguilar's photograph Grounded #114 as "suggestively queer connections between flesh and stone, between human and nonhuman."[2]

In "Nature Self-Portrait #4," Aguilar depicts herself alongside a deep pool, where the reflection of her torso forms a shadowy image of her lying beside the water. The serene pose of the artist seems to decrease the distance between viewer, subject, nature, and artifice as her own body blurs with the boundary of the water

Figure 1. Nature versus nurture: Laura Aguilar, "Center 78," 2001, © Laura Aguilar.
Courtesy the UCLA Chicano Studies Research Center

body. Similarly, in the series of images, some black and white, some color, Aguilar's body lifts out of the earth in comparable proportion to surrounding boulders, her back is often turned, and the cracks in the surfaces blend together with her own embodiment. This blending between land and her own crevices becomes a mode of seeing that blurs the dualities of the colonial divide and queers how we understand the female form, European aesthetics, Narcissus's reflection, and the objectifying logic of heteronormative attachment to the commons.

As the Navajo historian Jennifer Denetdale (2007: 296) writes, "Ironically, the American rationale for claiming these lands was to bring peace and stability to the region, but the United States only escalated the cycles of violence among Navajos, other Native peoples, and New Mexicans." Despite the fact that the US government promised to stop Indigenous dispossession, it expanded its practice of what the historian Frederick Jackson Turner ([1893] 1920) named the "frontier thesis," or the singular opportunity to access and acquire lands for US citizens. By ideologically representing the land as empty and free for the taking, Turner's ideology supported the normalization of violence against Native peoples and the expansion of private property ownership throughout the nineteenth century, contributing to the persistence of extractive speculation and dispossession. As Glen Coulthard's (2014) critique and reformulation of Karl Marx's primitive accumulation thesis illustrates, dispossession was not a singular event but a set of persistent and enduring practices of state violence that multiply coerced Indigenous peoples into the nation-state's colonial project.

Aguilar's mestiza and nonnormative corporality literally blocks the project of colonial occupation that is American expansionism. By including her own queer, mixed-race identity into the landscape, the artist's body calls attention to the invisibility of extensive networks of tribal communities, which in New Mexico include the Apache, Navaho, and Cohiti tribes, and the Pueblo peoples, like the Zuñi, Picuris, Laguna, and Ohkay Owingeh, all absented from landscape photography and from the narratives of national territorial cohesion. One need only address how ethnologists and photographers like Edward S. Curtis documented the Apache, Navaho, and Picuris through studio portraiture to understand how Aguilar's images block the extractive view. Through the technology of the camera, the studio became the extension of the nation-state, mediated tools of state violence and an ideological and physical space for an incorporative "taming of the Indian." Curtis's compulsive documentation of what he terms "American West Indians" was often accompanied by extremely stylized shots, where clothing, accessories, and stagnant poses accentuated stereotypical and binary gendered portrayals of Native populations. By unclothing herself, Aguilar unencumbers the queer mestiza body from these overdetermined portrayals, taking artistic agency to self-document her immersion within the landscape as its own looking back.[3] And, through images that eschew the formal qualities of the studio as a white settler and heteronormative aesthetic, Aguilar shatters the colonial objectification of Native portraiture and the making of the national visual archive. Michelle Rahejas (2013) refers to "visual sovereignty" as the capacity for Indigenous self-representation within overdetermined image histories. Aguilar's autonomous image production produces a kind of visual sovereignty as an exertion of mestiza queer embodiment that interrupts the conventions of landscape photography that depend so heavily on the enclosure view of the commons.

The extractive view reads the particular location of Aguilar's "Self-Portrait Nature series" outside time, place, and historical context, yet her images are bound by the specificities of American colonial violence and Indigenous dispossession. Aguilar complicates the unilinear narrative of national identity and Manifest Destiny, reminding us of the colonial past that bears the imprint of violence. Aguilar's queer mestiza body literally forces open a confrontation with amnesiac dominant narratives that ignore settler histories and the American myth of national innocence. Given these histories, is it even possible to thoroughly queer the concept of the commons? A queer decolonial episteme considers how the land has been violently fragmented by the legacies of US coloniality. Aguilar shows us that it is still (in)visibly saturated with Indigenous and mestiza presence.

Notes

1. The full quotation from Kaunaui's presentation is: "In the North American context, the concept of the commons was something English colonial subjects brought with them during the British imperial period, and the legal and ideological concept took root in towns across what is now considered 'New England' long prior to the formation of the United States. The concept of the commons is itself a historically racialized and gendered concept, as well as one implicated in colonial structures. English settlers in North America managed indigenous lands they expropriated as an asset under the concept of the commons. Settlers organized as proprietors under corporations—as collective shareholders seeking profit—managed lands as 'the commons' to serve collective resource needs of the early townships and plantations. Hence, the construct of 'the commons' in this context is bound to white male property owners in the English Empire in the service of settler colonialism—one that is inextricably tied to the corporation itself. So, to assert that these lands constitute 'the commons' is not outside of a property framework" (ibid.).

2. See the introduction to *Queer Inhumanisms* by editors Dana Luciano and Mel Y. Chen. As Luciano and Chen (2015: 192) point out, José Muñoz's concept of the "brown commons" is also central to the concept of organic: in its defiant queerness the "commons of brown people, places, feelings, sounds, animals, minerals, flora and other objects" refutes the form of the individual in favor of "a movement, a flow, an impulse, to move beyond the singular and individualized subjectivities." See Muñoz 2012.

3. On queer and women of color epistemes in relation to Laura Aguilar's oeuvre, see Luz Calvo's important article, "Embodied at the Shrine of Cultural Disjuncture" (2005).

References

Calvo, Luz. 2005. "Embodied at the Shrine of Cultural Disjuncture," in *Beyond the Frame: Women of Color and Visual Representation*, edited by Angela Y. Davis and Neferti X. M. Tadiar. New York: Palgrave Macmillan.

Coulthard, Glen. 2014. *Red Skin, White Masks: Rejecting the Colonial Politics of Recognition*. Minneapolis: University of Minnesota Press.

Denetdale, Jennifer Nez. 2007. *Reclaiming Diné History: The Legacies of Navajo Chief Manuelito and Juanita*. Tucson: University of Arizona Press.

Gómez-Barris, Macarena. 2017. *The Extractive Zone: Social Ecologies and Decolonial Perspectives*. Durham, NC: Duke University Press.

Huxley, Aldous. 1932. *Brave New World*. New York: Harper Brothers.

Kauanui, J. Kēhaulani. 2013. "Nothing Common about 'The Commons': Settler Colonialism and the Indigenous Politics of Land Dispossession." Paper presented at Brown University, October 9.

Luciano, Dana, and Mel Y. Chen, eds. 2015. Introduction to "Queer Inhumanisms," special issue, *GLQ* 21, no. 2: 182–207.

Morgenson, Scott. 2011. *Spaces between Us: Queer Settler Colonialism and Indigenous Decolonization*. Minneapolis: University of Minnesota Press.

Muñoz, José Esteban. 2012. "The Brown Commons: The Sense of Wildness." Paper presented at the annual convention of the American Studies Association, San Juan, Puerto Rico, November 16.

Rajehas, Michelle. 2013 *Reservation Reelism: Redfacing, Visual Sovereignty, and Representations of Native Americans in Film*. Lincoln: University of Nebraska Press.

Turner, Frederick Jackson. [1893] 1920. *The Significance of the Frontier in American History*. New York: Penguin Books.

DOI 10.1215/10642684-6957898

THE LONELY LETTERS

Ashon Crawley

"The Lonely Letters" is an autobiofiction in which I attempt to think the relationship of quantum theory, mysticism, relationality, and blackness together by considering the sound and noise of Blackpentecostal spaces. Building on the work in *Blackpentecostal Breath: The Aesthetics of Possibility*, "The Lonely Letters" attempts to think together what might seem to be disparate ways of thinking worlds known and unknown, the religious and the scientific, the noisy and the musical, with hopes of considering the epistemologies of quantum physics as Blackpentecostal. It is about love and heartbreak and hope and joy.

"The Lonely Letters" is about the capacity for what we study to work on us, to transform us, to change how we inhabit the world. It is about detecting connection in the most disparate of ways. These letters attempt to resist the epistemology of Western thought that privileges so-called critical distance, abstraction, rationality, the dispassionate, the neutral, and does so by moving intentionally and intensely with and into the feeling of the flesh, the way one can be moved to tears and joy and happiness and heartbreak. What if it were possible to resist the enclosure of emotion from thinking, to resist the enclosure of the flesh from the mind?

"The Lonely Letters" is an intentional exploration into something that is common, something that belongs to us all, something that we must share in to have such experience. Being moved to tears and joy and happiness and heartbreak is the beating heart of the flesh. And such movement is queer insofar as it is about the critique of the known world and its delimitation on thought and the capacity for movement: it is about a critique but also a way to imagine *otherwise possibility* for relationality. "The Lonely Letters" excerpted here are letters seeking to establish and maintain connection.

Not a narrative in terms of beginning, middle, and end of the story, the epistolary form is about the production of snatches and moments of conversation and the dance and play of emotion. The kind of love A seeks with Moth is about the celebration of the antagonism to sovereignty, an antagonism to an individual, individuated, liberal subjectivity. And similar to how one must attempt to touch a moth delicately lest it disintegrate into a kind of powder, A's ruminations on love and mysticism and renunciation of the one for the social, his ruminations on the renunciation of the subject for the entangled folds of blackness, a being together with others as the grounds for experience, are in the service of a delicate grasp of the other that withstands the risk of disintegration. A ruminates in the service of holding while being held within Moth. He wants an experience wherein they both are changed.

Dear Moth,

There are worlds. And the fact of our experiencing them is because we are impossibly vulnerable, open, as a way of life. The central nervous system isn't enclosed in the borders of the so-called body. But it's out there, in worlds, that which is central is kind of an ecstatic force, ecstatic being, existence beside or otherwise than, the self. Such that the idea of an outside and inside needs to be thought against. Maybe entangled. Maybe a system.

It's been a while since I've heard from you. You sent that text when you returned home that you shouldn't have come over, that you're sorry you cried, that you love me but can't. And then all this talk about god, mostly about god. You wrote to me about god and I had to think about it, had to think about what you think god is.

What quantum physics is discovering is a redefinition of spacetime as not linear or separable. If this is the case and god is the unfolding of all that is and is not detectual (of or pertaining to detection) by sensual capacities, that'd mean there is some something "behind" or that withdraws from even this quantum understanding of spacetime, some otherwise sorta relation, some sorta unity and convergence that would undo even the concepts of unity, convergence, together, sociality, unfolding. Does this make sense?

And, too then, love? Because don't we think love as the unfolding of possibility in time and space, or following quantum mechanics, in spacetime, that approaches a kinda sociality of experience? But then maybe also love would be that which necessarily withdraws through approach the very possibility of possibility? Because what does it mean for something or nothing to be *of*—from or marking relation to—possibility if "it" recedes from sense experience? Love as the sense experience beyond sensuality, beyond or withdrawing from experience? It's like when you said, "You are more than someone else's negation, someone else's exclusion." Because we exist in and as excess, as that which cannot be contained or engulfed or enclosed by *anything*, negation and exclusion included. It's as if we are the flesh of what quantum mechanics is discovering, what I just said about god and existence.

What I'm trying to say, imprecisely, is this: I think I love you? I watch *An Oversimplification of Her Beauty*, as you know, a lot. And I get why she sent the text she did, why it was a question that was also a statement, how it was tentative but also very sure.

I think I love you?

I finally understand because you, Moth, make me feel what I've just been afraid to say but I know to be true: I have never felt this way about anyone—*anyone*—in my life before. And that sounds like a platitude but this is what I mean:

You are, and my feeling for you, is black noise, is static, is sorta the background against which everything I do occurs. I don't consciously think about you all of the time, no, but I feel you. When I sleep, when I wake, when I cook, when I sing, as I breathe, as I breathe, as I breathe, it's you. A sorta quiet omnipresence, a soft enclosement, you are the sound, almost chant-like, I hear sorta far off in the deep recesses and furthest reaches of my flesh. And yet, you feel more than near, closer than anything I've ever known. I do not think *about* you as much as I think: you. It's as if you are bound to each thought, whatever it might be, that I think. It's as if you are the ground of all that is for me. I don't mean this in a way pathological or that I cannot exist without you, that I have some sorta weird codependence that is more about ego and narcissism than about your well-being or mine. I mean that I desire you. And I feel that we are one.

It's like what I said to you in that text message not soon after meeting you, it's as if in and with you I'd found the voice in my head to which I was constantly searching, the voice in my head to which I was always replying, as if meeting you confirmed that *we* already *were*, that *we* already *was*, as if meeting you were the promise and the fulfillment of the promise, a breakdown of simultaneity through a space-time rip or tear or break.

I understand David and Jonathan and being knit together. "Unlike weaving, knitting does not require a loom or other large equipment, making it a valuable technique for nomadic and non-agrarian peoples." They were knit together and were movers, nomadic. Nomads are wanderers, and I'm thinking about David's psalm, talking about walking through the valley of the shadow of death but not fearing, wandering in death's shadow but still feeling assured. And though this twenty-third is about the lord, I wonder if it's also about what had been backgrounded, his being knotted up and tangled with Jonathan.

What I mean is this: I think I love you. No question mark.

And what I mean is this: I have not stopped telling everyone about you, the joy you have brought and continue to bring me.

And what I mean is this: there is not only you in the world but you are my paraclete, or I, yours.

And what I mean is this: I want a consensuality with you, a continued consent to be together.

And what I mean is this: entanglement might be the best way to approach what I feel, that once bound together, we are a system. We maintain our uniqueness regardless of the nearness or farness, regardless of spacetime separation, we are indivisible, we are not separable in any easy way, we renounce the individual for the social, for and with and in each other.

And what I mean is this: it's as if dreamworlds were hallucinating otherwise universes as possible, and mine and your dreamworlds outpoured toward each other, enfolded into and collapsed within each other.

And what I mean is this: it's kinda beautiful, and mostly scary, because I don't know what this means and haven't since I first met you and am unsure what to do. I do not want to control you. Your consent is more necessary than my desire.

And what I mean, finally, is this: I don't want you to go to seminary if it means you will not, and cannot, be with me. I want to support you, but why the priesthood when they require celibacy? My stomach churns at the thought of us not being together, I literally get sick at the thought. Your T-shirt that you left here when you were here, I have not yet washed because the smell of sweat and Polo cologne and you and you and you linger on, in it. Don't do this. Please. I hate to even ask such a thing. Don't not go for me. But please don't go. I know Saint Sabina was formative for you, that you chose that space of care and were so compelled, you were able to get your parents to join too. I know you want to continue in the tradition of the folks there, that you too think the University of St. Mary of the Lake is the place to which you are called to study for a master's degree and all but, but . . . please. Do you think this will make you happy? Can you do the justice work and the preaching work in another tradition? I need you too.

Until the spacetime beyond whenwhere I no longer feel you, which will never be,

A

Dear Moth,

The occasion of the political climate, the occasion of the old but for many new thing about politics and disorganization, gave me a sorta explicit example. This is what I meant by renouncing the one for the many.[1]

These are folks that own and work at bodegas in New York City, all kindsa folks gathered together to argue in favor of their flesh, for the protection of their collective, improvisational, nondivisional, nonsingular identity, they moved and worked in the favor and protection of a nonliberal subjectivity, an intersubjective otherwise as possible.

Look at the sorta gracefulness with which they stand, then bow, then bend. Listen to the quiet, the quiet that makes the sound of wind and street noise apparent, a quiet that is not about the evacuation of sound but a refilling, an indwelling, of otherwise sound. Listen to how in that silence is the anticipation for the sounding out, the call, to bend again. It's, I don't know, beautiful to me.

They withdrew into the world, into worlds, made themselves available, open, by retreating into the outside. There, in the outside, they found through performance, the secret place of the most lowliness, the secret place of blackness—to echo a friend a bit—lowly against exaltation, they withdrew into the clearing. And there they worshipped. And there other theys stood and watched, rapt. They ascended into dissent, into descent. They left the bodegas and made themselves secret in public, and in such doing undid the distinction between private and public. They made apparent otherwise in flesh in the *thennowsoon* and *whenwhere* of spacetime. Entanglement. Entangled. They were not lonely. It is a mysticism of the social, the mysticism of sociality.

I've been listening to my breathing more as I sleep. Or, not necessarily listening but have become more aware of it as sound, as making noise, as displacement continually. I listened as I sleep or as I run on the treadmill or even as I walk down the street. Something about the constant movement of air in and out, in and out. Something about how we have to keep doing it to keep alive, how it is a biogenic fact, how flesh needs air to revive itself, sustain itself. That something from the so-called outside's gotta come and dwell with us, in us, maybe the dissent and descent of the holy ghost was just making this explicit: what keeps us alive, what holds us in embrace of the living, is something available and common and collective and social and outside oneself. It is ecstasy in the most explicit sense.

And I get this feeling as I watch these people pray in the middle of the city, as I watch them pray as staging protest. They're praying from positions physically, and from stations of life sorta theologically and philosophically, that are considered in the United States to be discardable, unnecessary, in need of conversion. But what their praying in the sorta secret place of blackness shows me is that they breathe and in the fact of such breathing we should cherish it.

I'll say more soon but this is getting to be too long,

A

Note

1.   "Instagram Post by Simone Leigh • Feb 3, 2017 at 1:27pm UTC," Instagram, www .instagram.com/p/BQDRUKCD-Tw/.

DOI 10.1215/10642684-6957912

THE JUBILEE OF 2033

Zach Blas

Recently, I have found myself reimagining Derek Jarman's 1978 queer punk film *Jubilee.* At its start, Queen Elizabeth I asks her adviser John Dee to summon forth a spirit in which to converse. After descending, the spirit Ariel offers Elizabeth a future vision of England. Through thick, black smoke, a collapsed and lawless London emerges, composed of fallen buildings, roaming, armed gangs, and a burning stroller. Here, the punk present of the late 1970s is rendered as a futuristic dystopia. Every time I watch this film, I find myself wondering how this scene could be rewritten for the early twenty-first century. What pressing question might a political leader ask the spirit Ariel now? After globalization, the rise of high-frequency trading, and the continued Googlification of public infrastructure, might knowledge be sought not about a particular country but about a major planetary structure or institution?[1]

One inquiry could concern the future of the Internet. In such a remake of *Jubilee*, Queen Elizabeth I would be replaced by a major Silicon Valley tech executive, like Elon Musk or Mark Zuckerberg; John Dee, the adviser, is now a computer programmer, seeking answers to the future in machines, not the heavens; and the spirit Ariel is an artificial intelligence, akin to IBM's Watson. Algorithmic predictions of the year 2033 are calculated, a time for the Internet's own jubilee, and two possible futures are disclosed: (1) The Internet has been killed. Governments have exacerbated their use of Internet Kill Switches in order to terminate Internet access during times of political unrest.[2] These Internet shutdowns are coupled with politically motivated blocks and bans of users and websites alongside rampant dataveillance. As a result, the Internet has been reconfigured solely as governance via networks. (2) The Internet has disappeared. First prophesied in 2015 by then Google chairman Eric Schmidt, the Internet has further dispersed into the world, fully realizing the Internet of things, which enacts a totalized integration, and therefore inseparability, of the Internet and the world. Capitalism and political unrest have thus accelerated.[3]

Beyond these two stalemates, might there be a third option, a queer utopian potentiality that could aid in escaping "the prison house" of the present, as José Muñoz (2009: 1) once put it? This third future could be understood as an infrastructural commons, what Keller Easterling (2014: 23) would term an "alternative extrastatecraft," suggesting a mode of infrastructure governance that is counter to "most global powers." In recent years around the world, technologists, activists, and artists have begun collectively building networks that do not rely on the corporate infrastructure of the Internet as we know it. From Hong Kong to New York, such network alternatives to the Internet are typically deployed to evade surveillance as well as remain functional during an Internet shutdown.[4] Additionally, community-oriented initiatives, like the Digital Stewards in Detroit, teach neighborhoods how to build and maintain their own autonomous mesh networks.[5] This "contra-internet" activity, as I prefer to name such endeavors, exposes a political horizon of transformation beyond the Internet, to an infrastructural commons that is beginning to thrive. Practically, an infrastructural commons—or "an open infrastructure of information and culture," as Michael Hardt and Antonio Negri (2009: 308) describe it—supports communication that is not proprietary and enables sharing, producing knowledge, and being together outside structures of privatization and surveillance.

What is the investment of queerness in an infrastructural commons? Tim Dean provides a unique starting point to consider this question, as his critique of networking is founded on a queer ethics of cruising. Concluding his book-length analysis on barebacking subcultures, Dean (2009: 176) offers up "cruising as a

way of life," which he defines as a promiscuous openness to alterity. To advance his
argument, Dean uses Samuel Delany's distinction between contact and networking.
Contact, Delany (1999: 129) explains, can be understood as the crossing of "class
lines in those public spaces in which interclass encounters are at their most frequent." Delany's examples for contact include conversation in a grocery checkout
line or bar as well as masturbation between two men in a public bathroom. Alter-
nately, networking consists of modes of social engagement that are "heavily dependent on institutions to promote the necessary propinquity" (ibid.). Parties, conferences, and classes are all instances of networking, according to Delany. Spaces
of networking, Dean continues, are often privatized and therefore narrow risk and
diminish pleasure. Crucially, Dean's use of networking is not restricted—or even
primarily oriented—around communications infrastructure. For instance, when
one cruises in a gym in which membership is required, one partakes in networking, not contact. Dean's critique of networking, then, is not strictly concerned with
a moralism of bodily presence over technically mediated interaction (even though
he ultimately favors bodily contact); rather, it is a critique of networking as a securitization against the public and the unknown. Preferring contact, Dean locates his
queer ethics of openness, risk, and alterity resolutely against networking's foreclo-
sure of potentiality.

    Yet if today's network infrastructures cut across myriad aspects of exis-
tence—queer and all—then perhaps another kind of queer ethics is needed. This
would be a position that no longer vies between contact versus networking but
networking versus contact *in* network infrastructures. Instead of only prizing the
physical contact of bodies, let us move the network forward—out of the Internet
and into the infrastructural commons!—by practically experimenting with forms
of queer life and relation that might come after the Internet. Such a project would
attend to questions such as how can filter bubbles be burst so that knowledge can
be circulated and shared beyond algorithmic personalization and individualism?
How can "platform capitalism" be thrown asunder, in order to build infrastructure
that operates like agoras (Srnicek 2017: 36)? How can policing be subtracted from
network infrastructure, in order to protect vulnerable populations from insidious
dataveillance? In the spirit of Delany and Dean, a queer infrastructural commons
may also foster new avenues for sexual encounters, far beyond the interface aesthetics of Grindr. These fantastic and nascent pursuits would undoubtedly stretch
the meaning of alterity in any queer ethics. Indeed, a queer infrastructural commons may even surpass the network form itself, opening up to other forms of organization yet unknown.

One of Queen Elizabeth I's encounters with the future in Jarman's *Jubilee* takes place in what appears to be an autonomous women's center. Equipped with a modified globe depicting geopolitical insults and a history book-cum-zine, the queer punk Amyl Nitrate delivers a lecture. She speaks on the histories of England but also fantasy, desire, and their relations to reality. Concluding her talk, Amyl Nitrate pronounces, "But I wanted to dance. I wanted to defy gravity." In the jubilee of 2033, I picture a renegade transhumanist turned feminist technoscientist delivering a queer futurist prophecy, disguised as a TED Talk. They mock Google's ethical slogan, "Don't be evil," critique Silicon Valley's colonization of the social, and challenge the audience to imagine a reality beyond networks. Yet they finish with the exact same words as Amyl Nitrate. Without a doubt, the flourishing of an infrastructural commons contra the Internet may indeed feel like defying gravity, but the desire for and work toward such a project is a commitment to a potential queer future worth cruising.

Notes

1. An example of Googlification is offered in a recent *New York Times* article that chronicles Google's impact on public education in the United States. See Singer 2017.
2. A fifty-year jubilee of the Internet is based on the date January 1, 1983, when ARPA-NET, a military forerunner to the Internet, adopted TCP/IP, a protocol suite used to link devices and transmit data, on which today's Internet still relies.
3. I have written more extensively on killing and disappearing the Internet in Blas 2016.
4. For example, in 2011 the artist Dan Phiffer developed a self-contained network named *occupy.here* for Occupy activists to use in Zuccotti Park during Occupy Wall Street.
5. More on the Digital Stewards can be found at www.alliedmedia.org/dctp/digitalstewards.

References

Blas, Zach. 2016. "Contra-Internet." *e-flux journal*, no. 74. www.e-flux.com/journal/74/59816/contra-internet/.

Dean, Tim. 2009. *Unlimited Intimacy: Reflections on the Subculture of Barebacking*. Chicago: University of Chicago Press.

Delany, Samuel. 1999. *Times Square Red, Times Square Blue*. New York: New York University Press.

Easterling, Keller. 2014. *Extrastatecraft: The Power of Infrastructure Space*. London: Verso.

Hardt, Michael, and Antonio Negri. 2009. *Commonwealth*. Cambridge, MA: Harvard University Press.

Muñoz, José Esteban. 2009. *Cruising Utopia: The Then and There of Queer Futurity.* New York: New York University Press.

Singer, Natasha. 2017. "How Google Took Over the Classroom." *New York Times*, May 13. www.nytimes.com/2017/05/13/technology/google-education-chromebooks -schools.html.

Srnicek, Nick. 2017. *Platform Capitalism.* Cambridge: Polity.

DOI 10.1215/10642684-6957926

QUEERNESS AND VIDEO GAMES:

Queer Game Studies and New Perspectives through Play

Bonnie Ruberg

*A*t the intersection of queerness and video games stands the experience of play. Though queer studies has yet to explore video games in depth, this digital interactive media form has much to say about queerness and the relationship between technology and contemporary LGBTQ lives. Video games represent an immensely popular and widely influential form of cultural production that both reflects and enacts social expectations around gender and sexuality. This makes games an important site of investigation for queer studies scholars. Yet the resonances between video games and queerness go far deeper than the representation of characters on screen or the identities of players. Queerness and video games share an ethos that can be fundamentally characterized through play. The language of play is not only the language of games; it is also the language of BDSM and other queer communities, where kink and sex parties are "play parties" and individual erotic practices are known by names like "anal play," "bondage play," and "puppy play." In an implicit sense, the importance of play already underlies much of queer experience and existing queer theory scholarship. Playfulness ties sexual expression to the queer desires of childhood in the work of Kathryn Bond Stockton (2009). It luxuriates in the *jouissance* of pleasure and rejects the use-value of sexual reproductivity in Lee Edelman's *No Future* (2004). The vibrant tomorrows, always "not yet there," of José Muñoz's *Cruising Utopia* (2009) are built through make-believe. Each of these examples demonstrates how play is already central to queer studies, and how play has the power to both disrupt and reimagine worlds.

Placing queerness in dialogue with video games brings play to the fore. The politics of play are complex and often contradictory—and no subject of study illus-

GLQ 24:4
DOI 10.1215/10642684-6957940
© 2018 by Duke University Press

trates this better than games themselves. The nature of play has long been a point of debate among scholars of game studies, the academic field dedicated to digital and analog games. Even the titles of the early works that have been foundational for the field, like Johan Huizinga's *Homo Ludens* (2016) and Roger Caillois's *Man, Play, and Games* (2001), make it clear that understanding play has been a central concern of game studies. Common lines of inquiry from game studies scholars include questions about how and why game players play (De Koven 2013; Sutton-Smith 1997), how they feel when they play (Isbister 2016; Juul 2013), how game play is structured and subverted (Bogost 2007; Consalvo 2007), and what cultural values play enacts (Flanagan and Nissenbaum 2014). Scholarship that explicitly ties video games to queerness is a relatively new—and fast-growing—addition to game studies. However, seen through a queer lens, video games become windows into both the powers and the pitfalls of play. On the one side is play as playfulness: a kind of free-form expression that allows game players to explore new ways of being in the world and by extension themselves. In this mode, players roam in-game terrains and try on the lives, bodies, and desires of others. On the other side is play as conformity to a system of rules. Video games appear to offer players infinite possibilities for interaction, but they are in fact highly structured. To play a video game the "right" way, the way that the game intends, is also to play along. In this way, video games complicate the notions of play that already underlie queer studies and queer pleasures.

This is only one of many new perspectives that video games bring to the study of queerness. As will become apparent below, the academic field of game studies is already being notably enriched by an increasing interest in queer studies. What about the other side of this interdisciplinary equation? What does queer studies stand to gain by turning its attention to video games? To date, conversations around LGBTQ issues and video games have taken place almost exclusively in game-related contexts, such as at game conferences and in publications on digital media. Now this work must cross over into the terrain of queer studies. Among the valuable critical tools that video games—and specifically the emerging scholarly paradigm of "queer game studies"—bring to queerness is this emphasis on play as an analytic framework (Ruberg and Shaw 2017). There are many reasons why queer studies scholars should attend to video games. Video games have overwhelming cultural influence across North America, Western Europe, Asia, and beyond, meriting them the same level of consideration as film, literature, and the performing arts. They also speak to a larger set of pressing questions about technology, identity, and belonging. The thread that links all these issues is play itself. Play can be a force of resistance or the tool of oppression. Thinking about queerness through play offers valuable opportunities for critiquing and reimagining the systems of power that shape LGBTQ lives, as well as for foregrounding play as key to the complexities of queerness.

Creating Dialogues between Queerness and Video Games

For those who are new to the study of video games, and even for many who know the medium well, talking about games in relation to queerness may seem counterintuitive. For decades, video games have wrestled with their reputation as mere entertainment for children, or as platforms for the enactment of mindless violence. The misinformed belief that games are devoid of cultural or artistic value has unfortunately overshadowed the richness of games themselves; however, this is not to say that video games, taken as a whole, are unproblematic. It is true that across their history, mainstream commercial games and the games industry have catered to an imagined white, straight, cisgender male audience (Fron et al. 2007). Heteronormative content remains standard in most game genres, homophobic language is commonplace in online gaming, and LGBTQ players often report feeling uncomfortable in game-related spaces, both online and off (Jones 2014). Recently, longstanding problems of discrimination in games culture have reached a boiling point, drawing national attention to the heated debates (and reactionary vitriol) that surround a rising push from game developers and game critics to bring more diverse representation to video games (Wingfield 2014). Yet, despite these problems, video games are and have long been important sites of queer expression. This is true for LGBTQ game makers and scholars, but also for LGBTQ game players—such as transgender players for whom video games may represent a safe space for identity exploration (Janiuk 2014).

Placing queerness and video games in dialogue is surprisingly controversial work. The current landscape of identity and diversity issues in video games positions queer games research against a backdrop of turmoil and change. This backdrop is made up of intersectional concerns that connect queer experiences of discrimination to the marginalization of people of color, women, people with disabilities, and others in games culture. It is well documented that mainstream video games underrepresent female characters and characters of color (Williams et al. 2009). Feminist game commentators like Anita Sarkeesian have also demonstrated the pervasiveness of misogynist tropes in video games. While companies like Electronic Arts have been vocal about their efforts to include more diverse content in "AAA" games (the industry term for games produced at the scale of Hollywood blockbusters), and distribution platforms like Steam have made nontraditional games an increasingly important part of the North American games scene, it would be misleading to say that games are simply improving in the realm of diversity and inclusion (Makuch 2015). Starting in 2014, large-scale online harassment campaigns unleashed a torrent of personal attacks, death threats, and hate speech against those who spoke publicly about bringing social justice to games. Yet many individuals and collectives are standing up in the face of this harassment—including organizations like I Need Diverse Games and a number of groups dedicated to teaching women and girls to build video games—foregrounding the importance of social justice in games, the games industry, and games culture.

Part of what makes the interplays between queerness and video games so rich yet so difficult to pin down is that the definitions of both *queerness* and *video games* are slippery. Like *queerness*, which operates both as an umbrella term for LGBT+ identities and a conceptual nexus, *video game* has multiple meanings. Speaking about video games in the most material sense, I define games as any designed, interactive experience that operates through a digital media interface and *understands itself* as a video game. By this definition, the category of video games encompasses a wide range of genres and platforms. Arcade games are video games, as are home console games, computer games, portable games for systems like the Nintendo GameBoy, social games played on Facebook and other networking sites, and mobile games played on smart phones. In the mainstream news media, video games are often equated with shooters, but in truth shooters represent only a small segment of the medium. Role-playing games, strategy games, puzzle games, adventure games, sports games, and racing games are all examples of popular video game genres. Different games emerge from different production paradigms. Video games can also vary greatly in their player bases and the communities that form around them. While my focus here is on digital games (commonly abbreviated to simply "games"), analog games are also an important component of the discussion around queerness and play.

This definition of "video game" is far from self-evident, however. In fact, the very history of game studies could be told as the ongoing struggle to establish a definition for video games. The longest-standing and best-known feud in game studies is between narratology and ludology; the former is founded on the belief that games should be understood as storytelling machines, the latter on the belief that games should be understood as play (Bogost 2009). Today, this feud is largely passé, but important new work continues to focus on redefining video games. Even (or perhaps especially) outside the academic context, debates about what does or does not count as a "real" video game continue to rage. A regular complaint expressed by reactionary gamers bemoaning the diversification of the medium is that video games that do not closely resemble established genres should not be considered games at all.[1] This question of how to define a game may sound rhetorical, but in fact it serves as a microcosm in which can be seen the often-unspoken biases that underlie the study of games and games culture more broadly. In both scholarly and popular contexts, policing the line between game and nongame is a tactic that has been used to delegitimize the work of women, people of color, and queer designers. Therefore defining video games as digital media objects that "understand themselves" as games is in fact a pointed political statement. Game studies, originally rooted in formalism, has traditionally cast itself as apolitical. Creating dialogues between queerness and video games is a way to insist on the politics of studying games. The multifaceted nature of queerness, along with the critiques from LGBTQ communities of notions of "realness," challenges the belief that a "real" video game can or should be defined. Just as video games expand definitions of queerness to account for play, queerness destabilizes the very ontologies of video games.

Queer Game Studies

What comes perhaps most readily to mind when one thinks of queerness in relation to video games is the representation of LGBTQ characters. The LGBTQ Video Game Archive, a project led by Adrienne Shaw, has demonstrated compellingly that LGBTQ characters have made appearances in games for more than three decades.[2] Yet the fact remains that few mainstream games have prominently featured queer characters—with a handful of notable, oft-cited exceptions. Some games in the *Sims* series (Electronic Arts, 2000–2016) allow for same-sex pairings, for example. *Mass Effect* (Bioware, 2007–2012), an epic sci-fi trilogy, offers players the opportunity to play as either a male or a female protagonist and to romance nonplayer characters (NPCs) of their choice regardless of their gender. The open-world game *Dragon Age: Inquisition* (Bioware, 2014) is beloved by queer gamers for its inclusion of bisexual and kinky characters. At the place where queerness meets video games, however, there is much more to unearth than the direct (and often highly limited) representation of LGBTQ romances. The complexities of queerness itself challenges game scholars to also look for nonheteronormative desires in how games are structured and how they are played.

That there are myriad ways to approach the relationship between video games and queerness is evidenced by the diversity of work taking place in the emerging paradigm of queer game studies. Though scholarship on gender (and, less commonly, sexuality) in games has appeared since the late 1990s, with early publications like *From Barbie to Mortal Kombat*, this work largely focused on the place of cisgender women in games, either as players or as characters (Cassell and Jenkins 1998). By contrast, queer game studies is interested in reimagining video games and games culture through a broad range of LGBTQ perspectives and queer theory. This area of research began taking form in 2012–13, alongside a handful of important coinciding factors that brought visibility, momentum, and a sense of community to the work. First, new software tools, like the online application Twine, were breaking new ground by allowing people without computer science training or large development teams to design and release their own video games (Anthropy 2012). Partly as a result, video games saw the rise of what might be termed the "queer games avant-garde"—a wave of explicitly queer, small-scale, highly personal games made by LGBTQ designers, including many transgender women. Some of these games, like Anna Anthropy's *Dys4ia* (2012), were widely reported on in the mainstream press, where news about LGBTQ issues in video games had rarely appeared before (Hudson 2014). Simultaneously, new events were being organized that focused on diversity issues in games, such as the "Different Games Conference" and the queer gamer convention "GaymerX," creating opportunities for those invested in queer games to meet and build connections.

In 2013 the event that has become the central hub for queer game studies, "The Queerness and Games Conference" (QGCon), was inaugurated. Now entering its fifth year in 2018, QGCon was originally founded by Chelsea Howe, Christopher Goetz, Mattie Brice, and me. What makes QGCon, and queer game studies in general, unique in its methodologies is its commitment to interdisciplinarity and interindustry collaboration. QGCon is run by a mixed group of academics, activists, and professional game developers. In this spirit, it is not uncommon for queer game studies scholars to work directly with the very same people who make the games they study. Just as the dangers of advocating for social justice in games are real and present, the creation of queer games is happening now—and at rates unprecedented in games history. For this reason, many queer game studies scholars believe it is important to go beyond the walls of academe and speak directly with game-makers: contemporary queer subjects whose experiences of identity, community, and marginalization deeply influence their work. These direct engagements have been formative for queer game studies. They keep this area of research, even in its most theoretical moments, rooted in the day-to-day realities of LGBTQ lives.

Because queer game studies scholars come from across a range of disciplines, they bring different frameworks through which to understand queerness in relation to video games. While some take ethnographic or data-driven approaches, the majority of scholars currently in this area are humanists: scholars of media studies, cultural studies, and sexuality studies trained to think about queerness conceptually. Many of these scholars, including me, are turning toward the idea of queerness "beyond representation"—that is, queerness as a function of video game systems themselves. This element of queer games research resonates with work by scholars like Kara Keeling (2014), Jacob Gaboury (2013), and micha cárdenas (2015), who have argued for conceptualizing technology more broadly in relation to queer experience. It is also linked to the queer digital humanities, with its alternative modes of meaning making, as well as to feminist data studies. Among the many goals of queer game studies is a rewriting of games history. Queer game studies changes the dominant narrative about the place of LGBTQ subjects in video games and aims to reclaim the medium by imagining video games themselves as queer.

Current Trends in Queer Game Studies

In only a few short years, an impressive array of queer game studies work has emerged, and much more is on its way. An overview of the current trends in this research area demonstrates some of the myriad ways that scholars and their collaborators are unpacking the relationship between queerness and video games. These key trends, surveyed here, give a sense of the diverse methodologies of queer game studies, yet they also speak to the common threads that unite this work. Chief among them is an interest in the transformative experience of play and play itself as an expression of queerness. Some of these trends include:

> 1. Identifying LGBTQ video game characters, either by pointing to lesser-known instances of explicit LGBTQ representation in games or by performing critiques that argue for characters' implicit queerness. Notable examples of this work include Amanda Phillips's writing on the hyper-femme queerness of Bayonetta, a character often mischaracterized as a mere object of desire for the straight male gaze who in fact uses her hyperbolic sex appeal as a weapon against the patriarchy (Ruberg and Shaw 2017). Conversely, queer game studies work has also pointed to the absence of meaningful LGBTQ representation in games, as in Edmond Chang's critique of same-sex marriage in the social media game *FrontierVille* (2015).
> 2. Arguing for a fundamental connection between queerness and games, such as by positing games themselves as queer or as spaces of queer experience. Notable examples of this include Naomi Clark and merritt kopas's 2015 QGCon keynote and subsequent article "Queering Human-Game

Relations," which proposes that play should be understood as the sort of queer excess described by Georges Bataille. Most recently, this interest in the inherent connection between queerness and games has begun to enter the thinking of established play theorists, such as Miguel Sicart. In his article "Queering the Controller" (2017), Sicart explores how game controllers can create opportunities for queer, erotic, and intimate experiences.

3. Reflecting on the connection between queerness and the game design process. Writing of this sort has most often been done by those who occupy a hybrid space between game design and academe. Colleen Macklin's "Where Is the Queerness in Games" (Ruberg and Shaw 2017), for example, explores the notion of queer game mechanics, while Avery Alder's tabletop role-playing game *Monsterhearts* (2012), about which she has given a number of interviews and talks, uses dice rolls to determine the vectors of player desire. Work like Alder's, while primarily creative, can itself be understood as a form of queer critical analysis through design. In a related vein, work like that by Robert Yang (Ruberg and Shaw 2017) and Evan Lauteria (2012) has posited "modding," the alteration of games themselves, as a mode of queer resistance.

4. Analyzing video games through queer theory, often with an emphasis on concepts of queer failure or queer affect. Jordan Youngblood's work on failures of masculinity in *Metal Gear Solid* falls into this category, as does my own writing on video games that flip the script on success by instructing players to lose (Ruberg 2017; Ruberg and Shaw 2017). Lisa Nakamura also makes this connection in her afterword to the collection *Gaming Representation: Race, Gender, and Sexuality in Video Games*, where she points to the work of queer theorists like Lauren Berlant as frameworks for reconsidering issues of identity and power in games. In addition to queer theory, feminist film theory is also coming directly into dialogue with video games, as evidenced by Diana Mari Pozo et al.'s (2017) writing in *Camera Obscura* on the mixed methodologies of queer game studies.

5. Studying the issues of community, culture, and history that surround queerness and video games. Shaw's monograph *Gaming at the Edge* (2014), in which she explores the ways that players discuss their own experiences with identification and video games, falls into this category, as does her work on the LGBTQ Video Game Archive, which seeks to catalog and thereby make increasingly visible the long but often-overlooked lineage of queer characters in video games. Less academic but nonetheless adjacent work has also contributed to these discussions of queer games communi-

ties, such as the documentary *Gaming in Color* (2014), developed by the creators of the annual event "GaymerX."

This overview is far from complete, but it offers a helpful starting point and a ready-made bibliography for scholars, instructors, and graduate students interested in incorporating queer games research into their writing or course design. Of course, as the work of queer game studies continues to progress, new threads are sure to emerge. Some of the topics on the horizons of queer game studies include the queer fandoms that surround video games, the ways that games engender or restrict queer forms of movement, and the nonheteronormative experiences that still remain largely absent from games, such as non-binary identities, polyamory, and queer of color perspectives. What unites these subjects is more than a thematic connection to queerness and video games. Play has a central part in all this work—whether it is addressing who players play as, how they play, how play is designed, or what play means. Though queer studies scholars conceptualize their work differently, the aim of this work is rarely the neoliberal "improvement" of video games. That is, while many scholars in this area hope to see video games do a better job of representing LGBTQ subjects, queer game studies is not itself in service of the games industry. This is another lesson that queer game scholars take from queer studies: that heteronormativity, oppression, and capitalism are all closely tied, and that the role of the scholar is to question rather than simply to promote the teleological narrative: "it gets better."

New Critical Perspectives through Play

It is clear from this diversity of work that queerness is bringing many important new perspectives to the study of video games. What does this work suggest that video games might bring to queerness? A few queer theorists have already begun investigating the answer to this question by bringing video games into dialogue with their existing work. Past QGCon keynotes Jack Halberstam and Kathryn Bond Stockton have each published articles in the area of queer game studies. In "Queer Gaming: Gaming, Hacking, and Going Turbo," Halberstam links video games to animation through the 2012 movie *Wreck-It Ralph* and suggests that both model "a queer orientation to reality" by "encouraging [players] to think in terms of parallel worlds" (quoted in Ruberg and Shaw 2017). For Halberstam, the video game "glitch" becomes a potent metaphor for the ways that "queer subjects have to hack straight narratives and insert their own algorithms for time, space, life and desire." Stockton in turn thinks about games as "highlighting two queer fires,"

sideways growth and excessive pleasure, which stand in the face of homonormativity and resist social legitimacy through an insistence on pleasure (Ruberg and
Shaw 2017). Halberstam and Stockton alike draw inspiration from video games
not because of the specific worlds or figures they represent but because they are
fundamentally structured around the experiences of play. Suggested in these two
pieces, as well as in the wealth of emerging queer game studies work, are many
connections between queerness and video games—connections through notions of
world building, agency, and counterhegemonic resistance. Each, however, returns
again to queerness as an experience of play.

Play is already central to queer theory, as in the examples of sexual and
theoretical "play" given at the start of this essay, but bringing video games into
direct dialogue with queerness highlights how play can itself be a framework for
queer critique. As a designed experience, play can offer opportunities for critical
reflections on how systems of power operate and how expectations for selfhood are
formed; it also creates opportunities for deconstructing and resisting these systems. Ultimately, what video games bring to queerness is new ways to think about
queerness itself. Considered through queer game studies, queerness emerges as
a set of desires and a way of being that are fundamentally linked to playfulness.
At the same time, queerness relates to games through its disruption of hegemony.
Queerness refuses to "play the game" of dominant culture. This speaks to the complexities of play, as well as the complexities of queerness: the game of queerness
is both queer experience itself and the forces that queerness rejects. Both queerness and play contain possibilities for resistance and for reinscribing norms. Much
as video games seem to offer infinite possibilities but in fact greatly limit player
agency, the lives of LGBTQ subjects can in fact be highly restricted by homonormativity and other culturally imposed expectations. Identifying the resonances
between video games and queerness does, however, imply a powerful potential for
imagining playing as a queer verb—not the verb "to queer," that is, but play as a
queer action.

In one sense, "playing queer" can mean playing video games in ways that
run counter to the intentions of their designers, reappropriating game play for the
pleasures of nonheteronormative players. Yet it also signifies the act of playing
queerness—whether playing at queerness or somehow playing that elusive thing
called queerness itself. The playing queer is also a subject, the queer who plays.
Like Huizinga's "homo ludens," the playing man (or playing human, depending
on how generous one is with the translation from the Latin), the playing queer is a
subject characterized by the fact that it is, in some sense fundamentally, at play.
Playing queer differentiates the study of queerness in video games from the study

of queerness in other media forms. Beyond the representation of LGBTQ subjects on the screen is the interactive experience of queerness, the experience called play. That play experience matters because it is individual as well as cultural, and because it is always felt in the body. Ultimately, it is in the body that queerness meets video games. Both approaching video games through queerness and approaching queerness through video games represent experiments in bringing the queer body—its desires, its loss, its expression of self—to press up against a game, to see where the two attract and where they repel, to form an intimate, erotic, and often subversive connection between the embodied experiences of queerness, the beauties and dangers of LGBTQ lives, and the medium of video games. The place where queer subjects and games meet is also a space of erotic play.

The work of queer game studies is only just beginning. In addition to the growing network of scholars taking part in research in this area, new voices must join this dynamic paradigm. Just as game studies is already expanding its horizons through its consideration of queerness, queer studies and queer theory can take on new forms through an engagement with video games. The bitter feud raging around diversity and video games makes it clear that there has never been a more important time for bringing LGBTQ perspectives to digital media. Conversely, when queer studies engages with video games, it does the important work of throwing itself into this fray—demonstrating a clear connection to the realities faced by queer subjects in cultural spaces related to technology. Queer game studies brings with it a spirit of activism that extends beyond academe. New complexities and new insights emerge at these boundary crossings between disciplines, as well as between scholarship and politics, creating opportunities to linger in liminal spaces and play.

Notes

1. Examples of this abound, but perhaps the most widely discussed is the independent game *Depression Quest* (2013), for which its designer, Zoe Quinn, has received ongoing harassment. Numerous forum threads and YouTube videos have been dedicated to angry diatribes about how this game should not have been made available through Steam, a game distribution platform—for example, the forum thread on Steam's own community section titled "This is not a game" (thread started from August 25, 2014, steamcommunity.com/app/270170/discussions/0/35221584654150330/).
2. See lgbtqgamesarchive.org.

References

Anthropy, Anna. 2012. *Rise of the Videogame Zinesters: How Freaks, Normals, Amateurs, Artists, Dreamers, Drop-outs, Queers, Housewives, and People Like You Are Taking Back an Art Form*. New York: Seven Stories.

Bogost, Ian. 2007. *Persuasive Games: The Expressive Power of Videogames*. Cambridge, MA: MIT Press.

———. 2009. "Video Games Are a Mess." Proceedings of the 2009 Digital Games Research Association Conference, London.

Caillois, Roger. 2001. *Man, Play, and Games*. Urbana: University of Illinois Press.

Cárdenas, Micha. 2015. "Shifting Futures: Digital Trans of Color Praxis." *Ada: A Journal of Gender, New Media, and Technology* 6, n.p.

Cassell, Justine, and Henry Jenkins, eds. 1998. *From Barbie to Mortal Kombat: Gender and Computer Games*. Cambridge, MA: MIT Press.

Chang, Edmond. 2015. "Love Is in the Air: Queer (Im)Possibility and Straightwashing in FrontierVille and World of Warcraft." *QED: A Journal of GLBTQ Worldmaking* 2, no. 2: 6–31.

Clark, Naomi, and merritt kopas. 2015. "Queering Human-Game Relations." *First Person Scholar*, February 18. www.firstpersonscholar.com/queering-human-game -relations/.

Consalvo, Mia. 2007. *Cheating: Gaining Advantages in Videogames*. Cambridge, MA: MIT Press.

De Koven, Bernard. 2013. *The Well-Played Game: A Player's Philosophy*. Cambridge, MA: MIT Press.

Edelman, Lee. 2004. *No Future: Queer Theory and the Death Drive*. Durham, NC: Duke University Press.

Flanagan, Mary, and Helen Nissenbaum. 2014. *Values at Play in Digital Games*. Cambridge, MA: MIT Press.

Fron, Janine, Tracy Fullerton, Jacquelyn Ford Morie, and Celia Pierce. 2007. "The Hegemony of Play." Proceedings of the 2007 Digital Games Research Association Conference, Tokyo.

Gaboury, Jacob. 2013. "A Queer History of Computing." *Rhizome* (blog), February 19. rhizome.org/editorial/2013/feb/19/queer-computing-1/.

Gaming in Color. 2014. Dir. Philip Jones. MidBoss.

Hudson, Laura. 2014. "Twine, The Video-Game Technology for All." *New York Times*, November 19. www.nytimes.com/2014/11/23/magazine/twine-the-video-game -technology-for-all.html.

Huizinga, Johan. 2016. *Homo Ludens*. Kettering, OH: Angelico.

Isbister, Katherine. 2016. *How Games Move Us: Emotion by Design*. Cambridge, MA: MIT Press.

Janiuk, Jessica. 2014. "Gaming Is My Safe Space: Gender Options Are Important for the Transgender Community." *Polygon.com*, March 5. www.polygon.com/2014/3/5 /5462578/gaming-is-my-safe-space-gender-options-are-important-for-the.

Juul, Jesper. 2013. *The Art of Failure: An Essay on the Pain of Playing Video Games.* Cambridge, MA: MIT Press.

Keeling, Kara. 2014. "Queer OS." *Cinema Journal* 53, no. 2: 152–57.

Lauteria, Evan W. 2012. "Ga(y)mer Theory: Queer Modding as Resistance." *Reconstruction: Studies in Contemporary Culture* 12, no. 2, n.p.

Makuch, Eddie. 2015. "'It Can't Be All White Males,' EA Exec Says about Diversity in Gaming: Electronic Arts Is Actively Looking to Increase Its Diversity." *Gamespot .com*, September 5. www.gamespot.com/articles/it-cant-be-all-white-males-ea -exec-says-about-dive/1100–6430348/.

Muñoz, José Esteban. 2009. *Cruising Utopia: the Then and There of Queer Futurity.* New York: New York University Press.

Nakamura, Lisa. 2017. "After: Racism, Sexism, and Gaming's Cruel Optimism." In *Gaming Representation: Race, Gender, and Sexuality in Video Games*, ed. Jennifer Malkoski and TreaAndrea M. Russworm, 245–50. Bloomington: Indiana University Press.

Pozo, Diana Mari, Bonnie Ruberg, and Chris Goetz. 2017. "In Practice: Queerness and Games." *Camera Obscura: Feminism, Culture, and Media Studies* 32, no. 2(95), 153–63.

———. 2017. "Playing to Lose: The Queer Art of Failing at Video Games," in *Gaming Representation: Race, Gender, and Sexuality in Video Games*, ed. Jennifer Malkoski and TreaAndrea M. Russworm, 197–211 Bloomington: Indiana University Press.

Ruberg, Bonnie, and Adrienne Shaw, eds. 2017. *Queer Game Studies.* Minneapolis: University of Minnesota Press.

Shaw, Adrienne. 2014. *Gaming at the Edge: Sexuality and Gender at the Margins of Gamer Culture.* Minneapolis: University of Minnesota Press.

Sicart, Miguel. 2017. "Queering the Controller." *Analog Game Studies* 4, no. 4, n.p.

Stockton, Kathryn Bond. 2009. *The Queer Child, or Growing Sideways in the Twentieth Century.* Durham, NC: Duke University Press.

Sutton-Smith, Brian. 1997. *The Ambiguity of Play.* Cambridge, MA: Harvard University Press.

Williams, Dmitri, Nicole Martins, Mia Consalvo, James D. Ivory. 2009. "The Virtual Census: Representations of Gender, Race, and Age in Video Games." *New Media & Society* 11, no. 5: 815–34.

Wingfield, Nick. 2014. "Feminist Critics of Video Games Face Threats in 'GamerGate' Campaign." *New York Times*, October 15.

LIVING ON

Leon J. Hilton

A Body, Undone: Living On after Great Pain
Christina Crosby
New York: New York University Press, 2016. xi + 208 pp.

Christina Crosby's beautifully constructed memoir spirals outward from a 2003 bicycle accident that left her largely paralyzed below the neck at the age of fifty-one. Crosby's account of the "violent and unceasing neurological storm" (18) set off by her spinal cord injury draws on insights from phenomenology and psychoanalysis, Victorian fiction and lyric poetry, and feminist and queer thinking about embodiment, pain, and the ethics of care. Composed of eighteen short, thematically organized chapters, the book intersperses vivid descriptions of the terrifying days and weeks that followed the accident (hospitalizations, surgeries, rehab, and physical therapy) with potent reflections on the arc of her life "before," from her tomboyish childhood in rural Pennsylvania to her entry into political consciousness by way of lesbian feminism as a college student, her fulfilling academic career as a professor of English and feminist studies at Wesleyan, and the rich domestic and intimate life she was in the midst of building with her partner, Janet, at the moment of the accident. Yet Crosby pushes back against the genre conventions of popular narratives about life-altering injury, disability, and illness; she insists on her need to mourn the loss of her previously able-bodied status and the kind of life that it allowed her to sustain. She equally departs from what she calls the "strategic elision" (7) of pain, loss, and grief that has sometimes accompanied disability studies' efforts to redescribe disability in social or political terms. Crosby takes exception to the way such accounts "almost always move toward a satisfying conclusion of lessons learned and life recalibrated to accommodate, even celebrate, a new way of being in the world" (189). Refusing catharsis, she gives voice to the depression and despair that she continues to experience in the face of such an utterly transformed and constrained mode of corporeal existence. "How could I be this body?" she recalls asking herself after the accident. "How could I bear what I had become?" (120). Yet if Crosby rejects sentimental self-heroizing and easy resolutions, neither is she fatally resigned or pessimistic. Her frank and brutal (at times wry) reflections on the realities of living in such a radically transformed body are accompanied by profound insights into the new forms of relationality and intimacy that have become necessary to sustain her daily existence, and she is especially attuned to the labor of others (both paid and unpaid) that she now relies on in order to move through the world.

Along with much else, the accident forced Crosby to confront the inadequacies of language in the face of traumatic injury—a particularly wrenching dilemma for a scholar and teacher of literature. She describes the "unassuageable loneliness" that comes from the realization that "I will never be able to adequately describe the pain I suffer" (31). All the same, she writes earlier in the book, "I begin in that leaden place where pain seems on the other side of language, and work toward living on" (12). For Crosby, the work of living on is inextricable from her resolve to find ways of accounting for her experience of pain and injury in writing, and *A Body, Undone* is the record of that hard-earned pursuit. Crosby's decades spent reading and teaching George Eliot and Jane Austen have sharpened her writerly sensibilities, and her impressively modulated prose is spiked with flashes of rage and bursts of deep sorrow. After the accident, she writes, "neurological destruction made a wilderness of my body. I was in an agony of grief" (117). The impress of Crosby's career as a literary scholar is also evident in her piercing insights into the ways that the lived experience of traumatic injury can become easily conventionalized according to a specific set of literary tropes and cultural genres. At one point, she notes that her embodied life after the accident seems to continuously exceed the "realist consensus" that governs the Victorian novels she teaches, and more closely resembles the reality-warping conventions of horror. (Yet as she also notes, "I'm not writing a horror story, I'm living one" [192].)

Readers interested in the burgeoning academic and cultural work emerging at the nexus of disability and sexuality will be particularly compelled by Crosby's insistence on maintaining a sense of herself as a sexual subject even as she observes how disability disrupts the normative and even queer codes of gender performance ("I no longer have a gender. Rather, I have a wheelchair," she writes at one point [60]). Perhaps most significant, Crosby draws from queer and feminist modes of thinking to reflect on the ethics of care and interference. She describes the deeply intimate and loving relationship she has developed with her care worker, Donna, even as she remains aware of the larger, structural constraints that fracture their bond across lines of race and class. She writes of how her friend and former student, the poet Maggie Nelson, accompanied her through the days and weeks that followed the accident, and wrote poems about this most difficult period that "suspend my life in the richness of poetic language" (9). Yet it is ultimately Crosby's relationship with her partner and lover, Janet, that lies at the book's emotional core and propels her to find ways of "living on." "You may not love your body," she quotes Janet telling her after an especially despair-fueled outburst, "but I do—and you should know by now that I want to be your physical lover" (196). Janet's insistence on the endurance of her desire is one of the book's most powerful and, indeed, radical insights, and Crosby shares this most vulnerable and intimate detail with the selfless impulse and generosity of a great teacher. *A Body, Undone* invites readers to consider how even a life so devastatingly transformed is never lived singularly, but bound to others through ties that are not always recognizable or even describable to ourselves.

Leon J. Hilton is assistant professor of theatre arts and performance studies at Brown University.

DOI 10.1215/10642684-6957954

KINKING RACE PLEASURES

Jordan Victorian

The Color of Kink: Black Women, BDSM, and Pornography
Ariane Cruz
New York: New York University Press, 2016. xii + 317 pp.

There is something sexy about racism, an unspoken erotic charge that animates the constant labor of racialization. The pleasures and performances imbricated in race underline the analytic work of *The Color of Kink: Black Women, BDSM, and Pornography.* In it, Ariane Cruz explores racialized performances in BDSM and pornography, arguing that these sites highlight the technologies of gender, race, sexuality, and pleasure that help constitute black female sexuality. Cruz contributes to feminist scholarship on representations of black women and expands the growing field of racial pornographics, offering a unique focus on BDSM performances in a contemporary porn archive. Throughout the text, Cruz responds to a body of black feminist work that considers racialization and the visual field as solely sites of violence. She instead argues that black women may encounter racial-sexual alterity, "the perceived entangled racial and sexual otherness that characterizes the lived experience of black womanhood" (33), as a site of both violence and pleasure. Cruz calls for a politics of perversion as a critical strategy to negotiate black female sexuality, one attuned to "the subversive, transformative power of perversion as the alteration of something from its original course and the *kink*—the sexual deviance—that perversion evokes" (11).

The weaving of feminist, queer, critical race theory, and media studies exemplifies Cruz's interdisciplinary background in African diaspora studies and women's studies. Cruz utilizes multiple methods including visual and textual analysis, archival research, and personal interviews. Analyses of pornographic performance engage film and web content across multiple pornographic genres: BDSM race play, interracial pornography, stag films, and "fucking machines." Beginning with a take on race play—a BDSM practice that uses race as an erotic stage for sexual encounters, a way of scripting domination and submission—Cruz considers BDSM and pornography not solely as sites of racism but also as stages in which black women and other actors engage the "labyrinthine pleasures" of race (133). BDSM and pornography are optimal sites of race play where racial difference and myths of black female sexuality are contested, rehearsed, and fucked with.

One of Cruz's great successes is her critical analysis and expansion of "race play." As a BDSM practice, race play takes pleasure in "the charged, complex, and contradictory relationship between racism and rapture" (71). Race-play pornography dramatizes racial scripts for consumption, enabling "a kind of pleasure pedagogy in and of race and racism" (115). While one might want to write off the perverse performances of race play as contained rehearsals of racism, Cruz complicates such a reading by asking us to "extend the theoretic aperture of race play to consider how the violent pleasure of the play of race is enacted in the larger venue of popular culture" (123). Beyond porn and BDSM, race constitutes a fluid project in which a range of actors coproduce racial difference, whether performing race through pornographic fantasy, BDSM practice, everyday interactions, or other moments of racialization. Race play itself may be figured more broadly as a "comprehensive performance with a more universal sociocultural currency and relevance" (78), offering an analytic to address varied modes of playing, and playing *with*, the real fantasy of race.

Cruz also highlights the queer pleasures of interracial pornography. Reading videos along with commentary from porn producers and performers, she argues that interracial pornography operates through queer race pleasures, "a simultaneous pleasure in race and queerness" (134). Cuckolding porn, for instance, involves a coproduction of queer race pleasure, as "the white male body co-produces the spectacle of its own racial-sexual humiliation" alongside the hypersexualized black male body that outperforms it (150). Here the play of race challenges static and binaristic views of sexuality. Domination and humiliation (of both black and white actors), race, and erotic pleasures intertwine as the social scripts surrounding material bodies animate the supposed "fantasy" of pornographic scenes: the "race and gender of the witnesses modulate the erotic currency of humiliation" (148). Cruz posits a queerness in the homoerotic resonances of these taboo fantasies and asserts that such scenes reveal BDSM as a lens for complex readings of racialized performance. Simply put, BDSM "helps us see debasement differently" (148).

Later, her reading of pornography with "fucking machines," or "mechanized phallic devices" (171), reveals a further breakdown of binaries such as fantasy/reality and human/machine. Performing as white masculine prostheses, fucking machines instantiate the erotic, narrative significance of racial-sexual alterity in pornography as the machines penetrate black women with techno-sexual supremacy and endurance, "winning" over them. While black women are not stereotypically or conventionally exoticized in these fucking machines videos, online comments demonstrate that codes of racial-sexual alterity still color spectatorship. Cruz observes that male viewers of these videos "often refer to the black body in relation to their own whiteness" (209), and racialized domination and consumption continue to mediate viewers' pleasure. The promise of color-blind pleasure that fucking machines may seem to offer is troubled; this techno-utopian fantasy remains tied to racial realities, as "fucking machines are programmed by and indeed reproduce racialized and gendered codes of sexuality" (209). In the process of spectatorship, male viewers engage queer identifications and pleasures with/through the fucking machines, such that Cruz experimentally extends the term *interracial* to touch on fucking and identifying across the human-machine divide—a sort of cyborg miscegenation. Again, her kinked black feminist critique reveals BDSM as an apt lens to analyze race as a technology of pleasure, domination, and difference.

The project critically refuses to (de)moralize or come to overly firm conclusions about the practices it engages, but for such a charged topic as race play, questions still loom on the political ramifications of these performances and acts. Further discussion could more thoroughly address the communal stakes of representation, particularly as far as black sexuality is concerned, or the political potential of such pleasures—all while avoiding pressures for moral judgment. Personal interviews might also further explore viewers' engagement with pornographic performances, adding texture to the included commentary from performers and producers and the short discussion of viewers' web comments. While at times the ambivalence of Cruz's readings seems to obscure rather than illuminate dynamics of racial-sexual pleasure, *The Color of Kink* lays definitive groundwork for analyzing the erotic economy of blackness and/in performance. Cruz joins scholars such as Jennifer C. Nash and Mireille Miller-Young in the growing area of racial pornographics, offering a critically kinky framework to bridge scholarship of black women's sexuality, BDSM, and pornography.

Jordan Victorian is a doctoral student in feminist studies at the University of California, Santa Barbara.

DOI 10.1215/10642684-6957968

IMPERMANENT LONGINGS

Brett Farmer

Ghostly Desires: Queer Sexuality and Vernacular Buddhism in
Contemporary Thai Cinema
Arnika Fuhrmann
Durham, NC: Duke University Press, 2016. xii + 255 pp.

In her classic sociological study of haunting, Avery Gordon suggests that ghosts, routinely dismissed as vestigial hangovers of premodern superstition, function as vital elements of contemporary social life. As obscene figures of liminal otherness, ghosts index the vast and often violent exclusions of modernity, reanimating the lost, conjuring the invisible, speaking the unutterable, and, generally, refiguring the taken-for-granted operations of social reality. "The ghost is not simply a dead or missing person," she writes, "but a social figure, and investigating it can lead to that dense site where history and subjectivity make social life" (Gordon 1997: 8).

Arnika Fuhrmann mines the rich materialist indexicality of ghosts to dazzling effect in her brilliant new study of queer sexuality and Buddhist-coded tropologies of desire in contemporary Thai cinema. After years of relative decline, Thai film experienced a marked renaissance in the turbulent historical aftermath of the 1997 Asian financial crisis that hit regional economies hard, Thailand in particular. The diverse corpus of film work that ensued—often denominated the New Thai Cinema—defies easy taxonomic assignment, but one of its common features is a striking fascination with the twin themes of ghostly return and the minoritized sexual personhoods of women, homosexuals, and *kathoeys* (Thai trans feminine subjects).

This concurrence of cinema, haunting, and queer sexuality is constitutively yoked by Fuhrmann to broader issues in the contemporary Thai polity, notably the postcrisis resurgence of nostalgic cultural nationalism that combined traditional Buddhist-coded appeals to social and economic discipline with novel state-driven modes of regulatory sexual attention. "After 1997," she notes, "new cultural and social policy took recourse to bodies and sexualities and national cultural identity and citizenship came to be closely articulated with normative prescriptions for sexuality" (6).

The recurrent stories, themes, and motifs of ghostly return that pervade Thai cinema of the past two decades signal cultural and aesthetic responses to the fraught sexualization of Thai national identity and citizenship. Occupying a dynamic nexus of textual representation, governmentality, and desire, these films blend issues of minoritized sexual identifications with "Buddhist-coded anachronisms of haunting [to] figure struggles over contemporary Thai sexualities, notions of personhood, and collective life" (7). The use of the word *struggles* is operative here, as Fuhrmann stresses the complex affective and political negotiations staged by these films around sexuality, desire, and selfhood. Surveying a broad range of texts from mainstream, independent, and avant-garde practices, *Ghostly Desires* is equally attentive to how these films support hegemonic discourses and how they constitute counternormative queer feminist possibilities "that represent sexual personhood in ways that challenge nationalist prescription" (6).

In theorizing the distinctive thematics of queer spectrality in Thai cinema, Fuhrmann advances her linchpin concept of "Buddhist melancholia," an affective and temporal configuration rooted in Buddhist conceptions of desire, loss, and impermanence. In doctrinal Theravadin Buddhism the doxa of impermanence is traditionally deployed to signal the futility of desire and prescribe a spiritual ideal of detachment. In popular form, however, its function is considerably more dynamic. The classic Theravadin practice of meditation on death is exemplary of the ambivalence of Buddhist melancholia, where a sustained contemplation of morbid decay services an ostensible pedagogy of erotic disavowal while advancing a phantasmic spectacle that actively engenders desire and allows for various modes of eroticized attachment. In this sense, Buddhist melancholia functions as "a trope of mobility" that "infuses prescriptive affective trajectories, in which attachment is the mere foil to inevitable expiration, with elasticity" (18). In turn, Thai films of ghostly haunting draw from the mercurial excess of Buddhist melancholia "to negotiate problematics of desire, sexual personhood, history, and the vicissitudes of attachment" and "furnish alternative models of sexuality for the present" (19).

This central argument about the counternormative productivity of Buddhist melancholia is developed in *Ghostly Returns* through four case studies, each addressed to a key film text or artistic configuration of the cinema of ghostly return. The first engages Nonzee Nimibutr's 1999 heritage film *Nang Nak*—a major commercial and critical success that was instrumental to the postcrisis renaissance of the New Thai Cinema—with a focus on how it (re)stages the celebrated folk ghost tale of Mae Nak in terms of Buddhist-influenced pedagogies of loss and negative female embodiment. The second mobilizes the Pang brothers' transnational coproduction *The Eye* (2002) to explore how the film's narrative of transnational haunting between two Chinese women—one Thai, the other from Hong Kong—indexes shifts in Thai conceptualizations of Chinese femininity from denigrated minority to cosmopolitan trans-Asian ideal. The third chapter advances a deft multileveled reading of Apichatpong Weerasethakul's arthouse masterwork *Tropical Malady* (2004), detailing how the film's rich tapestry of male same-sex desire, quotidian cross-gender sociality, and supernatural animism works to queer Buddhist notions of impermanence and forge utopian queer publics. The fourth and final chapter essays a brilliant analytic exploration of the important and hitherto critically neglected video work of avant-garde artist Araya Rasdjarmrearnsook, especially her provocative performance films with corpses and folk traditions of female lamentation, read here as the creation of feminist spaces of agency and intimacy between women.

This short summary could never do justice to the sophisticated theoretical commentary and insightful cultural analysis of *Ghostly Desires*. It is a singularly impressive achievement that stages valuable interventions in competing interdisciplinary debates about cinema, religion, and sexual publics. Fuhrmann brings to the project an admirable array of critical talents: extraordinary breadth of scholarly erudition, razor-sharp analytic acuity, and beautifully crafted writing. It is a dazzling debut from an important new voice in feminist, queer, and Asian cultural studies that deserves a wide and appreciative readership.

Brett Farmer is lecturer at Deakin University.

Reference

Gordon, Avery F. 1997. *Ghostly Matters: Haunting and the Sociological Imagination.* Minneapolis: University of Minnesota Press.

DOI 10.1215/10642684-6957982

A DEVIANT SEXUAL TYPE WELL BEFORE 1870

Emma Heaney

Heinrich Kaan's "Psychopathia Sexualis" (1844): A Classic Text in the History of Sexuality
Benjamin Kahan, ed.; Melissa Haynes, trans.
Ithaca, New York: Cornell University Press, 2016. vii + 193 pp.

Most students and teachers of sexuality studies take Michel Foucault's declaration that the homosexual as a distinct social type emerged in the 1870s as a start date for the emergence of sexual deviancy more broadly. But Foucault himself knew something that English-language readers can now also know thanks to Melissa Haynes's readable translation of Heinrich Kaan's *Psychopathia Sexualis*. Sexuality actually began to be systematized by 1844 with the publication of Kaan's book, the little-known precursor to Richard Von Krafft-Ebing's widely read 1886 medicolegal manual of the same title. Before homosexuality was identified as the definitional form of deviant sexuality, Kaan identified onanism, or masturbation, as the aberration of the sexual drive that was the gateway to all other deviations and that therefore urgently needed to be stamped out.

Kaan introduces his project in *Psychopathia Sexualis* as a "duty" to address a "difficult topic" that was thrust on him by the many patients who brought their struggles with sexual deviancy to his medical practice (31). The first half of part 1 outlines the reproductive function of plants and animals, relying heavily on citation of previous work by botanists and zoologists. Kaan pays particular attention to the sexual structures of both plants and animals, the role of these structures in reproduction, and the sexed structures (either male, female, or some blend of the two) of all life from the simplest plant to the highest order of mammals. The second half of part 1 turns to human anatomy, which reflects the "pinnacle of refinement in sexual differentiation," and traces the development of human sexuality from childhood to adulthood (52).

It is this "refinement" and sexual restraint that is violated when a person suffers from psychopathia sexualis, the umbrella term for the disease of excessive sexual drive. Kaan singles out onanism as the most medically significant form of psychopathia sexualis because it is the most common and therefore the most available for scientific study and also because it is the root of more advanced forms of sexual deviancy, including bestiality, pederasty, lesbianism (which is interestingly defined as sexual rubbing enacted by two women or by two men), necrophilia, and the violation of statues.

Kaan devotes part 2 to outlining the causes, symptoms, preventative measures, and cures for psychopathia sexualis. The causes include hereditary and acquired elements, from "lustful parents" to "too much sleep in soft bed covering" (84–85). The symptoms might include "sudden flush alternating with pallor" or, for boys, "traces of semen in the linens" (96–97). Prevention requires such measures as avoiding tight clothes and guarding children against friends who have had sexual experiences. The cures can include "ecclesiastical music," a range of homeopathic medicines, and Kaan's most highly recommended cure, cold water, applied in poultices or administered by dousing the whole body.

Benjamin Kahan's excellent introduction immediately focuses the reader's attention on the historical consequence of Kaan's book: this is the first instance in which a doctor taxonomizes sexual behaviors into types, laying the groundwork for the more elaborate taxonomies of sexuality that follow in the later nineteenth century. Kahan then outlines the intellectual foundation of the book, including studies of syphilis and anti-onanist tracts that surrounded Kaan as he wrote the book in early nineteenth-century Vienna, the center of the development of psychiatry. As Kahan notes, this new translation and critical edition of Kaan's text comes at a particularly good time, both because there has been such good work on sexology (Kahan provides a wonderful overview of the field) and because Kaan's text has been ignored in these accounts.

Of particular interest to readers of *GLQ* will be Kaan's declaration of biological bases for racial and sexed characteristics. For instance, Kaan claims that although excessive sexuality and onanism are present among all populations, they are more common among "Ethiopian" and "Mongoloid" races (77). Here Kaan toggles between an understanding of race as a characteristic of populations that live in primitive and colonial elsewheres and an understanding of race as inherent in racialized characteristics that possibly (and inappropriately) crop up as pathologies among white populations. This conceptual framework provides a clarifying distillation of a racial ideology that carries through in later sexological thought that connects the vices of European lowlifes to the common practices of Africa and the Orient. This ideology extends to the question of kinship when Kaan posits as scientific fact that polygamy is a form of sexual life proper to animals and practiced by "primitive people" but that "only monogamy which leads to marriage is suitable" for "humankind" (75). In this formation, moderate sexuality, European racial identity, and companionate monogamy are bunched together as mutually valorizing social goods.

Kaan also biologizes social sex roles, stating that the sexual instinct of men is geared to romantic pursuit and women to retreat with hopes of provoking pursuit. Further, men develop revulsion to women who allow sex before marriage. Without previous evidence or argumentation, Kaan states late in the book that "it is adequately clear that the end goal of feminine life is the propagation of the human race . . . : therefore sexual life creates a center for the entire life of women" (151).

Finally, Kaan's text offers an early resource for understanding the scientific approach to psychiatry and sexology that predominated before Sigmund Freud, which Freud both operated within and fundamentally challenged with his theories. We recognize Kaan's maturational narrative of sexuality, his association of maleness with sexual activity and femaleness with sexual passivity, and his claim that the taming of excessive sexuality is a necessary task for maintaining civilization as elements of the conceptual backdrop of Freud's theories. This new translation and critical edition expands our understanding of the form and content of medical claims about sexuality, race, and sex that Freud both identified and denaturalized.

Emma Heaney is assistant professor of English at William Paterson University.

DOI 10.1215/10642684-6957996

UNSETTLED TIME, SENSUOUS DURATION:

Methodologies of Native Becoming

Kara Thompson

Beyond Settler Time: Temporal Sovereignty and Indigenous Self-Determination
Mark Rifkin
Durham, NC: Duke University Press, 2017. vii + 277 pp.

To open *Beyond Settler Time* is to encounter the messy, uneven, and prismatic calculus of Native and non-Native spacetimes. The first chapter, "Indigenous Orientations," distills the book's central arguments and key interventions, including Mark
Rifkin's concept of *temporal sovereignty*: the experiences, collective and personal,
of time not reducible to—though not entirely set apart from—settler tactics and
temporalities. Native peoples remain oriented to homelands and territories as part
of their experiences of peoplehood, and as expressions of their sovereignty and
self-determination; such orientations both predate *and* endure genocide, dispossession, and the coercive policies attendant to settler civility and modernity. To
insist on designated and discernible boundaries between *modern* and *traditional*
is to cast Native peoples into a "natural" and "pure" before-time, where "conquest" serves as the clear line between *before* and *after*—and thus is assumed to
be over and done with.

And yet, efforts to *redress* the modern/traditional binary also take for
granted that time presents a neutral and mutual context for the unfolding and
sensations of events. To insist that Native people are indeed *coeval* and *modern*
is to assume settler legacies of violence and coercion as silent, but sanctioned,
backgrounds and frames of reference. Rifkin instead opens up a conceptual
space for expressions of temporal sovereignty, whereby "Native and non-native
trajectories . . . might be distinguished without resorting to a notion of shared
time," which is predominantly skewed toward non-Native framings (30).
Indigenous narrations of time, including periodization, the felt presence of human
and nonhuman ancestors, and the being-in-time related to land and occupancy,
may not accord with non-Native articulations of *the* past, *the* present, *the* future,
whereby time flows in a universal line of development. Rifkin argues for the

exertion of temporal sovereignty as an ongoing *re-creation*, oriented to the densities of history and the feelings of belonging to communities and territories, and to futures "that are neither equivalent to nor simply disconnected from the past" (32).

Rifkin takes an ambitious risk with *temporal sovereignty*. Though time's theoretical, perceptual, and political abstractions are cavernous and craggy, he offers clear and grounded readings of relativity theory, and captures time's dynamic and experiential contours. For instance, from Henri Bergson, Rifkin borrows *duration* to characterize forms of collective memory, experience, and engagement as, what he calls throughout, a *Native becoming*. The third chapter reads the histories of Osage land allotment (the settler nation's practice of dividing treaty lands into prescribed units to heads of households and individuals) through John Joseph Mathews's 1934 novel *Sundown*. The characters in *Sundown* inhabit multiple copresent temporal modes, and the novel's queerness—less homoeroticism than emplacement and duration alongside settler colonial impositions—captures the densities of Osage life, "particularly the ways postallotment political economy racializes and renders anomalous sensations emerging from the dynamics and duration of Osage inhabitance" (125).

This chapter shows what happens when settler allotment policies meet the counterforce of extant Osage modes of becoming. And the chapter that follows turns settler projections of inertia and surrender into modes of becoming and prophecy, with readings of Sherman Alexie's *Indian Killer* and Leslie Marmon Silko's *Gardens in the Dunes*. Silko, for instance, unsettles the straight time and fixed points of chronologies, generations, and histories with nonnuclear modes of pleasure; the novel offers up a grammar of time that exceeds the chronobiopolitics of settler historicity and realizes instead the queerer syncopations of enmeshment, multiplicity, and syncreticism.

Throughout, the book focuses on the dynamic motions of *storying*. Stories provide backgrounds for Indigenous experiences of time; they shape perceptions and orientations, and influence the horizon. Readers who work at the junctures and crossing vectors of Native/Indigenous, settler colonial, and queer studies will be especially invested in Rifkin's method of thinking Indigenous storying through queer time, or the modes of being-in-time that do not adhere to linear, normative, heteroreproductive timelines. Theories of queer time demonstrate the imposed straightness of time, but also engage alternative modes of existing in and across time. Crucially, though, Rifkin also shows how even the insights of queer studies, which enrich the meanings of *continuity* and *historical density*, tend to assume a settler background and frame of reference. Queer approaches to time, in other words, are ill equipped to account for intergenerational storying, the duration and renewal of connections to place and community, and the modes of continuity that might serve the exercise and experience of temporal sovereignty.

Rifkin makes clear early on that as a non-Native scholar, he offers the book in a speculative, negative dialectical mode to investigate what kinds of intellectual and political possibilities emerge by positioning time in the register of sovereignty and self-determination. In Audra Simpson's (2010: 107) words, "nothing is simultaneously so certain and yet so fraught with precariousness as the practice of sovereignty—globally or locally." Perhaps understandably, then, the book's coda claims deferral as a strategy for determining what temporal sovereignty might mean in the context of Native institutions of governance. As Rifkin points out, "Modes of governance officially recognized by the United States as sovereignty can express forms of temporality that differ from dominant Euramerican frames of reference" (179). The term *temporal sovereignty* might at first seem misleading if readers expect to learn how it could be operationalized as part of an Indigenous juridical apparatus. Nevertheless, I take the form of the coda seriously—these final pages are an offering, an opening to others, especially Native scholars, to theorize what temporal sovereignty means for Indigenous governance.

Those familiar with Rifkin's impressive and prolific body of work know that he is a model close reader. And because this book offers itself up as a hermeneutic, an intellectual account of time with a set of interpretative possibilities, his readings here are especially careful and well tuned. *Beyond Settler Time* makes its readers newly aware of how settlers manage time and create the illusions of its coherence. Beyond this, Rifkin shows us that simply to *recognize* multiple, even queer, experiences and impressions of time is still to instantiate the clocks of settler colonialism as stable referents against which Native peoples must react or respond. Rifkin productively and necessarily disorients the tenuous stabilities of settler colonialism to make way for temporalities, sensations, and densities that constitute the being and becoming of Native sovereignty and self-determination.

Kara Thompson is assistant professor of English and American studies at the College of William and Mary.

Reference

Simpson, Audra. 2010. "Under the Sign of Sovereignty: Certainty, Ambivalence, and Law in Native North America and Indigenous Australia." *Wicazo Sa Review* 25, no. 2: 107–24.

DOI 10.1215/10642684-6958010

SEXUAL UNRULINESS IN COLONIAL LATIN AMERICA

Ramón A. Gutiérrez

Sexuality and the Unnatural in Colonial Latin America
Zeb Tortorici, ed.
Oakland: University of California Press, 2016. xiv + 239 pp.

Here is a fascinating new anthology on the history of sexuality in Latin America that studies how nature was imagined and understood in the late colonial Iberian world. The book explores theological and juridical definitions of how human bodies reproductively reflected God's divine natural order, but also how free will created disorderly deviates who through behaviors against nature (*contra natura*) subverted that design. According to the Catholic Church, procreation was the only natural goal for which the reproductive body should be used. When the body's postures and dispositions did not maximize impregnation, when its genitals and fluids were used in ways that could not bear human fruit, when its desires and actions were deemed inappropriately focused simply on satisfaction and declared unnatural, the full force of the church's and state's disciplinary regimes were used to investigate, interrogate, and punish acts with purely erotic ends.

The book's two halves are based on the legal documents the authors mined. Essays in the first half, "Unnatural Heresies," reference Inquisition records and their orthodox definitions of sodomy, heresy, and bestiality. Here we learn of the 1779 suicide of Estaban Sobrino, a friar imprisoned by Cartagena's Holy Office. He was found guilty of seducing African slaves and free persons of color, usually in the confessional. Sobrino's defense: yes, he was a sinner and a joker, with a "cheerful and lively temperament." Though he admitted to arousing six boys to orgasm, his actions were not, he claimed, *contra natura*, because they stemmed from "sincere and honest love." Nicole von Germeten herein offers a subtle and complex reading of politics of the Inquisition, describing how after Sobrino's suicide, his inquisitor constructed a narrative that hid the clerical brother's sins. Nora Jaffary studies the Mexican Inquisition's 1797 investigation of Getrudis Arévalo for heresy because she doubted Christ's embodiment in the consecrated host. Eager for proof of God's existence, Arévalo confessed her escalating eroticized acts of profanation, placing rosaries, sacred images, even the Eucharist in her shameful parts. Jaffary urges contemporaries not to impose our understanding of sex on those who lived in the eighteenth century. The Holy Office was mainly concerned that a host had been profaned, not how it had occurred.

Was carnal consort with the Devil unnatural? This is the question Jaqueline Holler explores in her study of eighteen Mexican Inquisition dossiers of women with demonic pacts. What is particularly fascinating here is how the Inquisition defined the Devil as natural and unnatural, operating in individual lives in complex ways, particularly in natural form as a lover. The Inquisition believed such sins were female, rooted in humors (too much black bile), which produced melancholy and its madness. Ronaldo Vainfas and Zeb Tortorici turn our focus to twenty-nine women accused of sodomy in colonial Brazil between 1591 and 1595, a sin the Holy Office prosecuted fully, expecting that on interrogation its officials would also discover profanations of a heretical sort. Female sodomy required evidence of anal intercourse with a penis, dildo, fingers, or some penetrative object in the anus or vagina. Here we read explicit testimony on girls being seduced by older women, of lower-class women satisfying each other, sometime for lack of male partners but equally by preference.

The anthology's second half uses a broader swath of civil and ecclesiastical records, which yield more complicated, less formal, local juridical landscapes for the late colonial period. Chad Thomas Black studies two female sodomy cases from Quito in the 1780s. The women were found guilty because their behavior—public drinking, rowdiness, behaving as if a couple, sleeping in the same bed, preferring the company of females—was appropriate only for male-female couples. Though no evidence of anal or vaginal penetration existed, the women were punished for public disorder and depravity based on the complaints and suspicions of neighbors, families, and friends.

The tome's best essay is by Fernanda Molina, who challenges the reductionism explicit in describing sexual acts as simply "natural" and "unnatural," contesting the active-passive dichotomy in studies of male sodomy. Based on 123 cases from the Viceroyalty of Peru, Molina urges scholars to probe beyond those theological and juridical discourses of power focused on sin and crime, chronicling too the complex identities, subjectivities, and range of behaviors that archives reveal. Though many of the men accused of sodomy in colonial Peru were of unequal status (men/boys, masters/slaves, priests/parishioners, Spaniards/Indians), their relations were rarely merely sexual, coercive, or unequal. They involved public kissing, holding hands, gift giving, declarations of love and affection, which equalized or inverted their status differences. Many were long-standing relations marked by overt cohabitation. Of these men, 54 percent were anal receptive, 35 percent were insertive, and 5 percent flipped. Sodomites transvested their bodies to attract particular types and in some towns shared a common identity rooted in desire, persecution, and visibility.

Lee M. Penyak studies incest in Mexico between 1740 and 1854, showing how the Catholic Church sanctioned unions it defined as incestuous to perpetuate elite status, upholding patriarchal privileges even when violent assaults occurred. Mílada Bazant examines fourteen Mexican bestiality cases between 1800 and 1856. The accused were usually young peasant men from rural communities who had little or no sexual access to women; the exception: two older married men who preferred it to their wives. Martín Bowen Silva studies the confessional of José Ignacio Eyzaguirre, a Chilean elite young man as he came of age from 1799 to 1804. In this notebook, which José kept in preparation for the sacrament of penance, he painstakingly chronicled every bodily sin of self-discovery as he masturbated and explored the bodies of other boys and girls, overcome with desire but simultaneously wracked by shame. Absent in José's lexicon: the natural-unnatural divide.

This volume is rich, engaging at the empirical level with ample testimony on how sins against nature were defined by high tribunals, such as the Inquisition, and by lower ecclesiastical and civil courts. The majority of the cases studied come from the late colonial and early national periods, from 1750 to the 1860s, when Enlightenment ideas were already influencing educated elites who increasingly eschewed clerical assessments of what was unnatural and disorderly. This seems to be the recorded but unreported class subtext of this anthology, where elites rarely appeared before tribunal for their peccadillos. The sins of priests were sanitized. And those who suffered the full consequences of engaging in unnatural sins were society's lowest groups.

Ramón A. Gutiérrez is professor of history at the University of Chicago.

DOI 10.1215/10642684-6958024

About the Contributors

Arlen Austin is a PhD student in the Department of Modern Culture and Media at Brown University. His research addresses the relation of postwar social movements to the imbrication of mass media in neoliberal backlash. He is coeditor with Silvia Federici of *The New York Wages for Housework Movement, 1972–1979: History, Theory and Documents*, recently published by Autonomedia.

Zach Blas is an artist, writer, and lecturer in Visual Cultures at Goldsmiths, University of London. He has exhibited internationally, recently at Art in General, New York; Gasworks, London; Institute of Modern Art, Brisbane; and the 68th Berlin International Film Festival. He is a recipient of a 2016 Creative Capital award in Emerging Fields.

Gavin Butt is Attenborough Chair of Drama, Theatre and Performance at the University of Sussex. He is the author of *Between You and Me: Queer Disclosures in the New York Art World, 1948–1963* (2005), and coauthor, with Irit Rogoff, of *Visual Cultures as Seriousness* (2013). He is codirector of *This Is Not a Dream* (2013), a documentary film exploring queer artists' DIY use of moving image technology, and between 2009 and 2014 he was codirector of *Performance Matters*, a creative research project addressing the cultural value of performance. He is editor of *After Criticism: New Responses to Art and Performance* (2005) and coeditor, with Kodwo Eshun and Mark Fisher, of *Post-Punk Then and Now* (2016).

Beth Capper is a doctoral candidate in the Department of Modern Culture and Media at Brown University, where she is completing a dissertation on social reproduction and post-1970s feminist media cultures. Her articles have been published in *Art Journal*, *Media Fields*, *Third Text*, and *TDR: The Drama Review*. She is also part of a collaborative effort to build a digital archive of materials from the North American branch of the 1970s Wages for Housework movement.

Ashon Crawley, assistant professor of religious studies and African American and African studies at the University of Virginia, is the author of *Blackpentecostal Breath: The Aesthetics of Possibility* (2016), an investigation of aesthetics and performance as modes of collective, social imaginings otherwise.

Vivian A. Crockett is a New York–based independent researcher, scholar, and curator focusing largely on art of African diasporas, (Afro)Latinx diasporas, and the

Americas at the varied intersections of race, gender, and queer theory. She is a PhD candidate in art history at Columbia University.

Amalle Dublon received a PhD from Duke University's Program in Literature, with a Certificate in Feminist Studies. She teaches at the New School and New York University, and is the author of published essays on Pauline Oliveros and disco; on gossip and girl talk in recent artwork by Jessica Vaughn, Carolyn Lazard, and Hannah Black; and, with Constantina Zavitsanos, on the work of Lorraine O'Grady and Ellen Cantor.

José Esteban Muñoz (1967–2013) was professor and chair of performance studies at New York University. He was the author of the forthcoming *The Sense of Brown*, as well as *Disidentifications: Queers of Color and the Performance of Politics* (1999), *Cruising Utopia: The Then and There of Queer Futurity* (2009), and coeditor of *Pop Out: Queer Warhol* (1996) and *Everynight Life: Culture and Dance in Latin/o America* (1997).

Macarena Gómez-Barris is chairperson of the Department of Social Science and Cultural Studies at Pratt Institute and director of the Global South Center. She is the author of *The Extractive Zone: Social Ecologies and Decolonial Perspectives*, which theorizes social life through five extractive scenes of ruinous capitalism upon Indigenous territories (2017). She is also the author of *Beyond the Pink Tide: Art and Politics in the Américas* (2018), *Where Memory Dwells: Culture and State Violence in Chile* (2009), and coeditor, with Herman Gray, of *Towards a Sociology of a Trace* (2010).

Christina B. Hanhardt is associate professor in the Department of American Studies at the University of Maryland, College Park. She is the author of *Safe Space: Gay Neighborhood History and the Politics of Violence* (2013), which won the 2014 Lambda Literary Award for Best Book in LGBT Studies.

Tara Hart has lived in Brooklyn since 2005 and works as an archivist in the Meatpacking District.

Diarmuid Hester is a Leverhulme Early Career Fellow in English at the University of Cambridge. He is writing a critical biography of Dennis Cooper for the University of Iowa Press. Other projects include a counterhistory of New York's art and culture in the twentieth century from the perspective of waste, broadly conceived. His work is published or forthcoming in *American Literature*, *Critical Quarterly*, the *Journal of American Studies*, and other venues.

Leeroy Kun Young Kang is an archivist, independent curator, and artist based in Los Angeles. His research interests include experimental cinema, belated archives, and queer sexual subcultures.

Amira Khusro is a musician, poet, and writer.

Dragon Mansion is a writer living in New York.

Nadja Millner-Larsen is lecturer in Visual Cultures at Goldsmiths, University of London and 2017–2018 NEH Postdoctoral Fellow at the Getty Research Center in Los Angeles. She has previously taught at the Center for Curatorial Studies at Bard College and in the Department of Media, Culture and Communication at New York University, where she received her PhD. Her work has appeared in *Grey Room*, *Women's Studies Quarterly*, *Art Monthly*, and *Triple Canopy*. She is currently completing a book titled "Up against the Real: Black Mask from Art to Action."

Cenk Özbay is associate professor of sociology and gender studies at Sabanci University. He received his PhD from the University of Southern California. His books include *Yeni Istanbul Calismalari* (2014), *The Making of Neoliberal Turkey* (2016), and *Queering Sexualities in Turkey: Gay Men, Male Prostitutes and the City* (2017). He is currently working on his new book project about retail work, shopping malls, class, gender, and sexuality in Istanbul.

Bonnie Ruberg ("Bo") is an assistant professor of digital media and games in the Department of Informatics at the University of California, Irvine. From 2015–2017, Bonnie was a provost's postdoctoral scholar in the Interactive Media and Games Division and a member of the Society of Fellows at USC. In 2015, Bonnie received their Ph.D. in Comparative Literature from UC Berkeley in conjunction with the Berkeley Center for New Media and the Department of Women and Gender Studies.

Evren Savcı is assistant professor of women's, gender, and sexuality studies at Yale University. Her work on the intersections of language, knowledge, sexual politics, neoliberalism, and religion has appeared in the *Journal of Marriage and the Family*, *Ethnography*, *Sexualities*, *Political Power and Social Theory*, and *Theory & Event*. She is the coeditor of *PPST* special issue "Perverse Politics? Feminism, Anti-Imperialism, Multiplicity." She is currently finishing her first book, "Queer in Translation: Sexual Politics under Neoliberal Islam."

Eric A. Stanley is assistant professor in the Department of Gender and Sexuality Studies at the University of California, Berkeley. They are the coeditor of *Trap Door: Trans Cultural Production and the Politics of Visibility* (2017) and *Captive Genders: Trans Embodiment and the Prison Industrial Complex* (2015).

Julie Tolentino creates performance, installation, and objects.

DOI 10.1215/10642684-7175500

My Butch Career
A Memoir
ESTHER NEWTON

Little Man, Little Man
A Story of Childhood
JAMES BALDWIN
YORAN CAZAC, illustrator
Jennifer DeVere Brody and
Nicholas Boggs, editors

Comfort Measures Only
New and Selected Poems, 1994–2016
RAFAEL CAMPO

Desire Work
Ex-Gay and Pentecostal
Masculinity in South Africa
MELISSA HACKMAN

None Like Us
Blackness, Belonging, Aesthetic Life
STEPHEN BEST
Theory Q

Mobile Subjects
Transnational Imaginaries
of Gender Reassignment
AREN Z. AIZURA
Perverse Modernities

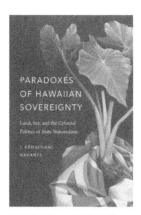

Trans Exploits
Trans of Color Cultures and
Technologies in Movement
JIAN NEO CHEN
ANIMA

Infrahumanisms
Culture, Science, and the Making
of Modern Non/personhood
MEGAN H. GLICK
ANIMA

Exile within Exiles
Herbert Daniel, Gay
Brazilian Revolutionary
JAMES N. GREEN

Paradoxes of
Hawaiian Sovereignty
Land, Sex, and the Colonial
Politics of State Nationalism
J. KEHAULANI KAUANUI

Unruly Visions
The Aesthetic Practices
of Queer Diaspora
GAYATRI GOPINATH
Perverse Modernities

dukeupress.edu

DUKE
UNIVERSITY
PRESS

Printed and bound by CPI Group (UK) Ltd, Croydon, CR0 4YY

25/03/2025

14647326-0002